WHERE THE DOVE CALLS

La vida Cucurpeña.

Where the Dove Calls

THE POLITICAL ECOLOGY OF A PEASANT CORPORATE COMMUNITY IN NORTHWESTERN MEXICO

Thomas E. Sheridan

THE UNIVERSITY OF ARIZONA PRESS
TUCSON

ARIZONA STUDIES IN HUMAN ECOLOGY

Editor
Robert McC. Netting (University of Arizona)

Associate Editors
Peggy F. Bartlett (Emory University)
James F. Eder (Arizona State University)
Benjamin S. Orlove (University of California, Davis)

Note: When fieldwork was conducted in preparation of this book in 1980–81, the exchange rate was approximately 25 Mexican pesos per U.S. dollar. The values utilized herein are based on that ratio.

THE UNIVERSITY OF ARIZONA PRESS
Copyright © 1988
The Arizona Board of Regents
All Rights Reserved

This book was set in Linotype Palatino.
Manufactured in the U.S.A.

Library of Congress Cataloging-in-Publication Data

Sheridan, Thomas E.
    Where the dove calls.

    (Arizona studies in human ecology)
    Bibliography: p.
    Includes index.
    1. Human ecology—Mexico—Cucurpe.   2. Natural
resources—Mexico—Cucurpe—Management.   3. Cucurpe
(Mexico)—Economic conditions.   4. Economic anthropology—
Mexico—Cucurpe.   I. Title.   II. Series.
GF517.C87S54   1988   304.2'0972'17   87-30139
ISBN 0-8165-1055-5 (alk. paper)

British Library Cataloguing in Publication data are available.

To Chris

Contents

REFERENCE MATERIAL

Illustrations

Maps

Tables

Acknowledgments

I first went to Cucurpe in 1975 after dropping out of law school—three of the most tedious weeks of my life. When I did, a friend—ethnobotanist Gary Nabhan—said, "Welcome back to chaos." We threw our camping gear in Gary's 1962 Valiant with the push-button transmission and headed for Sonora. Chaos was never more welcome.

After that initial trip to the Río San Miguel country, I kept returning—sometimes to do research, other times just to get out of town. I also entered graduate school in anthropology, and through all the courses and exams I kept promising myself that if I made it over the academic hurdles, I would do my dissertation fieldwork in Cucurpe. Some anthropologists hate the field. Living in Cucurpe during 1980–81 was one of the best years of my life. I loved the country and I loved the people. Their life was hard, but it made sense.

I've made a lot of friends in Cucurpe during the last thirteen years, and I thank a few in particular for their hospitality and their generosity: Beto, Ana, and Teri Cruz, Luis and Angelita Montijo, Juan and Amanda Montijo, Gel and María Elena Montijo, Alejandro and Guadalupe Arvizu, Jesús and Teresa Montijo, Francisco and Rita Miranda, Francisco Mariscal, Gabriel Escalante, Jorge Denton, Sergio Palomino, Gilberto Quiñones, Monino Palomino, Trini Arvizu, and Socorro Palomino. I also remember with affection and gratitude those friends who have died: Manuel Arvizu, José Quevedo, and Octavo Palomino, who gave my wife and me a place to live and kept us constantly amused with his incomparable sense of humor. I miss them; they were the best of company.

I also thank the people in Hermosillo, Tucson, and points north who helped me with the research: Conrad Bahre, Tom Barnes, Dave Bradbury, Connie Cronin, Hank Dobyns, Bob Erskine, Steve Falconer, Dick Felger, Bunny Fontana, Eric Henderson, Jane Ivancovich, Fritz Jandrey, Martha Martin, Paul Martin, Gary Nabhan, Tom Naylor, Charlie Polzer, Cynthia Radding de Murrieta, Dick Reeves, Marty Senour, Glenn Stone, Bud Surman, Carmen Villa Prezelski, and Tony

Zona, the computer wizard and cutthroat poker player who wrote the programs which allowed me to enter and analyze my data. Above all, I thank Bob Netting, who served as dissertation chairman, editor, and friend. His unflagging scholarship and decency were exemplary.

My research was partially supported by the Wenner-Gren Foundation, the Inter-American Foundation, and a very special friend of the Southwestern Mission Research Center who wishes to remain anonymous. The Centro Noroeste of the Instituto Nacional de Antropología e Historia in Hermosillo graciously provided institutional affiliation in Mexico.

John Kohl printed the photographs. Charles Sternberg drafted the charts and graphs. To both John and Charles, I offer my heartfelt appreciation.

Finally, I thank my wife, Chris Szuter, for her humor, patience, and support. She lived through the best times and the worst times and knows better than anyone else what this book means to me.

Introduction

THE CORPORATE CONTROL OF SCARCE RESOURCES IN PEASANT SOCIETIES

According to legend, the name Cucurpe means "where the dove calls" in the language of the Opata Indians. If you get up early enough on a summer morning, before the desert sun blazes and the tractors and diesel pumps break the ancient riparian spell, you realize that the name is not just some forgotten Indian's poetic flight of fancy. As you walk through the mesquite and saguaro along the mesas bordering the Río San Miguel, the sound of the floodplain begins to seep into you: a soft, constant murmur of doves. You hear them in the cottonwoods and willows. You see them flying across the patchwork fields. White-wings, mourning doves—their riverine plainsong is older than the Opatas, older than the Spaniards, far older than the farmers and their families lighting woodstoves and drinking their strong black coffee below. More than three hundred years ago, when the Jesuits first established a mission in Cucurpe, the floodplain must have sounded much the same. And if the *Cucurpeños* (inhabitants of Cucurpe) ever leave, the doves will remain, nesting in remnant fencerows, calling from the mesquite *bosques* (forests) as the trees reclaim the abandoned fields.

This is not a study of doves, however, but of the people who hear them and take them for granted as they try to make a living from a harsh land. To those of us who have grown up in the cities of modern Mexico or the United States, a place like Cucurpe seems idyllic, offering us a vision of a distant agrarian past. But if we bother to go beyond that vision, we see that life in Cucurpe is predicated on struggle, not pastoral harmony: struggle to raise crops when the rains won't come or when the floods wash away the topsoil; struggle to keep cattle from turning into emaciated ghosts; struggle to prevent neighbors from diverting your irrigation water or fencing your pasture or stealing your land. The struggle is rarely violent. It is interspersed with laugh-

The pueblo of Cucurpe, looking southwest across the floodplain of the Río San Miguel.

ter, kindness, and cooperation. But the impressions of rural tranquility fostered by romantics from Rousseau to Redfield break down into a series of harder, sharper images: a farmer slumped in his chair after finding out the government wells have failed; an angry quarrel over irrigation water on a bone-dry April afternoon; a hot, bitter meeting to decide whether to take away the land of a woman whose father fled Bolshevik Russia so his daughter could battle *bolshevikis* of her own.

This book, then, is an attempt to record the patterns of that struggle—a struggle for and with the land. It is also an exploration of the reasons why certain participants in the contest, especially the less powerful ones, join together to hold certain resources like grazing land and irrigation water in common. What I have tried to do is to write an ethnography of resource control, to describe how people battle aridity and one another in order to survive in an agrarian society characterized by economic inequality and political conflict. Borrowing a phrase from Eric Wolf (1982), I call this study a "political ecology" because I have endeavored to wed the approaches of political economy, which focus upon a society's place in a region, nation, or "world system," with those of cultural ecology, which examine adaptations to local environmental and demographic factors. To understand peasant societies, I think you need to investigate both sets of linkages. The ecology of any human community is political in the sense that it is shaped and constrained by other human groups. The exploitation, distribution, and control of natural resources is always mediated by differential relationships of power within and among societies. At the same time, however, the resources being exploited impose certain constraints as well—constraints that modify the political force fields emanating from outside the community in question. Peasant societies are neither isolated "little communities" nor helpless pawns in an international power struggle. On the contrary, they are constantly engaged in a creative dialectic between both local and external forces.

That dialectic is the underlying theme of this book. I chose to explore it in the *municipio* (roughly analogous to a U.S. county) of Cucurpe, Sonora, in northwestern Mexico, for two reasons. First, Cucurpe is a region where peasant farmers and stockmen continue to exist despite the expansion of large-scale private ranching. Second, Cucurpe has a history of long-standing conflict between peasants and private ranchers, conflict exacerbated in recent years by the federal reconfirmation of two traditional peasant land-holding associations (the *comunidades* of Cucurpe and San Javier) and by the creation of an entirely new organization (the *Ejido* 6 de Enero) in 1976. The municipio, therefore, offers an excellent opportunity to analyze the peasant corporate control of scarce resources in an arena where those resources are a bitterly contested prize.

Cucurpe also demonstrates that peasant corporations—or corporate communities, if you will—are not merely historical curiosities or marginal survivals from a pre-capitalist past. Such organizations once dominated the countrysides of much of Europe, Latin America, and Asia, prior to the commercialization of agriculture in the sixteenth, seventeenth, and eighteenth centuries. As late as the 1890s, village communes controlled over ninety percent of peasant land in Great Russia. Even today, traditional peasant corporations continue to exist in areas of highland Mesoamerica, Andean South America, Alpine Europe, and Spain.[1] More importantly, these organizations have provided the pattern for the modern Mexican *ejido*, an institution that plays a critical role in the rural sector of that nation.

Despite their historical importance, however, peasant corporations such as the Russian *mir*, the Spanish *común de vecinos*, and the Latin American *comunidad*, among others, rarely receive the historiographic or ethnological attention they deserve (Menegus Bornemann 1980). Detailed case studies are few, theoretical syntheses even fewer. Within the anthropological literature, in fact, the most widely known formulation regarding these institutions remains Eric Wolf's concept of the closed corporate community, which Wolf (1955, 1957) elucidated in several influential articles published in the 1950s.

As his retrospective on the corporate community makes clear, Wolf (1986) was primarily interested in analyzing the structural relationships between different types of peasant communities and the larger societies in which they were embedded. In Mesoamerica and central Java, for example, he called the corporate community a "child of conquest" created by the subjugation of indigenous populations by the Spaniards and the Dutch (Wolf 1957). He believed that peasants developed corporate communities as defensive responses to external conquest or domination by internal elites, exercising jurisdiction over important natural resources and restricting access to those resources to members born into the communities themselves. By communally controlling land, by redistributing potential forms of wealth, and by severely limiting immigration, corporate communities attempted to keep external political and economic forces at bay while at the same time reducing conflict within their own boundaries, thereby maintaining a precarious balance between themselves and the outside world.[2]

Wolf's model represented a major advance in anthropological peasant studies. In an era when Robert Redfield's notions about the "little community" still held sway in many circles, Wolf demonstrated that peasants do not live in a "traditional," ahistorical vacuum. On the contrary, they are part of much larger social systems, responding to powerful political and economic currents that shape their institutions, their ideologies, and their daily lives. In a very real sense, Wolf anticipated Wallerstein's impact upon anthropology by nearly two decades.

Nevertheless, Wolf's concept of the corporate community suffers from a number of limitations that need to be recognized if the peasant corporate control of scarce resources is to receive the attention it deserves. First of all, his model is overly centrist, focusing attention upon the linkages between peasants and elites while ignoring local ecological and demographic factors that may influence peasant society in a more immediate fashion. In this regard, it suffers from many of the same problems that plague world-systems analysis when it is uncritically applied to local societies (Nash 1981). Secondly, as Wolf (1986) himself admits, his formulation is far too schematic, making a number of assumptions about the nature of closure, corporateness, and community that often do not correspond to the empirical realities of peasant life. Dow (1973) argues that Wolf merges juridical and sociostructural definitions of corporateness in muddled and misleading ways. As Greenberg (1981:5) points out:

Properly, corporateness in a jural sense and closure in a sociostructural sense should be treated as independent variables. The apparent fusion of these definitions in Wolf's typology seems to be responsible for some misunderstanding and confusion over what constitutes a closed corporate community.

Finally, and most importantly, Wolf never really pays much attention to the economic foundation of corporate communities: the corporate control of scarce resources themselves. His contention that corporate communities are primarily defensive responses to encroachment is an important insight, but it also begs a number of questions about the nature and functions of corporate tenure. Peasants have been subordinated and exploited by elites throughout history, but not all peasant societies retaining control of their own land and labor have developed corporate organizations or communal tenure. It becomes necessary, therefore, to ask whether defense against outside forces is a necessary and sufficient explanation for the existence of corporate communities, or whether other more localized variables influence these institutions as well.

Perhaps the most detailed investigation of the ecological basis of corporate tenure is Robert Netting's work on the peasant community of Törbel in the Swiss alps (1976, 1981). Taking issue with Wolf, Netting (1976:137) argues that the long-standing local autonomy of Törbel "suggests that corporate features may be less oriented to resisting external domination and more closely related to environmental conditions and subsistence requirements." In other words, adaptation to local environments may determine the configurations of peasant economies more directly than the actions of external elites.

Netting's conclusions about land tenure in Törbel deserve close attention because, in effect, they constitute a hypothesis about the corporate control of scarce resources that can be tested across the world. According to Netting, the agropastoralist economy of Törbel was shaped by a number of environmental factors, particularly altitudinal zonation. Each individual household in Törbel needed access to resources ranging from grain fields and meadows occurring at elevations of 900–1950 meters (m) to forest and alp summer grazing lands at altitudes of 1950–2400 m. What Netting found was that the types of land which could be effectively utilized in small, fixed amounts and whose use could be intensified were privately owned. Types of land where the frequency and dependability of exploitation were low, and which were difficult to intensify and improve, on the other hand, were held by the corporate community itself. As a result, communal tenure prevailed on higher-altitude forest, wasteland, and alp, while individual tenure characterized lower-altitude pastures, gardens, grain fields, and vineyards. In a mixed economy of agriculture and stock raising such as Törbel's, households had to possess both private fields and rights to corporate forest and pasture in order to survive.

Guillet (1981) discovered similar patterns in a sample of rural communities in the central Andes. There, communal control with indivisible use rights was restricted to high-altitude grazing lands. Irrigated, intensively cultivated farmland, in contrast, was privately owned. Even when corporate communities legally held arable land in common, this land was usually divided among individual households who held firm usufruct rights to the fields they cultivated. Based upon ethnographic information from Alpine Europe and Andean South America, then, it seems that corporate tenure does indeed develop in response to certain definite ecological constraints, in particular, the need for access to resources that are not evenly distributed, whose dependability and frequency of use are low, and which cannot be intensively exploited by individual households. Such ecological variables are, of course, influenced and mediated by political, economic, demographic, and technological factors. Nevertheless, the resources themselves impose limitations upon the ways they can be utilized, distributed, and controlled.[3]

This brief discussion of agrarian ecology brings us to the second point we must consider, which is the nature of "community" itself. The corporate communities Wolf discusses are not just networks of people who hold certain resources in common. On the contrary, they are all-encompassing social systems that regulate most aspects of their members' lives, including the disposition of property and the accumulation of wealth. As such they constitute fundamental units of resource control.

Such a notion of "community" has a long tradition in Western thought, harkening back to Tönnies' *Gemeinshaft* and Durkheim's mechanical solidarity. As many social scientists have pointed out, however, this concept of community embodies a number of assumptions about human interaction that may not correspond to empirical reality. Pahl (1968:293), for example, argues:

> Whether we call the process acting upon the local community "urbanization," "differentiation," "modernization," "mass society," or whatever, it is clear that it is not so much communities that are acted upon as groups and individuals at particular places in the social structure. Any attempt to tie patterns of social relationships to specific geographical milieux is a singularly fruitless exercise.[4]

Such caveats force us to ask ourselves whether "communities" are the best place to begin an investigation of peasant resource control. Wolf implies that such is the case, but historical and anthropological research carried out since his articles appeared suggest that corporate communities may be little more than legal constructs whose functions vary considerably through space and time. Gibson's (1964) pioneering analysis of Aztec society in the Valley of Mexico supports Wolf in many respects, demonstrating how the Spanish policy of *congregación* created Indian corporate communities during the early colonial period.[5] Nevertheless, Gibson also provides examples of how individual Indian leaders exploited community structures to their own advantage. Taylor (1972) goes even further, arguing that private ownership of land in Oaxacan Indian communities was far more pervasive than Wolf's model suggests. According to Taylor (1972:75):

> An individual Indian in colonial Oaxaca had much more freedom in disposing his lands than the modern ejido tenure allows. Wills from the sixteenth and early seventeenth centuries reveal that *macehuales* and *principales* distributed land at their personal discretion, implying at least an incipient form of private ownership. As well as to members of the nuclear family, lands were willed to cousins, uncles, nephews, in-laws, servants, the Church, and even non-relatives living outside the community.

Taylor's analysis indicates that Indian land tenure in colonial Mesoamerica was considerably more complicated than any single, unitary notion of "community" could encompass, a point Wolf himself (1986) concedes. Wolf also recognizes that his model often obscures stratification and conflict within corporate communities themselves. Corporate communities are not necessarily egalitarian institutions.[6] Considerable levels of inequality may exist and even be increased within corporate structures. More to the point, important resources may be controlled by other social groups within or outside of the "community" itself. Consequently, it is necessary to search for more basic units of resource control in any given peasant society. Then and only then is it possible to understand the competition for land and water that occurs among peasants as well as between peasants and elites.

A growing number of researchers are arguing that just such an entity is the peasant household. Netting (1981:202) states that, "The basic social unit for production, control of agricultural resources, and consumption in peasant Törbel was the household." Orlove and Custred (1980:33) come to similar conclusions for Andean South America, claiming that "the household is the basic unit of economic activity. Although many goods are individually owned, and rights to land and irrigation water are frequently based on membership in larger corporate groups, the household is the locus of decision-making with regard to production, exchange, and consumption. Its component members engage in economic activities as part of the overall budgeting and allocation of household resources to meet the needs and goals of the household."

Orlove and Custred, in fact, propose an "alternative model" of Andean social organization that views the household, not the community or the hacienda, as the "fundamental element of peasant society" (1980:33). They contend that households are the basic building blocks that make up other, secondary institutions such as corporate communities. And even though communities may perform vital political and economic functions, the households composing them remain "autonomous economic decision-making units" competing as well as cooperating with each other for resources within the boundaries of the communities themselves (Orlove and Custred 1980:48).

A research strategy starting with households rather than communities eliminates many of the problematical assumptions of Wolf's model. First of all, it allows for a much more flexible and fine-grained analysis of peasant resource control; rather than positing a sociostructural corporateness that may or may not be present, it forces us to search for the reasons—ecological, economic, and political—why groups of peasants exercise corporate tenure over certain basic resources in the first place. Such an approach allows us to see the great diversity in community structure and function—and the limitations on community power—that Wolf's formulation tends to obscure.

Secondly, it helps to reveal the economic inequality and political conflict that may be masked by corporate structures and the corporate ideologies they engender. The importance of class differences between peasants and elites has long been recognized, but too little attention has been paid to the class structure of peasant society itself. Nonetheless, not all peasants share the same relations to the productive forces, even within bounded corporate communities. As Mintz (1973) points out, peasant society is not communistic or egalitarian; peasants are among the exploiters as well as the exploited.

Thirdly, and most importantly, it disentangles corporate tenure from specific social and cultural manifestations of "corporateness" that occur in certain parts of the peasant world. In the years that have followed Wolf's presentation of his model, far more attention has been focused upon Mesoamerican fiesta cargo systems than upon communal land tenure or water control.[7] But peasants have held land and water in common without developing civil-religious hierarchies or even closing their societies to outsiders. Consequently, we need to determine what is the more fundamental phenomenon—the corporate control of scarce resources, or the ideological expressions of social cohesion that may or may not exist in any given corporate community itself.

The following analysis, therefore, considers the household to be the basic unit of production, consumption, and resource control in the municipio of Cucurpe. I begin by examining the ecological and economic constraints which scarce and necessary resources, particularly arable land, grazing land, and irrigation water, place upon households in Cucurpe. I then investigate why many such households have formed corporate communities to insure their access to resources they cannot control on their own. In the process, I seek to identify the class differences that exist within the corporate communities as well as between members of those organizations and the private ranchers who surround them. "Class" in this case is defined in the Marxist sense as those members of a given society who share the same relation to the productive forces such as land, capital, and labor. Class differences are usually reflected in different levels of economic status, but wealth in and of itself is not necessarily a determinant of class.[8]

The reader will note that I have also chosen to retain the term "corporate community" even though I am employing it more narrowly than Wolf and others do. By "corporate community," I mean an organization of peasant households that controls certain basic natural resources, and that preserves its corporate identity through time. In Mexico, there are two major types of federally chartered corporate communities—*comunidades* and *ejidos*. Far fewer in number, comunidades are organizations whose existence predates the Mexican Revolution and the Constitution of 1917. Ejidos, on the other hand, may be entirely new peasant corporations. Nonetheless, both comunidades and ejidos exercise corporate tenure over resources such as land, water, firewood, and wild plants within their borders. (For a more extended discussion of the similarities and differences between the two types of organizations, *see* chapters 8 and 9.)

Such a definition precludes many of the assumptions about corporateness and closure that Wolf makes. It also applies to organizations that may not be isomorphic with actual geographic communities. In some places, such as the Swiss village of Törbel, nearly all permanent inhabitants belonged to the peasant corporation. In other areas, the corporation encompassed only a segment of the local population (Lewis 1951; Keatinge 1973; Brandes 1975). My use of the term presupposes that such groups are first and foremost communities of interest rather than communities of place. In other words, their basic characteristic is the corporate control of certain resources, not the degree of social solidarity or geographic proximity they may or may not possess.

Viewing the corporate community as an organization of households rather than as an all-embracing "little community" in the Redfieldian sense of the term is more than an academic exercise in typology. As Wolf and others have pointed out, external elites often try to impose corporate structures upon subordinate populations in order to control and exploit them more effectively. One such example was the policy of *congregación* in New Spain, which amalgamated Indian groups decimated by Old World diseases into nucleated settlements with their own political authorities, liturgical organizations, and juridical identities (Gibson 1964; Wolf 1986). Another was Julius Nyerere's program of *ujamaa* in Tanzania, which endeavored to create communal production villages by extending the cooperative principles of *ujima* found in peasant households to the level of the rural community itself (Hyden 1980). Socialist and Marxist intellectuals and government officials, in particular, often view communal organization as a major goal of agrarian policy. As a result, they frequently confound the limited forms of corporate tenure among peasants with true collectivism, engendering confusion and resistance in the process.

What both Marxist and non-Marxist social scientists need to understand, however, is that the "peasant mode of production," as Hyden (1980) and others call it, represents an enduring adaptation to certain ecological, economic, and political constraints. That mode takes different forms in different historical and environmental circumstances, but it is characterized above all by the existence of the peasant household as the fundamental unit of both production and consumption. Such households may, out of coercion as well as choice, join together to form larger organizations like corporate communities. Nonetheless, they always strive to maintain their autonomy within such institutions. Consequently, any attempts to weaken or destroy that autonomy are met with opposition ranging from passive resistance to physical violence, as the following study of one such peasant society in northwestern Mexico reveals.

WHERE THE DOVE CALLS

No quiere llover, pero ni modo. Así es la cosa.
No quiere llover y no vale llorar.

It doesn't want to rain, but that's all right. That's the way it is.
It doesn't want to rain and its not worth crying about.

Cucurpe farmer

1. *Donde Canta La Paloma*

CUCURPE IN HISTORICAL PERSPECTIVE

We reach an oak-studded basin called Agua en Medio after dark, the heavy clouds of a winter storm settling around us like an animal bedding down for the night. As soon as we pull up, the ejidatarios materialize out of their ocotillo jacales and climb into the back of my pickup. At least half of them are younger than twenty, hardly more than boys. Their faces are the faces of modern Mexico—young, poor, and unemployed. I ask if they were frightened during the brief gunbattle. "No hay miedo en la defensa de la libertad" *(There's no fear in the defense of liberty), one replied without a trace of irony in his voice.*

The municipal síndico (investigator), his deputy, and I crawl back into the cab of the pickup and drive the ejidatarios out to a "y" in the road where the incident occurred. The day before, twenty-six members of Ejido 6 de Enero caught up with a party of eight men who were cutting their fences. The leaders of the fencecutters were two ranchers who had lost land to the ejido when it was created in 1976.[1] *They were accompanied by four of their cowboys, a lawyer, and a heavy-set man who claimed to be a state policeman. When the ejidatarios tried to stop them, the policeman pulled his pistol and opened fire, shooting out the windshield of a truck. He also put a bullet through the hat of one of the ejidatarios. The ejidatarios disarmed him anyway, capturing one of the ranchers and two of the cowboys in the process.*

By the time we return, a cold winter rain has begun to fall, so we crowd inside a hut made of cartón *(corrugated cardboard) where a fire is burning. There we drink coffee the color of oil and eat tortillas, potatoes, and a thin stew ladled from a pot resting on the dirt floor. People drift in and out, their faces illuminated for a moment by the firelight before they slip back into the darkness. Time and again we hear the story of the capture, especially the part about how quickly the bravado of the policeman dissolved into abject fear. One old man laughs and says the policeman was scared to death because he didn't know whether the ejidatarios were going "to kill him or to fuck him." "I'm nothing," he kept repeating as he cried and begged for mercy. "I have a family. I have*

1

The president of Ejido 6 de Enero and the municipal síndico investigating the cutting of the ejido's fences by private ranchers.

children." The ejidatarios replied that they had children, too, which was why they were defending their land.

Earlier that day, the rancher and the policeman had been turned over to the authorities unharmed. The two cowboys, on the other hand, remain prisoners of the ejidatarios, who gather now to decide what to do with them. Most of the men are drinking lechuguilla, the local bootleg mescal, and the excited crowd mutters about the "pinche ricos" (fucking rich men) who refuse to leave them in peace. But their anger does not extend to the cowboys waiting in another hut. As the discussion progresses, most of the ejidatarios agree with one of their spokesmen, who concludes that the cowboys "are not guilty. They're workers, nothing more. They had to follow the orders of their bosses or lose their jobs."

Finally, after a consensus is reached, the cowboys are brought before the informal tribunal. The ejidatarios ask them to sign an acuerdo (resolution) in which they admit their guilt and implicate the ranchers. One of the cowboys is a short, cocky little fellow whose every third word is pinche. The other is taller, thinner, and more reserved. The acuerdo is read to them and both scrawl their names on the paper. The ejidatarios then formally pardon them of their crimes.

Later that night, as we are driving back to Cucurpe in the rain, I ask the síndico what will happen to the two ranchers. "Well, nothing," he answers. "Here in Mexico, money is what runs things. Money is what moves the *world"* (Pues, nada. Aquí in México, el dinero es lo que manda. El dinero es lo que mueve el mundo). *I then ask how the conflict over land will be resolved. He replies that it never will be.* "Este problema sigue toda la vida" *(This problem lasts your whole life)*.

Throughout Mexico's history, one basic theme emerges like a long and bloody thread: the struggle for land. Silver mining may have fueled her economy during the colonial period (MacLachlan and Rodríguez 1980); urban problems and oil prices dominate the nation today. But the peasants who raised their scythes in response to Hidalgo's *Grito de Dolores* or followed Emiliano Zapata into Mexico City were motivated by a hunger for land, not precious metals. Mineral wealth flowed out of Mexico to support the imperial ambitions of Madrid, London, or New York. Agriculture and stock raising sustained Mexico itself. In 1980, after decades of rapid industrialization, 35 percent of Mexico's work force continued to labor in the agrarian sector. What happens in the countryside, then, will affect the destiny of the Mexican republic for a long time to come.

A key element in that countryside is the widespread existence of peasant corporate communities. As chapter 8 points out, there were more than 21,000 ejidos and 1,200 comunidades in Mexico in 1970. Since then, the number has undoubtedly increased. Peasant organizations like the comunidades of Cucurpe and San Javier and the Ejido 6 de Enero play an enormous role in Mexican rural society, protecting millions of small farmers and stockmen who otherwise would be driven off the land. These organizations, therefore, draw the wrath of private landowners, who argue that their corporate resources would be more efficiently exploited in private hands.

The conflict between corporate and private tenure is not a new one. On the contrary, it has disrupted Mexican rural life since the Conquest, if not before (Gibson 1964). It has also attracted considerable attention from social scientists, who have investigated the rise and fall of haciendas during the colonial period (Chevalier 1963; Gunder Frank 1969; Florescano 1971), and explored the intricacies of Mexican peasant life today (Cline 1952; Schwartz 1978; Chambers and Young 1979; Hewitt de Alcántara 1984). Until recently, however, historians and anthropologists have paid little attention to the struggle for land in the Mexican northwest, including Sonora. Nonetheless, the struggle there has been just as acute, and just as encompassing, as in other areas of Mexico. In 1975, for example, Sonora attracted international attention when state police and federal soldiers opened fire on a group of campesinos at San Ignacio, Río Muerto, in the Yaqui valley (Sanderson 1981; McGuire 1986). At least six campesinos were killed. Their deaths made everyone aware that Sonora—booming, bustling, entrepreneurial Sonora—still had peasants who were willing to challenge both landowners and the government for a piece of ground.

In Cucurpe, fortunately, no one has died yet, but the possibility for violence exists and has existed for a long time. Ever since the colonial period, each generation has fought its own variation of the same battle, a battle that pits peasants against private ranchers. A brief synopsis of Cucurpe history is therefore necessary to trace the origin and development of the conflict wracking the municipio today. And since the historical record on Cucurpe is often mute, we must occasionally turn to the history of Sonora as a whole in order to infer what may have happened in Cucurpe itself at certain times in the past.[2]

Perhaps the most significant fact about Cucurpe is its long-standing marginality, a marginality it has shared for much of its history with the rest of Sonora. As Voss (1982) points out, Sonora, until the late nineteenth century, was the periphery of a periphery, an arena where the full weight of colonial exploitation and capitalist penetration did not fall. Another important fact is Cucurpe's proximity first to New Spain and then to Mexico's northern frontier. Until the nineteenth century, great landed estates developed only sporadically in northern Sonora, their entrenchment impeded by chronic Indian hostilities. A few large ranches were carved out along the frontier, but other areas were either periodically depopulated by Seri and Apache Indian raids, or they remained in control of Indian communities buffered by the Jesuit and Franciscan mission systems. As a result, the huge haciendas of central and north-central Mexico did not take root in Sonora until relatively late in its history. Communities like Cucurpe, on the other hand, managed to retain corporate control over their land and water through Mexican independence, the chronic civil wars of the nineteenth century, the oppressive modernization of the *Porfiriato*, and the bloody chaos of the Revolution itself.

Sonora's history differed in many respects from that of central Mexico from the beginning of the colonial period. After the fall of the Aztec Empire in 1521, for example, conquistadores like Hernán Cortéz and Pedro de Alvarado swept across the rest of Mesoamerica in the relatively short span of several decades. Most of the Indians they subjugated were already organized into states and chiefdoms that had long paid tribute to more powerful neighbors. Consequently, it was a relatively easy task for the Spaniards to replace Native American elites with European ones. In some cases, the conquerors relied on the same tribute rolls that the Aztecs had compiled. Spanish conquest was also

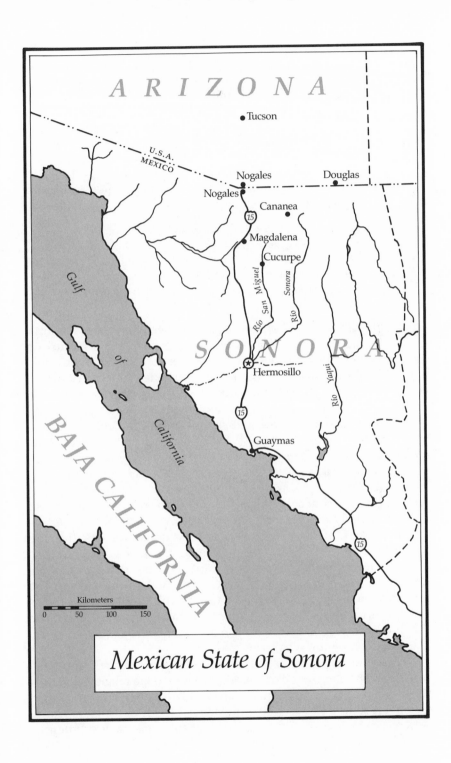

ARIZONA

• Tucson

U.S.A.
MEXICO

Nogales   Douglas
•   •
Nogales •
        Cananea
        •
(15) Magdalena
     •
        Cucurpe
        •

Gulf

of

California

BAJA CALIFORNIA

Río San Miguel

Río Sonora

SONORA

Río Yaqui

(☆)
Hermosillo

(15)

Guaymas
•

(15)

Kilometers
0   50   100   150

Mexican State of Sonora

facilitated by epidemics of Old World diseases such as smallpox, measles, and influenza that ravaged Indian populations throughout the Americas (Dobyns 1966; Crosby 1972).

One of the most ruthless of these *adelantados* was Nuño de Guzmán, a rival of Cortéz who became the second governor of Nueva Galicia, the colonial province encompassing western Mexico. Under his command, the Spaniards slashed their way to the Pacific, devastating the small chiefdoms of coastal Jalisco, Nayarit, and southern Sinaloa in their wake. Historical geographer Carl Sauer (1932:7) writes:

> By a single entrada, in 1530–31, Nuño de Guzmán ruined the native scene. The conquest was cheaply won. Mostly he met no resistance. Often he was received with open arms. Behind he left a trail of smoking ruins and shambles. Survivors were driven out in gangs and sold as slaves; in a few years the lowlands of Sinaloa and Nayarit became almost a wilderness.

In 1531, Guzmán had plundered and pillaged his way as far north as central Sinaloa, where he established the villa of San Miguel de Culiacán. There his rapacity stalled, however, and Culiacán remained the northwesternmost outpost of Spanish society for the next fifty years. In the deserts and river valleys to the north, the Spaniards encountered a different type of Indian society—Cáhita-speaking groups who successfully resisted conquest until the end of the sixteenth century (Spicer 1962, 1980; Hu-DeHart 1981). Ancestors of the modern Yaquis and Mayos, the Cáhita peoples were floodplain farmers, but they lived in small, scattered rancherías rather than in nucleated settlements. They also were among the most effective warriors in arid North America, and the Spaniards who followed Guzmán to Culiacán simply did not have the manpower to break them to the Spanish yoke (Sheridan 1981). During subsequent decades, the only Spaniards venturing north of the outpost were explorers like Francisco Vásquez de Coronado or Francisco Ibarra, restless men chasing their chimeras of wealth and glory as far north as modern-day Kansas. The tiny settlements they left behind—Coronado's San Jerónimo de los Corazones in central Sonora, Ibarra's San Juan Bautista de Carapoa on the Río Sinaloa—survived a season and then were destroyed by Indian attacks (Bannon 1974).

The quest for souls, not slaves or gold, impelled the first permanent Spanish colonization of Sonora. As heirs to the religious fervor of the Reconquista, the Spanish monarchs believed that it was their duty to convert as well as to conquer the native groups of the New World. As a result, the mission became one of the fundamental institutions of colonization on the northern frontier. Gray-robed Franciscan friars accompanied miners and soldiers into the silver-mining regions of Zacatecas, Guanajuato, San Luis Potosí, and southern Chihuahua. The black-robed Society of Jesus, on the other hand, received permission to proselytize northwestern New Spain. By 1591, the Jesuits had established a base of operations in Culiacán. From there they launched the missionization and colonization of Sonora itself (Dunne 1940; Bannon 1955).

These early Jesuits did their best to adapt Roman Catholicism to the cultures of the Indians they encountered. They learned and preached in the native languages. They incorporated aboriginal music and dance into Christian rituals. Perhaps more importantly, they served as extension agents for European agrarian technology, introducing a wide variety of plants and animals that revolutionized Indian life in northwestern New Spain. According to Sheridan and Nabhan (1978:6):

> Along with their pantheon of saints and strange Christian doctrines, the missionaries brought material benefits which the Indians could see, touch, and eat. Old World grain, pulses, and vegetables allowed them to cultivate their fields during the cooler months when New World crops would have failed. Domestic livestock, especially cattle and goats, gave them a reliable source of animal protein and expanded their exploitation of the uplands, where these animals grazed. Metal plows and draft horses, burros and oxen made possible regular tillage of the soil and increased productivity per acre.

It is extremely important to emphasize that missionaries rather than Spanish colonists pioneered the initial settlement of Sonora. Along other stretches of the northern frontier, such as New Mexico or Chihuahua, soldiers, ranchers, and miners dominated the conquest and colonization of the Indians. Settlers there were often awarded land grants, called *mercedes*, or grants of *encomienda*, which gave the *encomendero* the right to extract labor or tribute from Indians living in a certain area. By the time the miners and ranchers entered Sonora, however, much of the land and Indian labor was controlled by the Society of Jesus (Spicer 1962; Hu-DeHart 1981; Voss 1982; Deeds 1985). As a result, the encomienda system never became widespread, and a secular mine-ranch complex, characteristic of mining districts in Nueva Vizcaya (West 1949), did not develop except in a few important mining communities like Alamos, San Juan Bautista, and the Bacanuche valley. The Jesuit presence, therefore, prevented the evolution of large private estates in many areas of Sonora, including Cucurpe, during much of the seventeenth and early eighteenth centuries.

Unfortunately, the precise dynamics of land tenure within the Jesuit mission system have never been adequately explored. In some cases, the Jesuits ran enormously productive haciendas, often under a variety of legal guises (Polzer 1972a). Mission lands, on the other hand, belonged to the Indian communities themselves. The Jesuits held no royal title to those domains even though they often exercised considerable control over both the Indians and their fields. The absence of Jesuit ownership makes sense when we realize that missions were designed to be transitional institutions, transformed into parishes run by secular clergy once the Indians had been converted and Hispanicized. Although such a progression rarely took place in northwestern Mexico, the idea remained an important part of the Spanish philosophy of conquest.

The Jesuits jealously guarded their missions nonetheless. As Spicer (1962) points out, the missionaries wanted to create self-sufficient Indian communities isolated from secular Spanish settlements, a goal of the regular orders from the beginning of the conquest of Mexico (Lafaye 1976). The Jesuits believed, with reason, that if Spaniards or *castas* (individuals of mixed race) were allowed to settle among the Indians, the Native Americans would be exploited, corrupted, and destroyed. And since royal stipends were not sufficient to cover mission expenses, the Jesuits—out of necessity as well as inclination—attempted to turn the missions into economic units that stockpiled supplies for emergencies and provided surpluses for the expansion of the mission system into territory beyond the Spanish pale.

To support such endeavors, a portion of each mission's arable land was set aside to be worked communally under the direction of the missionary. The rest of the fields were apportioned among individual Indian households, who held them in usufruct for as long as they worked them. Adult males were required to devote three days a week to the mission lands or livestock herds and three days to their own fields and animals. In return, the Indians usually received rations rather than wages, a point of controversy between the Jesuits and their enemies throughout the colonial period (Ortega Noriega 1985).

Such a well-defined system of land tenure and communal labor, of course, represented the ideal and not necessarily the reality of mission life on the northwestern frontier. Detailed case studies undoubtedly will reveal more complex patterns of ownership and resource control within individual missions themselves. Nevertheless, preliminary evidence suggests that the corporate control of Indian land and water was recognized and reinforced by both the Jesuits and their Franciscan successors (Polzer 1976; Radding de Murrieta 1977, 1979; Deeds 1981).

That control did not go unchallenged, however. During the seventeenth century, the rise of colonial mining centers like San Juan Bautista, Ostimuri, and Alamos attracted a growing number of Spanish settlers. At the same time, a series of Indian rebellions among the Pueblo, Suma, Tarahumara, and Northern Pima Indians resulted in the creation of a number of new *presidios*, or military garrisons, along New Spain's northwestern frontier (Naylor and Polzer 1986). The militarization of that frontier progressed even further as Spanish officials attempted to grapple with the increasing hostility of the Western, Chiricahua, and Mescalero Apaches, who began raiding both Spanish and Indian settlements in Sonora and Nueva Vizcaya in the late 1600s. The development of presidios and mining communities created nuclei around which congregated stockmen, farmers, and traders. Moreover, these secular Spanish settlements weaned many Indians away from the missions themselves (Hu-DeHart 1981; Voss 1982). As a result, Jesuit hegemony over Indian land and labor in the northwest was weakened, and a counterbalance to the Jesuit mission system arose.

What followed was rising tension between Jesuits and Spanish settlers. The dichotomy was not a simple one, because many Spaniards continued to support the missionaries. Prominent *Sonorenses* like Juan Mateo Manje and Juan Bautista de Anza (the Elder), for example, joined forces with the Jesuits to protest the corruption of Gregorio Alvarez Tuñón y Quirós, captain of Fronteras presidio.[3] More to the point, important colonial officials like Brigadier Pedro de Rivera, the presidial inspector who removed Tuñón y Quirós from office, continued to view the Jesuit mission system as a vital part of northwestern New Spain's defensive alignment. To soldiers like Anza and Rivera, the missions kept the pacified Indians under control and provided the presidios with necessary supplies (Voss 1982). Nonetheless, profound economic and political conflicts between the missionaries and the colonists were already manifesting themselves as Sonora moved toward the mid-eighteenth century.

Those conflicts deepened as Jesuit energy and imagination flagged. In the words of Voss (1982:12):

> With the passing of years, a growing pessimism among the missionaries had begun to take hold beneath the surface as expectations were not met and discipline was increased to compensate for it. The visible, marked decline in the mission population between the 1670s and the 1720s was indication enough that all was not nearly as well as it should have been. And the decline was not arrested thereafter in most districts. Disease was the major culprit, but many neophytes simply drifted away. This man-

ifestation of a general problem of the Indians straying from the straight and narrow path was attributed by the padres to the neophytes' ignorance, laziness, and irresponsibility. Nevertheless, the real snake in their Garden of Eden was the settlers, who, with increasing success, tempted the Indians with the material goods of European culture in exchange for their labor.

The Indians, it must be emphasized, played an active role in this process. If the missionaries and settlers viewed them as pawns in a power struggle, the Indians themselves manipulated Spanish political and legal systems to achieve their own ends. To avoid taxation and preserve their corporate lands, for example, they resisted the secularization of the missions (Spicer 1980; Hu-DeHart 1981, 1984; Voss 1982). To escape missionary paternalism, on the other hand, they complained about individual priests and frequently migrated to non-mission settlements to work for wages as miners, cowboys, farm laborers, or pearl divers. And when all else failed, they took refuge in the deserts and mountains, rebelling against both the missionaries and the settlers. Beginning with the Yaqui revolt of 1740, in fact, many Indians in Sonora adopted a pattern of guerrilla warfare that devastated the province for the next thirty years (Nentvig 1971; Sheridan 1979; Rowland 1930).

The result, not surprisingly, was a growing demand for bureaucratic and military solutions to Sonora's problems. Such solutions culminated in what historians label the Bourbon reforms of the late eighteenth century, but the impetus for those reforms began much earlier—in the increasing dissatisfaction over Jesuit control of Indian land and labor, in a series of inconclusive efforts at reform ranging from Rivera's realignment of the presidios in the 1720s to Rodríguez Gallardo's disastrous attempts to deport the Seri Indians in the 1740s (Sheridan 1979). As Indian populations declined under the impact of Old World diseases, and as Indian hostilities intensified as competition for Indian land and labor rose, Spanish officials began to question the importance of the Jesuit mission system. They began to challenge the special status of mission Indians as well. In 1767, the Jesuits were expelled from all Spanish dominions, including northwestern New Spain. Thereafter, the most enduring economic legacy of the Jesuits— the corporate control of Indian land and water—came under increasing attack.

The Spanish colonization of the modern municipio of Cucurpe did not deviate much from the general pattern discussed above. Even though the first Spaniard to settle in the San Miguel valley was a miner and military commander named Pedro de Perea, Perea concentrated most of his activities in the vicinity of Tuape to the south (Polzer 1972b). The Jesuits, on the other hand, founded successful missions at Cucurpe in 1647 and at Opodepe in 1649 (Almada 1983; Roca 1967). By the early 1650s, most of the Eudeve Indians living along the San Miguel river had been reduced to mission life.

At contact, the San Miguel was an ethnic frontier. The Eudeves, who spoke a language closely related to Opata, occupied the middle portions of the watershed from Opodepe to Cucurpe. Upper Pimas, known as Hímeris, lived along the Río Dolores, which joins the Río Saracachi to form the Río San Miguel just north of Cucurpe, while Lower Pimas inhabited the southern stretches of the San Miguel from Nacameri (modern Rayón) to the vicinity of modern Hermosillo. West of Nacameri, nomadic Seri-speaking groups occasionally camped along springs in arroyos that drained into the San Miguel, trading with and perhaps occasionally raiding the riverine settlements of the San Miguel and Sonora valleys.[4]

Interestingly enough, there is no recorded instance of San Miguel Eudeve armed resistance to the Spaniards. Other Opata groups initially opposed the missionaries and their soldier escorts (Decorme 1941), but the San Miguel Indians apparently welcomed the Jesuits into their midst. During much of the colonial period, in fact, the Eudeve missions remained the northwesternmost haven of Spanish control, serving as refuges and supply centers for the colonization of the Pimería Alta in the late seventeenth and early eighteenth centuries. Along with their Opata brethren to the east, the Eudeves constituted the backbone of the Sonoran mission system, winning reputations as "the best Christians and the most loyal vassals of Our Lord the King" among missionaries and Spanish officials alike (Nentvig 1971:114).

There are a number of possible reasons to explain Opata and Eudeve receptiveness to Spanish rule. Significantly, the first missionaries to enter the San Miguel valley described Eudeve communities as "pueblos." Upper Pimas north of Cucurpe, in contrast, were said to live in "rancherías," implying a more scattered, less permanent settlement pattern. If the Eudeves were in fact occupying relatively compact, organized villages at contact, they may well have been living a more sedentary existence with a greater dependence upon riverine agriculture than their Piman neighbors. Consequently, Spanish agrarian technology and Old World crops and livestock would have intensified rather than conflicted with an aboriginal tendency toward sedentism. Missionization and *reducción*—the policy of concentrating dispersed Indian groups into nucleated communities—may not have interfered with Eudeve settlement patterns and subsistence practices as much as it did among more mobile groups like the Hímeris, the Seris, or the Lower Pima groups (Sheridan and Nabhan 1978).

Whatever the situation at contact, missionization proceeded smoothly at Cucurpe, and by the end of the seventeenth century, Jesuits stationed there were regularly supporting other missions throughout northwestern New Spain. In 1689, for example, the mission of Cucurpe sent 1,000 head of cattle to Jesuits in the Tarahumara country.[5] Several years later, during the Upper Pima revolt of 1694–95, Cucurpe served as temporary headquarters for General Domingo Jironza Petrís de Cruzat as well as refuge for Padre Agustín de Campos, who fled there after his mission of San Ignacio was attacked and burned by Pima rebels (Naylor and Polzer 1986). Its proximity to the Pimería Alta, therefore, made Cucurpe a center of Jesuit activity, at least during the late seventeenth century.

Nevertheless, Cucurpe was not immune to the pressures of Spanish frontier society. In 1684, for example, the Indian governor of the community was ordered to send eight men to work twenty-day shifts in the mines of Bacanuche, located along a tributary of the Río Sonora to the northwest.[6] Such an order indicates that Cucurpe's mission Indians were occasionally being parcelled out to Sonoran miners under the *repartimiento* system, a labor draft that supplied Indians to Spanish mines and farms. Many of the Eudeves and Northern Pimans of the San Miguel undoubtedly labored in the mines around Tuape, discovered as early as the 1630s, as well as in the important mining *real* of Saracachi, situated upriver from Cucurpe itself. The presence of such settlements and the demands of the *repartimiento* system clearly demonstrate that Cucurpe never functioned as an isolated mission community. On the contrary, while its mission status afforded Cucurpe's Indians a measure of protection against Spanish encroachment, that protection was far from absolute.

Interestingly enough, pressure came not just from Spaniards but from other Indians as well. Consider, for example, the case of Cucurpe versus the infamous El Pintor. In 1723, Juan Bautista Quigue, the Indian governor of Cucurpe, presented Spanish authorities with a lengthy petition asking for redress against one Francisco Montés, alias El Pintor. El Pintor was a Pima Indian from Ures who had married a local woman and settled along the floodplain of the Río Dolores about one league north of Cucurpe. He was also something of a reprobate, accused of being an *hechicero* (sorcerer) and a mescal distiller who once had assaulted Jesuit missionary Luis Velarde in the Pimería Alta. Whatever his past, El Pintor proved to be a formidable adversary of the Cucurpeños, diverting their irrigation water onto his own fields and then disarming them with mescal whenever they called to complain. Finally, after seven years of watching their harvests shrivel, the Cucurpeños decided to protest. The resulting documents provide a glimpse into the local politics of land and water during the colonial era.[7]

In the original petition itself, Governor Quigue argued that the fields occupied by El Pintor "are ours by native right."[8] This claim was reiterated by a series of local inhabitants who testified that the land in question had always been cultivated by the *hijos del pueblo* (native inhabitants of the community). Through an interpreter, one eighty-year-old *indio natural* told the judge hearing the case that ever since he had reached the age of reason

> the lands that El Pintor possesses today have belonged to the pueblo, as well as those farther north (along the Río Dolores) up to the estancia known as the estancia of Padre Kino about four leagues north of this pueblo.[9]

In other words, the residents of Cucurpe had enjoyed jurisdiction over floodplain land extending from Cucurpe to the mission of Dolores for as long as any of the Cucurpeños could remember. Moreover, these same people were organized into a *común*—a community or association—that acted as a group whenever their control over the land was threatened. Unfortunately, the depositions do not reveal the exact nature of this body, even though the witnesses refer to it again and again. Nevertheless, the común of Cucurpe clearly exercised some form of corporate control over irrigated land lying along the San Miguel and its major tributary, the Río Dolores.

At the same time, however, several of the depositions noted that a small parcel (*un pedacito*) of the land claimed by El Pintor belonged to his wife, a local woman who had inherited the field from her parents. According to her brother, who also testified against El Pintor, the plot of ground had been cleared (*desmontó*) by their father, an activity which apparently gave the family ownership rights to it.[10] Therefore, it seems that corporate dominion was not absolute, coexisting with limited forms of private ownership or at least transgenerational usufruct rights.

The case against El Pintor also indicates the permeability of community boundaries in Cucurpe. Even though the Cucurpeños did not want to admit El Pintor as a *vecino* (neighbor or citizen) into their común, the wily Piman was still able to remain in the area and to monopolize both land and water for at least seven years. Native-born residents may have wanted to keep their community closed to outsiders, but such closure was very difficult to achieve.

Like many other settlements in northwestern New Spain, Cucurpe was not an isolated "little community." On the contrary, it was part of a frontier where ethnic and geographic boundaries were even more fluid than in the mestizo society taking shape to the south (MacLachlan and Rodríguez 1980). In 1772, for example, the Franciscan reformer Antonio María de los Reyes, stationed in Cucurpe, wrote, "The Indians themselves say they are of the Eudeve and Opata nations, but the truth is that they are a composite and mixture of Spaniards, mulattoes, natives, and other castes."[11] Despite attempts by both missionaries and local inhabitants to restrict immigration into the village, Cucurpe was becoming an ethnic melting pot rather than a closed indigenous community.

These trends were reinforced by major economic and political changes sweeping across New Spain. During the mid-eighteenth century, the Spanish empire suffered a series of shocks that forced colonial officials to rethink their concept of the northern frontier. The first was the growing unrest of the Indians themselves, stimulated in part by changes in the balance of power in the southern Great Plains. French expansionism in the trans-Mississippi area led to a brisk trade in arms, livestock, and slaves. Among groups obtaining weapons from French traders were the Comanches, who began to score victory after victory over the Lipan and Mescalero Apaches. Pushed west and south, the Apaches, in turn, put pressure on other groups. They also began raiding Spanish settlements in Coahuila and Chihuahua with greater frequency, contributing to the instability of those provinces. At the same time, the Western and Chiricahua Apaches were intensifying their forays into Sonora at a time when Sonoran presidial garrisons and militias were attempting to suppress rebellions among the Yaquis, the Pimas, and the Seris. As a result, Sonoran mining and ranching were devastated, leading to the depopulation of many communities (Nentvig 1971; Sheridan 1979).

Then, in the aftermath of the Seven Years' War, the French presence on New Spain's northeastern frontier suddenly disappeared, replaced by the even more aggressive English. Meanwhile, Russian fur traders were creeping down the Pacific coast, threatening the northwest. Spanish officials not only began to fear that their frontier might buckle but that the vital silver-mining provinces of Zacatecas, Guanajuato, and San Luis Potosí might be threatened as well. Consequently, they decided it was time, long past time, to reorganize frontier society in order to protect those mines (Navarro García 1964; Bannon 1974).

The results were the fiscal, administrative, and military changes known as the Bourbon reforms. First came a major inspection of the northern presidios under the command of the Marqués de Rubí (1765–69). Then the Jesuits were expelled (1767). Finally, northern New Spain itself was restructured as a semi-independent entity known as the *provincias internas* (1776). Modified continuously for the rest of the colonial period, the *provincias internas* represented a sustained attempt to streamline and militarize the northern frontier.

When viewed in strictly military terms, the Bourbon reforms were a success. Beginning in the late 1760s, major Spanish military expeditions pacified the Lower Pimas, wore down the Seris, and forced a number of Apache and Comanche groups to surrender and settle near Spanish garrisons. The general reduction in Indian hostilities allowed the region's economy to expand once again, attracting many non-Indian settlers. And since those settlers needed both Indian land and Indian labor, the mission system came under increased attack.

Immediately after the Jesuit expulsion, in fact, colonial officials toyed briefly with the idea of secularizing all of the missions. They quickly found out there were not enough secular clergy to minister to the Indians, however, so the reformers were forced to ask the Franciscans to replace the Jesuits. Nevertheless, they still attempted to destroy the political and economic power of the missions by restricting the Franciscans to purely religious affairs. Civil commissioners, on the other hand, were to administer mission properties themselves (Kessell 1976; McCarty 1981).

The ideological justification for such restrictions, grounded in the ideals of the Enlightenment, was to free the Indians from the tyranny of their missionaries by turning them into full-fledged citizens of Spanish society. A more basic motivation was the desire for Indian land and labor. In a very real sense, the Bourbon reforms represented a regional manifestation of the expansion of European capitalism under the protection of the absolute Spanish state. Part of that expansion was an official emphasis upon individual initiative rather than corporate responsibility. The privatization of mission property, including land and livestock, therefore became a major goal.

Luckily for many Indian communities, the full force of those intentions was never felt. At Cucurpe, for example, Antonio de los Reyes, who went on to become the first bishop of Sonora, quickly abandoned any pretext of restricting himself to spiritual matters, distributing seed to the Cucurpeños and urging them to plant their communal fields (McCarty 1981). Rather than viewing such actions as rebellious, colonial officials soon realized that Reyes and his fellow missionaries needed to wield economic as well as religious authority over their Indian charges. On June 1, 1769, in fact, José de Gálvez, the greatest reformer of them all, officially abolished the civil commissioner system and gave the Franciscans control over mission lands and livestock. Two weeks later, he sternly informed the governor of Sonora that mission properties had not been confiscated from the Jesuits. On the contrary, they continued to belong to the Indians themselves, just as they had in the past. The missionaries were simply better qualified to administer those properties than colonial officials at the present time (Kessell 1976; McCarty 1981).

For the rest of the colonial period and beyond, then, the Franciscans exercised some economic control over the missions they inherited. Nonetheless, they never dominated Indian land and labor the way the Jesuits had. The Yaquis, for example, received only three Franciscan missionaries, and for the rest of the colonial period, they largely took charge over their own religious, political, and economic affairs. They also began to migrate in even greater numbers to mines and haciendas throughout northwestern New Spain (Spicer 1980; Hu-DeHart 1981).

Similar forces must have been at work in Cucurpe as well. Even though the mission continued to provide an institutional umbrella protecting the community's land and water, individual Cucurpeños during the late 1700s worked in mining centers like the placers of Cieneguilla or fought the Apaches under commanders like Juan Bautista de Anza. Moreover, a rising stream of outsiders poured into the Cucurpe region, first to search for gold at Saracachi during the 1760s, then to settle along the San Miguel itself. By the end of the century, a census taken in 1796 revealed that only 49.1 percent of Cucurpe's population were Indians, while 43.4 percent were mestizo or mulatto, and 7.3 percent were Spaniards.[12] The indigenous community of Cucurpe no longer was so indigenous. Instead, it was becoming a community of peasant farmers and stock raisers confronting a society that increasingly emphasized private property and the ascendancy of the state.

It is not surprising that one of Cucurpe's largest private estates—the *predio* of Torreón—began as a land grant in 1793 (*see* chapter 4). With Apache hostilities decreasing and the mission system weakening, private ranchers and farmers moved into the upper San Miguel drainage to occupy land not held by the Indians. Actually, the process had begun half a century earlier after Kino's mission headquarters at Dolores was abandoned in the 1740s because of Apache attacks and epidemics. Private ranchers began to occupy the fertile Dolores valley, beginning a pattern of occupation that still exists today. From at least the mid-eighteenth century, then, both private and corporate landholders settled the same general region. Whether they came into conflict with one another during the rest of the colonial period we do not yet know. Nonetheless, the stage was set.

Mexico's independence from Spain did little to stabilize the situation. Not much is known about events in Cucurpe during the chaotic nineteenth century, but Cucurpe undoubtedly was affected by the same contradictory forces that shaped land tenure and resource control in areas better documented. One of the most destructive consequences of independence for the entire northwestern frontier was the resumption of Apache raiding. With its mining industry reeling and its economy in shambles, the young republic no longer could afford to maintain the Apache rationing program that had kept many of the Athabascans pacified during the late 1700s and early 1800s. Even the more established mission and presidio systems decayed as funds ran short. As a result, the Western and Chiricahua Apaches began preying upon Sonoran communities with renewed vigor, causing both ranching and mining to contract or disappear from many stretches of the frontier.

A second factor that impeded Sonora's economic development was the chronic civil wars among the Sonorenses themselves. From the 1830s until the 1870s, Sonoran politics were dominated by a handful of *caudillos* who fought one another for control of the state (Voss 1982). During the ensuing power struggles, these military and political leaders attempted to manipulate Indians and peasants like the Cucurpeños to keep themselves in power or depose their adversaries. At the same time, however, the frequent coups and conflicts allowed organized groups like the Yaquis to keep the *hacendados* and the state at bay, at least for a while (Spicer 1980; Hu-DeHart 1984).

Nevertheless, the major thrust of Sonoran development during the nineteenth century was the ascension of interlocking urban elites based in cities like Alamos, Guaymas, and Hermosillo, and their gradual penetration of the Sonoran countryside (Voss 1982; Balmori et al. 1984). These entrepreneurs resented the protection the Indians had enjoyed under the colonial regime, often cloaking their true intentions beneath the ideals of nineteenth-century liberalism. Indians were declared to be citizens of the new republic, freed from the bondage of the past. To the Indians, however, that freedom meant little more than taxation and an end to local autonomy. It also represented a serious threat to their corporate control of mission property. According to Voss (1982:50):

> The new republican regime expressed much less concern about protecting the Indians' lands. In fact, it desired to break up their communal lands

and make them individual farmers. In the new federal system such questions were left to the states, whose governments were in the hands of those who at best believed such communal ownership unproductive, and at worst desired to obtain such lands for their own use. Mexico City not only was unsympathetic to the maintenance of the Indians' communal lands, but also abdicated responsibility in the matter. It did not take the tribal Indians in the region long to realize the implications of this new republican order—that they were being given the short end of the stick.

The nineteenth-century struggle for land among the Yaqui is well-known (Spicer 1980; Hu-DeHart 1984). What happened in Cucurpe, on the other hand, remains to be documented if, indeed, such documentation still exists. The fragments collected by the federal Department of Agrarian Reform during the past decade provide only the smallest insight into the development of land tenure in the upper San Miguel valley (*see* chapter 8). Regardless of the exact details, however, one fact is clear: somehow the Cucurpeños managed to retain control of at least some of their corporate grazing lands as Sonora lurched from one government to another.

The struggle was probably not an easy one. During the first half of the nineteenth century, the Sonoran state government made a number of attempts to destroy corporate tenure and divide up Indian land. Such efforts were met with resistance if not outright hostility by many communities; occasionally that hostility even flared into widespread rebellion. For a brief time in the late 1820s, in fact, a Yaqui leader known as Juan Banderas tried to create an autonomous pan-Indian nation in the northwest, one that united Yaquis, Mayos, Pimas, and Opatas (Spicer 1980; Hu-DeHart 1984). The union never came about, but for the first time since the seventeenth century, some Opatas and Eudeves took up arms against rather than for the state (Spicer 1962; Voss 1982; Hu-DeHart 1984).

Cucurpeños did not seem to be among the rebels. In 1832, for example, Cucurpe was counted among the nine "patriotic pueblos" whose representatives met in Cocóspera to form a militia to fight the Apaches under the command of Ignacio Elías (Kessell 1976). Fifty years later, the president of Mexico, Manuel González, rewarded ninety-two Cucurpeños with parcels of 145 ha of land for military service (*see* chapter 8).[13] The grant does not specify against whom the Cucurpeños fought. In the chaos of the mid-nineteenth century, it could have been the Apaches, the Yaquis, the Seris, the French, or even the Americans.[14] Whoever the enemy was, however, the Cucurpeños apparently remained faithful to the Mexican republic.

The Cucurpeños evidently ignored González' decree; 145 ha of semi-arid rangeland could never have supported a household, so the local inhabitants must have continued to run their stock on the old *egidos* (sic), as the common lands were called. Nonetheless, the grant itself was another manifestation of the prevailing ideological winds blowing across Mexico during the nineteenth century. In 1856, for example, the federal government promulgated the famous Ley Lerdo, which prohibited civil and ecclesiastical corporations from owning most types of real property, including arable land. A year later, the law was incorporated into Mexico's new constitution. Aimed primarily at the Church, Ley Lerdo also undermined the legal status of peasant corporate communities throughout Mexico, including the northwest (Meyer and Sherman 1979). Civil war and the French intervention of the 1860s prevented the constitutional provision from taking effect in many areas of Mexico for several decades. Beginning in 1876, however, the privatization of corporate lands—a goal ever since the Bourbon reforms—became a reality throughout much of the Mexican countryside.

The architect of this profound structural transformation was a hero in the war against the French named Porfirio Díaz. From 1876 until 1910, Díaz was president of Mexico with only one interruption (1880–1884), and during that four-year term, the presidency was held by Díaz' colleague, Manuel González. During the *Porfiriato*, as the period came to be called, Díaz suppressed banditry and ended civil war, providing Mexico with the stability it needed to carry out many of the goals the Bourbon reformers had striven for a century before. Chief among these objectives was the "rationalization" of the Mexican economy and the capitalization of Mexico's natural resources. Ley Lerdo was applied, causing many Indian and peasant communities to lose their lands. In their place, vast private holdings, or *latifundias*, locked up land and labor under a system of debt peonage that turned thousands of campesinos into virtual serfs. Moreover, private capital, much of it foreign, came to dominate major industries like railroads and mining, leading many disaffected intellectuals to call Mexico "the mother of foreigners and the stepmother of Mexicans." Under Díaz, then, Mexico entered the twentieth century on the backs of its peasants, and progress and misery walked hand in hand.

Perhaps even more than the rest of the republic, Sonora experienced the Porfiriato in all its contradictory dimensions. The Apaches were pacified, mining was revived, and ranching and agriculture prospered. For the first time in its history, Sonora's marginality was breached as transportation networks linked it closer and closer to Mexico City and the southwestern United States (Gracida Romo

1985a). During the same period, however, a brutal war against the Yaquis culminated in the widespread deportation of Yaquis and other Indians to the henequen plantations of the Oaxaca Valley and Yucatan (Spicer 1980; Hu-DeHart 1984). As both foreign and domestic capital penetrated Sonora, land and water became enormously valuable resources (Gracida Romo 1985b). Not surprisingly, competition for those resources grew ever more intense, resulting in the dispossession of many Indian and peasant communities.

The division of corporate lands has been documented for numerous Pima and Opata pueblos in the Sonora, Yaqui, Moctezuma, and Bavispe river valleys (Figueroa Valenzuela 1985). What happened in Cucurpe, on the other hand, is not well understood. The González decree discussed above certainly indicates that attempts were made to break up the old corporate community, but the survival of that community into the twentieth century suggests that those attempts failed. Nonetheless, other elements of the Porfirian economy did entrench themselves in Cucurpe, creating conditions that led to the conflict over land as documented in chapter 8.

Perhaps the most significant economic change was the expansion of the local mining industry. As noted earlier, both gold and silver mining had been important during the colonial period. By the 1770s, however, the placer boom at Saracachi had ended (Pfefferkorn 1983), and no strike of similar magnitude apparently took place in the region during the late eighteenth or early nineteenth centuries.

Beginning in 1863, however, a number of the most prominent business families in Hermosillo formed the *Compañía Explotadora* to work the mines at La Brisca upriver from Saracachi. Capitalized at 210,000 pesos, this venture focused the attention of the Sonoran state capital's urban elite on Cucurpe's mineral wealth (Balmori et al. 1984).

That wealth soon attracted the attention of foreign investors as well. As chapter 5 points out, several large British and North American concerns like the Cerro Prieto Mining Company began extracting gold and silver ore in Cucurpe during the 1890s and early 1900s.[15] And since these highly sophisticated operations employed hundreds of Mexican and even Oriental workers, local agriculture and ranching thrived as well, providing the mines with beef, cheese, wheat flour, vegetables, and *panocha*, or brown sugar. Water-powered mills sprang up along the San Miguel and its tributaries, and Cucurpe artisans produced everything from saddles to soap. In the words of one old man, "There were jewelry shops, palm-weaving shops, shoe shops, mills." Unlike today, many goods were manufactured locally rather than purchased in Magdalena, Nogales, or the United States.

Another consequence of Porfirian prosperity was the development of large estates. Although the municipio did not have abundant stretches of arable land like other Sonoran river valleys, several latifundias were established in the region during this period, the largest being the hacienda of Agua Fría along the Río Saracachi east of the pueblo of Cucurpe. Agua Fría was the creation of a man who inherited one *rancho* from his father and expanded that patrimony into a 28,000-hectare domain between 1900 and the 1930s. At its height, the hacienda employed at least eleven families and supported a chapel and a school. Agua Fría also made its owner the most powerful man in the region, a power broker who was often able to bend local politics to his own design.[16]

Significantly, the founder of Agua Fría was a member of one of the families who invested in the La Brisca mines. As Balmori et al. (1984) point out, flexibility and diversification were essential strategies for Sonora's emerging elite during the Porfirian period. Few of these powerful families confined themselves to one sector of the economy, putting their money instead into a wide variety of industries as Sonora developed and grew.

The Indian and peasant families of the region, on the other hand, found their situation increasingly precarious. Although no documents for the period have yet been located, oral history suggests that the modern struggle for land between the comunidad of Cucurpe and its neighbors originated in the expansion of the mining and livestock industries that took place during the early 1900s (*see* chapter 8). With the introduction of barbed wire, ranchers began fencing land that had previously been open range. At the same time, wealthy farmers and mill-owners absorbed the milpas of many of their less powerful neighbors. As a result, much of the floodplain land and perhaps a third of the corporate range fell into private hands.

This erosion of corporate tenure was matched by an accelerated erosion of ethnic identity as well. During the colonial period, it often made sense to identify yourself as an Indian, even if your genetic makeup was mestizo or mulatto. During the Porfiriato, however, Indians were exploited and despised, their cultures denigrated and their lands seized. In Sonora, moreover, state and federal troops were conducting a genocidal war against the Yaqui Indians, killing or deporting Opatas, Pimas, and Mayos in the process (Spicer 1962, 1980; Hu-DeHart 1984). Being Indian no longer entailed the protection of the mission system. On the contrary, it often meant peonage or death.

Out of sheer desire for survival, then, many Sonoran Indians attempted to assimilate themselves into the mestizo mainstream of

Mexican society. The famous physical anthropologist Aleš Hrdlička (1904:74) described this process in the Cucurpe area when he wrote:

> Along the San Miguel valley the Opatas do not like to be regarded as Indians; they prefer to be called "Mexicans". Very few under thirty years of age can speak their native language; even if they understand it they do not like to employ it, and if anyone addresses them in Opata, they answer in Spanish.

The processes of *mestizaje* (racial mixture) and assimilation did not begin with the Porfiriato. As noted earlier, more than half of Cucurpe's population was already non-Indian by the end of the eighteenth century. Nonetheless, Porfirian policies and Porfirian attitudes completed the transformation. Today a few families in the municipio retain Eudeve surnames, but no one speaks Eudeve anymore. On the contrary, the Cucurpeños are mestizo in both language and custom, their Indian cultural heritage little more than a handful of place names or the memories of a few Opata customs like *gomi*, a stickball game that was last played in the late 1940s.[17]

Nevertheless, the people themselves survived, weathering both the Porfiriato and the Mexican Revolution that followed. And even though one of the major goals of the Revolution was to destroy *latifundismo* and redistribute land to the peasants, agrarian reform rarely happened overnight, nor was it universally applied. In many places like Cucurpe, for example, there was no sharp break between the Porfirian and the post-revolutionary eras. On the contrary, powerful private ranchers like the owner of Agua Fría and his first cousin, who owned the adjoining Rancho Santo Domingo, not only preserved but increased their holdings after the Revolution. It wasn't until the 1950s, in fact, that peasant stockmen began to take advantage of the provisions encoded in Mexico's revolutionary Constitution of 1917 or the Federal Law of Agrarian Reform it engendered.[18] One could argue, in a sense, that the Revolution did not really reach Cucurpe until 1976, when the federal government finally recognized the existence of the municipio's two *comunidades* and created Ejido 6 de Enero. Then and only then were corporate resources like grazing land finally secured under the law (*see* chapter 8).

Meanwhile, the expansion of the Sonoran livestock industry was making both peasant and private ranchers in Cucurpe more dependent upon economic developments on the other side of the international border. Ever since the Porfiriato, Sonoran stockmen had produced for the U.S. market, driving their cattle to railheads and exporting them across the line. This exchange diminished during the

Revolution, revived the following decade, slowed again in the early years of the Great Depression, and accelerated during World War II. A devastating epidemic of hoof-and-mouth disease (*fiebre aftosa*) closed the border between 1947 and 1954, but by the end of the decade, the United States was once again importing thousands of Sonoran cattle (Machado 1981; Peña and Chávez 1985).[19]

Most of this demand was met by private stock raisers, who also received much of the financial and technological assistance. Beginning in the late 1950s, major Arizona banks began making loans to Sonoran cattlemen to increase and improve their herds. Those linkages grew even stronger in the 1960s as feedlots proliferated across the southwestern United States. And as the feedlots devoured more and more animals, many peasant stockmen were incorporated into the international livestock industry for the first time.

Prior to this growth, small producers like the Cucurpeños raised cattle primarily for their own consumption. Dairying was more important than the production of beef, and the animals were said "to have no price" since so few of them were sold on a regular basis (Peña and Chávez 1985). The growth of the feedlots, on the other hand, outstripped the capacity of private ranchers to meet U.S. demand. Feedlot operators wanted calves that they could purchase cheaply and fatten quickly. Cattle buyers, therefore, turned to the small stockmen as well, driving their trucks into the mountains, fording streams, fanning out across the isolated river valleys of central and eastern Sonora in search of calves wherever they could be found. By the 1970s, even the smallest of peasant ranchers were selling nearly all their male calves to these itinerant merchants, who served as intermediaries in a complicated transaction that extended from the corrals of rural Sonora to the dinner tables of the United States.

As a result, many small producers became part of an international division of labor that placed peasant stock raisers in northern Mexico at the base of an economic pyramid whose apex jutted into the United States. In the process, peasant households bound themselves ever more tightly to a cash economy that rarely worked to their own advantage. People like the Cucurpeños may have won a tiny slice of the feeder calf market, but they lost much of their self-sufficiency in the bargain. Suddenly their livelihoods, like those of their private neighbors, depended upon the demand for beef in the United States. When the market was good and both governments permitted calves to cross the border, Cucurpeños had money in their pockets. But if demand slackened or bureaucrats in Mexico City or Washington, D.C., decided to limit exports, the cash flow slowed down.

Perhaps the most visible consequence of this economic transformation was a major change in local cropping patterns. Prior to the 1960s, Cucurpe households grew most of the wheat they needed for tortillas, one of the staples of their diet. Following the expansion of the livestock industry, however, it made more sense to purchase wheat flour and devote your fields to forage crops such as barley, alfalfa, or sorghum. People began eating less of their own produce and their own beef, as they became integrated as consumers as well as producers into an international market economy (*see* chapters 3 and 4).[20]

And as international markets intruded, local markets inevitably declined. The wheels of the mills that once lined the banks of the San Miguel no longer turned, and so the buildings themselves slowly weathered away, symbols of a regional vitality that had been sapped by the economic "miracle" of post-war Sonora. Contributing to this atrophy was the collapse of the mining industry, which had largely abandoned Cucurpe by the early 1950s. The only operations that remained were tiny pick-and-shovel affairs employing handfuls of men at most (*see* chapter 5).

As a result, population in the municipio declined at a time when Sonora and the rest of Mexico were experiencing tremendous growth. Between 1940 and 1950, for example, the number of Cucurpeños fell by more than 50 percent as an evanescent placer mining boom disintegrated and people left for more dynamic areas of Sonora or the United States. The following three decades witnessed declines of 16 percent, 18.5 percent, and 11 percent respectively, indicating that Cucurpe was becoming another of those donor areas so characteristic of rural society across the world (*see* Figure 2.2).

Despite demographic decline and economic stagnation, however, Cucurpe's peasantry did not disappear. On the contrary, the reconfirmation of the two comunidades and the creation of Ejido 6 de Enero culminated years of struggle to protect corporate boundaries from the invasions of private ranchers. As the vignette at the beginning of this chapter attests, legal recognition did not bring the battle for land and water to an end, but it did give the peasant rancher-farmers of Cucurpe a stronger foundation from which to make their stand.

It also brought them under the umbrella of the federal Department of Agrarian Reform, a development that engendered conflicts of its own. For more than three centuries, the Cucurpeños suffered and survived a series of governments that all tried to impose their visions of agrarian society upon them. The Jesuits converted them to Christianity and revolutionized their economy by introducing Old World crops and livestock. The Bourbon reformers of the late eighteenth century and the Porfirian positivists a century later attempted to destroy the economic heritage of missionization: the corporate control of grazing land and water. Since the Revolution, the Cucurpeños have received mixed signals, encountering bureaucratic inertia or collusion between government officials and private ranchers much of the time, winning support for their struggle on other, less frequent occasions.[21] Regardless of the actions of Madrid or Mexico City, however, they have endured, running their cattle, raising their crops, fighting among themselves, and fighting their neighbors in an effort to maintain a precarious political and ecological balance. It is a balance between corporate and private tenure, between household autonomy and communal solidarity, between economic marginality and the uncertain opportunities of the outside world. As the following chapters attest, external political and economic forces shape Cucurpe life in a multitude of ways. At the same time, however, longstanding adaptations to the local environment cause the Cucurpeños to resist many of the blueprints for change drawn up in Hermosillo or Mexico City. Cucurpe's continuing history, then, must be seen as an interplay between internal and external factors. The interplay may be asymmetrical at times, but the Cucurpeños have never been passive pawns.

La fiesta y la fe: Holy Week in Cucurpe.

2. *La Vida Cucurpeña*

MODERN AGRARIAN SOCIETY IN CUCURPE

El sábado de la gloria—Easter Saturday—10 A.M. A small group of men are sitting under the big mesquite in Beto's backyard, drinking Coors or Tecate or bootleg lechuguilla while Beto and his oldest son butcher a pig. The son drove in from Tucson late last night in his brother-in-law's 4 × 4. The pig was killed at dawn. Bloody to the elbows, Beto supervises the last stages of the slaughtering while his wife and daughters fry chicharrones and slice the pork into long, thin strips.

The male guests of the house—son-in-laws, friends, compadres—joke with Beto while they cure their hangovers and listen to Los Alegres de Terán blaring joyously from the pickup's tape deck. It is Semana Santa (Holy Week), the biggest celebration of the year in Mexico, a time when people return to the pueblos of their birth to eat, drink, and visit with relatives and friends. It is also a time to follow the Vía Cruz (Way of the Cross) and to laugh at the antics of the fariseos (Pharisees), a time to renew ties with a rural way of life that has survived in the Sonoran Desert for more than three hundred years. By late afternoon, everyone at Beto's will pile into the 4 × 4 and join the long, sweaty caravan to the airstrip across the river to wait for the horse races to begin. But for now the men are content to drink beer and watch the women prepare the meal, a carne asada in celebration of the Resurrection and the return of Beto's emigrant sons and daughters, if only for a few short days. The centripetal pull of family versus the centrifugal tug of the United States. Fathers who spend their days in a saddle or behind a plow. Sons who work as landscapers in Tucson or roofers in L.A. All come to pay homage to la vida Cucurpeña this warm spring morning, none dwelling upon the contradictions that life entails.

The modern municipio of Cucurpe is a collection of contradictions—a bucolic little corner of Sonora that is also an agrarian battleground, a region of declining population in a nation bursting its Malthusian seams. Cucurpe is less than a half day's drive from the United States, yet its way of life reflects the colonial period as much as it does the twentieth century. Visiting a Cucurpeño's home, you realize you are surrounded by the artifacts of at least three centuries: burro-powered *taunas* (grinding stones) and dilapidated pickup trucks, wooden *bateas* (bowls for mixing flour) and K-Mart crockery. Old women in mourning (*guardando luto*) may wear black dresses or brown *hábitos* tied with rope at the waist, but young girls apply the latest cosmetics and dress in tight-fitting slacks. To outsiders, the juxtapositions can be jarring. To Cucurpeños, they are simply the stuff of daily life.

Many of these apparent paradoxes arise from the municipio's marginality. During the colonial period, Cucurpe was both a mission and a mining center, a relatively secure pocket of Spanish settlement poised on the edge of the northwestern frontier. Today, by contrast, the upper San Miguel watershed is a political and economic backwater, largely bypassed by the agricultural and industrial development that have transformed Sonora into one of the most prosperous states of the Mexican republic. Cucurpe's major connection with the outside world is a winding, occasionally impassable dirt road leading to Magdalena, a regional center of approximately 15,000 inhabitants where most Cucurpeños go to sell their cattle, to purchase supplies, and to seek health care. Located along both Highway 15 and the Mexican Pacific Railroad, Magdalena straddles the nation's major west-coast arteries of transportation. Cucurpe, on the other hand, is penetrated neither by rail or paved road. In 1985, an electric line was finally extended from Magdalena to the pueblo of Cucurpe itself, ending the town's reliance upon a diesel-powered generating plant that only operated seven hours a night. During the last two *sexenios* (six-year presidential administrations), the Mexican government has also been building a paved highway between Cucurpe and Magdalena. Construction proceeds in fits and starts, however, and at present, the municipio remains outside the commercial mainstream of northwestern Mexico.

This isolation undoubtedly explains why small rancher-farmers have survived in a region of rapid change. For a number of ecological as well as political reasons, the municipio has never attracted large-scale capitalist agriculture. And while private ranchers do control much of the grazing land, they have never grown powerful enough to destroy the peasant corporate communities, the most enduring legacies of Cucurpe's colonial past. A majority of the municipio's population, then, is organized into peasant households who cultivate small fields and raise a few head of cattle. These are the households that dominate municipal daily life.

SETTLEMENT PATTERNS

Where these households live is determined in large measure by ecological constraints that have operated since prehistoric times. Most of
the municipio's 1,789 square km—some 99.5 percent of it—are simply
too dry or too rocky to farm. The only topographical locations where
irrigated agriculture is possible are the narrow alluvial floodplains of
the San Miguel watershed. These riparian oases—where the doves
call and the cottonwoods rustle, and where, above all, the water
flows—are the ecological foundations of agrarian society in Cucurpe.
Without them, the riverine communities of the Eudeves, the Spaniards, and the modern Cucurpeños could never have taken root.

Municipal settlement patterns reflect the floodplain's importance.
According to the 1980 federal census, 1,160 people live in Cucurpe—
averaging less than one person per square kilometer. A survey of 251
resident households yielding a sample population of 1,071 (92.3 percent of the total) reveals that 71 percent of all Cucurpeños dwell along
the banks of the three major drainages or on the small mesas above
them (page 30). Of these, 64 percent are found along the San Miguel
proper, while 17 percent live along the Dolores and nearly 19 percent
along the beautiful but serpentine Saracachi. The pueblo of Cucurpe
itself with a sample population of 357 inhabitants is the largest of these
communities, embracing one-third of the municipio's population. The
remaining riparian settlements—El Pintor and El Carrizal along the
Dolores, El Júparo and La Calera along the Saracachi, El Potrero and
San Javier along the San Miguel—consist of little more than a few
scattered households. During colonial times, these hamlets would
have been described as rancherías rather than pueblos, small clusters
of farmsteads located near stretches of surface water and pockets of
arable floodplain land.

Between these settlements, solitary households are strung up and
down the rivers like adobe beads. Hispanic society in the New World,
like its Iberian progenitor, has always been largely urban, its inhabitants living in towns and cities rather than on isolated farms or
ranches.[1] While Cucurpe conforms in part to this cultural model, its
rugged landscape and low population densities have imposed a frontier overlay on this basic Mediterranean pattern. Nearly 30 percent of
the sample population occupy the uplands or side canyons of the San
Miguel watershed. And except for Agua en Medio, a community of
eleven households in the northeastern portion of the municipio, most
of these people live on secluded ranches or near small, isolated mines.
Roads lead to these places, but they are crudely constructed and

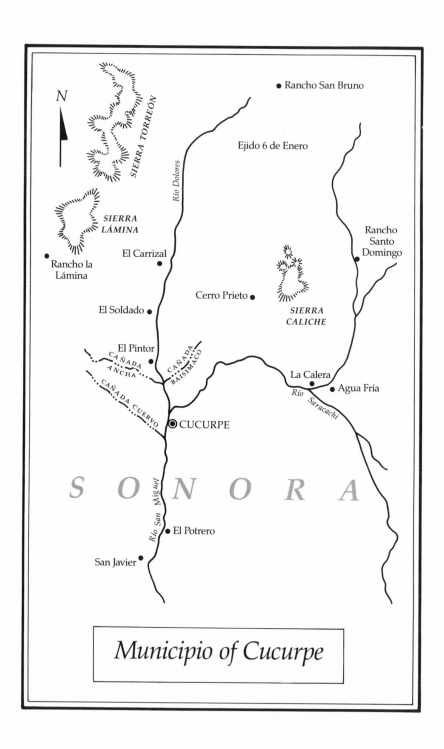

N

Rancho San Bruno

Ejido 6 de Enero

Río Dolores

SIERRA TORREÓN

SIERRA LÁMINA

Rancho la Lámina

El Carrizal

Rancho Santo Domingo

Cerro Prieto

SIERRA CALICHE

El Soldado

El Pintor

CAÑADA ANCHA

CAÑADA BAISIMACO

CAÑADA CUERVO

La Calera

Agua Fría

Río Saracachi

◉ CUCURPE

S O N O R A

Río San Miguel

El Potrero

San Javier

Municipio of Cucurpe

irregularly maintained. Ranchers and miners are, therefore, frequently cut off from vehicular communication with the outside world, especially after heavy rains. Like much of the rest of northern Mexico, Cucurpe is a region where Iberia met the great North American desert. The result was a hybrid settlement pattern combining urbanism with solitary ranch and mine life.

An interesting manifestation of this hybrid is the relatively widespread existence of dual residences. Of the 251 households interviewed, 64 (25.5 percent) reported that they possess at least two dwellings. Eighteen of these domestic units maintain both a house in Cucurpe and an outlying *rancho*. An even greater number (37) divide their time between ranches in the municipio and homes in Magdalena. In the late nineteenth and early twentieth centuries, dual residence characterized Hispanic ranching society in other rural areas of the Greater Southwest, including southern Arizona (Sheridan 1986). Rising land prices and increasing economies of scale drove most Mexican ranchers off the ranges and into the cities north of the border, but in Cucurpe, this pattern still survives.

It does so in part to relieve the isolation and monotony of ranch life. While some men and women enjoy the solitude and tranquility, others crave more human contact—drinking, gossiping, dances, baseball games, and the constant interaction with neighbors and relatives that enlivens daily life in a Mexican town. A house in Cucurpe or Magdalena allows families to punctuate long stretches on the ranch with more urban activities. Furthermore, *muy ranchero* is a derogatory term, signifying that people are too shy or too rustic to move comfortably in human society. The only antidote is prolonged exposure to life in town.

A more immediate motivation among Cucurpeños, however, is a strong desire to educate their children. Except for the one-room, one-teacher schools at La Calera, Agua en Medio, and Rancho Santo Domingo, the only place in the municipio to obtain a full six-year primary education is the pueblo of Cucurpe, where the federal government operates *La Escuela Federal Cuauhtémoc*. Secondary schooling is even more difficult to attain; prior to 1981, when a *secundaria* was established in Cucurpe, students had to move to Magdalena to progress beyond the sixth grade. Parents in the countryside are confronted, therefore, with a serious dilemma: whether to keep their children at home, thereby denying them an education, or to send them away to school. Realizing that the days of pick and shovel work (*trabajo de pico y palo*) are waning, many Cucurpe families choose the latter alternative.

The choice is not an easy one. While some ranch families board their children with relatives, this arrangement imposes considerable burdens on everyone involved, especially those kinsmen with their own families to support. Consequently, most households temporarily split up, the wives and younger children moving to Cucurpe or Magdalena, the husbands and older sons remaining on the ranch. Despite the separation and financial burdens dual residence entails, many Cucurpeños are willing to make considerable sacrifices to send their children to school.

DIET AND HOUSING

Families who divide their time between town and ranch experience one of the basic paradoxes of *la vida Cucurpeña* on a daily basis. Most homes in Magdalena, no matter how humble, possess the amenities of twentieth-century life: electricity, running water, refrigerators, gas stoves. Few households in the municipio, by contrast, enjoy such conveniences. In 1980–81, for example, only 67 of 251 households (26.7 percent) were illuminated by electricity. And those households were all located in the pueblo of Cucurpe, where the diesel-powered generating plant was fired up at four in the afternoon and shut down at eleven at night. The countryside, on the other hand, remains without electric power except for the headquarters of a few wealthy ranchers who have installed generators. In the coming years, the new electric line from Magdalena to Cucurpe may be extended into rural areas. For the time being, however, ranches and mines glow at night with the soft light of kerosene lanterns rather than with the glare of electric bulbs.

An even more basic limitation concerns the preservation of food. Thirty-eight families (15.1 percent) own propane refrigerators, but the other 85 percent of the Cucurpeños continue to rely on methods of food preservation that were ancient by colonial times. Such limitations impose considerable constraints on the Cucurpe diet. About the only major dietary changes since the eighteenth century, in fact, have been the introduction of coffee as the most common beverage and the substitution of wheat for maize as the most important starch. Other than that, Cucurpe meals are not much different from what they were like when Padre Ignatz Pfefferkorn was stationed there in the 1760s (Treutlein 1949).

Not surprisingly, pinto beans and wheat-flour tortillas, supplemented by potatoes, remain the staples of the Cucurpe diet. These inherently bland foodstuffs are enlivened by the liberal use of spices, the most celebrated of which is the tiny wild chile known as *chiltepín*, a berry-like gustatory explosion that has inflamed Sonoran palates for centuries. Locally grown garlic and red onions also relieve the monotony of most meals. Fresh vegetables, on the other hand, are rarely served. Except for squash, lentils, haba beans, and peas, vegetables are not cultivated on any scale in the municipio, and Cucurpe's small grocery stores (*abarrotes*) import very little fresh produce other than cabbage, onions, and an occasional sack of puny fruit.

Even more infrequent is the consumption of fresh meat. Although Cucurpe's major industry is cattle ranching, almost all of the cattle are exported rather than butchered locally on a commercial scale. Households occasionally slaughter their own animals, but rarely more than once or twice a year. In a study of 48 households in the pueblo of Cucurpe, for example, Szuter (1984) discovered that only 58 percent had killed a cow in 1980, while fewer than half had killed a pig. In short, livestock are simply too valuable to be butchered for domestic consumption on a regular basis.

Because of the expense, the slaughtering of large animals such as cows or pigs is usually reserved for celebrations—formal holidays like New Year's or Easter, or rites of passage such as baptisms and weddings.[2] All the more special because of their infrequency, these occasions are feasts in every sense of the term, times when food, beer, and music overflow and the normal constraints are suspended while everyone eats and drinks his fill. Once the celebration is over, however, the uneaten meat has to be given away to relatives or sliced into thin strips and hung up to dry in the sun. This later becomes *carne machaca*, meat that is tenderized by pounding and mixed into soups and stews. Nonetheless, many families may go weeks without eating beef or pork, whether fresh or dried. During such hiatuses, chickens may occasionally be killed, but even poultry is scarce in the Cucurpeño diet. Forty percent of all municipal households (102), in fact, raise no chickens whatsoever. Meat of any kind is a luxury few Cucurpe households can routinely afford.

Diet will undoubtedly change as electricity makes modern conveniences more available in the municipio. The preparation of the food itself also will undergo some transformations, decreasing the present reliance upon wood stoves which make woodcutting such an important and time-consuming task. At present, however, modern artifacts for the most part serve traditional ends. Every girl spends hours learning how to mix tortilla dough in wooden bateas passed down from generation to generation. Then, more often than not, she deftly flips that dough over a hot *comal* (griddle) consisting of a worn-out tractor disk. But contemporary touches do not change the basic pattern. The huge, paper-thin tortillas remain the pride and glory of Sonoran cuisine, and any woman who fails to master the art of tortilla-making exposes herself to gentle but continual ridicule. Her lumpy, ill-formed products are dismissed as *huaraches* (sandals with soles cut from tire tread), or labeled derisively as *guadalupanas*, a derogatory comparison between the rays emanating from the Virgin of Guadalupe and the ragged edges of a tortilla gone awry.

Housing also juxtaposes the traditional and the modern. As it has been for centuries, sun-dried adobe is the basic building material; of the 251 households surveyed, 183 (72.9 percent) occupy adobe homes. Because of its remarkable insulating properties, adobe protects Cucurpeño families from the extremes of their climate, keeping them reasonably warm in the winter and cool in the summer. Moreover, it provides a graceful and subtle presence that makes many of these homes elegant in their simplicity, refuges as well as extensions of the desert with their clean-swept yards, their flowers, their herb gardens, their shade trees, and their *ollas* of water cooling on the porch.

Nonetheless, brick and slump block are beginning to make inroads as they become cheaper and more available. About 14 percent of all Cucurpe dwellings are now constructed primarily from these materials, while an increasing number of additions to older houses utilize such ready-made products. Even within adobe homes, modern touches are being adopted, the most widespread of which is the cement floor, found in two-thirds (167) of all Cucurpe dwellings. Another ubiquitous modernization is the sheet-metal (*lámina*) roof. Nearly 78 percent of the houses in Cucurpe are covered with this material, followed a distant second by corrugated cardboard (*cartón*) (17.9 percent). Only three homes still utilize earthen roofs, and no one in the municipio lives in abandoned mining tunnels or caves anymore, despite the fact that local Indian families occupied rock shelters south of the pueblo of Cucurpe as late as Porfirian times. Twenty-one families do inhabit ocotillo *jacales* roofed with cartón, a sure sign of those households' poverty. But their poverty has a modern, slapdash, impermanent quality to it, one that will undoubtedly change as those people either build more substantial dwellings or move away.

The material aspects of domestic life, then, are in visible, often bemusing transition. Propane stoves stand next to cast-iron ones in the same kitchen, while pickups are gradually replacing horse-drawn wagons. Even a few used television sets have been smuggled into Cucurpe by relatives from the United States. Curiously enough, these sets pick up Nogales, Arizona, stations better than stations from the

Sonoran side of the border. Wedded in many respects to a colonial technology, Cucurpeños nevertheless are able to bring bits and pieces of the twentieth century—and fragments of *el otro lado* (the United States)—into their homes.

HOUSEHOLD ORGANIZATION

The demographic composition of the households themselves displays to an even greater degree the tensions and incongruities generated by marginality in the modern world. Consisting primarily of biological relatives, Cucurpe households perform the most important functions of an agrarian society—the rearing of children, the raising of livestock, the cultivation of the land. And since they are units of production as well as consumption, their size and type influence a whole series of basic economic decisions ranging from what to grow to when to sell. But Cucurpe's domestic units also respond to forces that have little to do with the fertility of the land or the fluctuations of the regional livestock market. Nearly all of these households are affected by developments beyond Cucurpe's borders. Nearly all are plugged into networks of kinship that link them not only with urban Mexico but with the urban United States as well.

As Table 2.1 reveals, the most common household type is what the British historian Peter Laslett (1972) calls the "simple family household": a married couple, or its remnant, with biological offspring. Sixty-two percent of the sample (156 households) fall into this category, which is dominated by 106 simple nuclear families (42.2 percent of the total) consisting of husband, wife, and unmarried children. Variations on the nuclear family comprise the remaining simple family households—widowed spouses with children, married couples with children as well as unrelated household members, and married couples living alone. Despite the purported importance of the extended family household in rural Mexico, the nuclear family constitutes the most widespread domestic unit in Cucurpe.

In contrast, only 41 households (16.3 percent) embrace extended or multiple families of one sort or another, that is, households consisting of three or more generations of a family or more than one nuclear family. Most children establish their own domiciles soon after they marry, and hardly any married siblings reside together. Cucurpe therefore lacks any analogues to the repressive patriarchal families of late nineteenth-century Ireland (Arensberg and Kimball 1940) or the communal *frèreches* of fifteenth-century France (Le Roy Ladurie 1974).

Nearly 18 percent of the households (44), on the other hand, can

Table 2.1. Types of Cucurpe Households

Solitary Households		
Widows/Widowers	10	3.9 %
Single	16	6.4
Married men, families elsewhere	18	7.2
SUBTOTAL	44	17.5 %
No-Family Households		
Siblings	2	0.8 %
Relatives other than siblings	5	2.0
Unrelated persons	3	1.2
SUBTOTAL	10	4.0 %
Simple Family Households		
Married couples alone	23	9.2 %
Married couples with child(ren)	106	42.2
Married couples, children, unrelated	8	3.2
Widows with child(ren)	6	2.4
Widowers with child(ren)	1	0.4
Other	12	4.8
SUBTOTAL	156	62.2 %
Extended Family Households		
Extended upwards (*ex.* married couple with single surviving parent)	8	3.2 %
Extended downwards (*ex.* married couple with children, grandchildren)	6	2.4
Extended laterally (*ex.* married couple with unmarried sibling)	9	3.6
Other	11	4.3
SUBTOTAL	34	13.5 %
Multiple Family Households		
Multiple generations (*ex.* married couple with married children)	5	2.0 %
Same generation (*ex.* married siblings)	2	0.8
SUBTOTAL	7	2.8 %
TOTAL	251	100.0 %

be characterized as "solitaries"—widows or widowers, unmarried males, and married men whose families live elsewhere. The relatively large number of households (18 or 7.2 percent) in this latter sub-category reflect Cucurpe's rural isolation. A century ago, these men would have kept their families with them. Today the men live alone while their wives and children live in the pueblo of Cucurpe or in Magdalena. The municipio has not yet experienced the massive out-migration that has transformed other rural areas of the world into sad, ghostly pockets of the isolated and the old (Brody 1973; Brandes 1975). Nevertheless, declining population and dual residence patterns have imposed a solitary life-style on a number of Cucurpe adults.

Despite the predominance of nuclear family households and the fairly high frequency of solitaries, however, extended family networks remain vitally important components of Cucurpe society. Adult relatives care for one another's children, share cash and machinery, and occasionally labor in one another's fields. More to the point, municipal residence patterns frequently incarnate such networks on the ground. If they remain in the municipio, married children often settle near their parents, especially if they dwell outside the pueblo of Cucurpe. Most rural areas, in fact, consist of little enclaves of parents, children, or married siblings. One stretch of San Miguel floodplain known as El Caporachi, for example, harbors the households of three married brothers and one married sister. Just around the bend, the canyon of the Río Saracachi looms over a fertile little hollow called La Pulsera, where an eighty-year-old patriarch and his two married sons maintain their separate homes. Family members may not reside together, but they often live within hailing distance of one another. Such kinship units in many respects resemble the "sets" of Appalachian mountain people in the United States (Batteau 1982).

INHERITANCE

The reason for such proximity is the prevailing system of partible inheritance. According to both local custom and Mexican law, the property of an individual who dies intestate is divided equally among male and female offspring. This is especially true of arable land, which is carefully parceled out among surviving heirs. El Caporachi—the example cited above—was once the estate of a single man. When he died, his seven sons and four daughters each received roughly equal portions of his patrimony, which consisted primarily of floodplain fields scattered along all three rivers. His older children chose land along the Río Dolores, but three sons and three daughters inherited slightly less than one ha apiece at El Caporachi itself. Because two of the daughters had already emigrated from Cucurpe, however, they sold their shares of the estate to their brothers for a nominal fee. In this way, El Caporachi stayed in the family, even though it is now being farmed by four households rather than one.

Similar patterns of inheritance characterize many other local families as well. In a random sample of 74 households belonging to the comunidad of Cucurpe, 18 of the 50 domestic units who possess irrigated fields (36 percent) inherited all of the land they farm, while 7 more cultivate a mixture of inherited and purchased land. Inheritance is clearly one of the most important ways in which land is transmitted within the municipio.

Such a system sounds very egalitarian, and in some cases, it is. Nonetheless, partible inheritance Cucurpe-style somehow manifests a pronounced patrilineal trend. Among the same sample of comunidad households, 19 work land bequeathed them by the parents of the husband. Only 3, in contrast, farm fields that once belonged to the parents of the wife. Even though female heirs are entitled by law to their fair share of the estate, a number of factors ensure that the transmission of land generally moves from father to son.

One of these factors, of course, is differential emigration: more females leave Cucurpe than males. Another is a bias towards patrilocality; married sons settle near their parents more often than married daughters. In addition, inheritance practices themselves sometimes stray from strict partibility and overtly concentrate land in male hands. When one wealthy landowner in Cucurpe died many years ago, for example, his wife received half his estate while the other half was apportioned equally among his five sons and three daughters. After the wife passed away, however, only the sons inherited her share. Descent may be reckoned bilaterally, but property tends to remain within the male line. Equable in theory, partible inheritance does little in practice to redress the economic balance between men and women in the municipio.

At the household level, by contrast, partible inheritance does serve as a rough but effective leveling mechanism. Through luck, ruthlessness, or hard work, a Cucurpeño may carve out a sizeable estate for himself, but if he has many children, individual patrimonies may be quite modest. More than any other factor, partible inheritance has prevented the entrenchment of a hereditary landed elite in the region.

The most dramatic case in point concerns the hacienda of Agua Fría, once the largest private ranch in the municipio. During his lifetime, Agua Fría's founder amassed a latifundo of nearly 30,000 ha straddling a wide, fertile valley watered by the Río Saracachi. Related by blood or marriage to the most prominent families in Sonora, this determined individual continually added to his estate by engulfing surrounding properties, operating his empire from a headquarters that resembled a small town. He and his family resided in an elegant country home with a walled courtyard and a private telephone line to

Magdalena. In addition, there were much smaller homes for fifteen to twenty workers and their families as well as a school for their children and a chapel where they and their patron could worship together.

After Agua Fría's founder died, however, the hacienda was broken up into eight parcels and distributed among his children. Five of these parcels are now being rented by a powerful ranching family from the Altar Valley in northwestern Sonora. Only one original heir—an aging son—actually works the land himself. This man raises cattle from the old hacienda, which is slowly decaying because his share of the estate cannot support such an imposing physical plant. Meanwhile, his own son ekes out a meager income from less than 1,000 ha— his portion of the great ranch—supplemented by wage work for a North American mining company at nearby La Brisca. Within the space of three generations, then, members of this once-powerful family have either moved away or seen their status drop from *hacendado* to virtual proletarian. The laws and customs of partible inheritance simply do not encourage the preservation of large estates.

EMIGRATION

If all heirs remained in Cucurpe, partible inheritance would have disastrous consequences for the municipio. With each successive generation, fields would become more and more fragmented, and *minifundia* (the progressive fractionization of agricultural land) would plague the San Miguel as harshly as it does so many other rural areas of the underdeveloped world. But Cucurpe's great counterbalance to partible inheritance is emigration. By the time a man dies or retires from active farming, most of his children have grown. And if they have not already acquired land of their own, they probably have left the municipio in search of other livelihoods. Once settled outside Cucurpe, a share of their parents' estate is rarely enough to lure them back. Instead, they may sell or even give their fraction of milpa or temporal to the siblings who remain behind.

Emigration's political and ecological importance cannot be overestimated. Cucurpe has no industry, no tourism, no nonagrarian sector of the economy to absorb its surplus population. Therefore, the land has to bear any increase in numbers. Without emigration, marginal fields would be pressed into production, ranges would deteriorate, and stands of hardwood would be depleted. And because of all these pressures on scarce resources, political conflict would undoubtedly intensify. Consequently, emigration is the demographic safety valve that allows Cucurpe's peasant agrarian society to survive.

Nevertheless, this safety valve has bittersweet consequences for the people who stay behind. Parents who expect to grow old surrounded by children and grandchildren often find their hopes dashed as sons and daughters move away. Beto—the patriarch in the vignette at the beginning of this chapter—is relatively prosperous by Cucurpe standards. He runs about twenty head of cattle and cultivates seven ha of floodplain land, much of which he inherited from his father. A careful, innovative farmer, Beto wants to pass this land on to his sons, but both of them, as well as three of his five daughters, have left Cucurpe for the United States. His two boys would rather work for minimum wages as gardeners in Tucson than follow in their father's stead. And so Beto and his wife have to content themselves with visits back and forth across the border—holidays in Arizona or southern California, fiestas like Semana Santa back home. There are compensations—remittances from his children, occasional wage work for Beto himself in the United States—but the pain of separation still exists.

Moreover, the international border is not the only border crossed by the emigrants and their families. Many of the contradictions of *la vida Cucurpeña* are embodied in these countless individual journeys—journeys from the rural to the urban, the peasant to the proletarian, the world of the horse to the world of the freeway. In *Hunger of Memory*, Richard Rodríguez (1982:5) writes about the loss he felt as a "scholarship boy who returns home one summer from college to discover bewildering silence, facing his parents." Rodríguez was raised in Sacramento, California, not even on the Mexican side of town. How much greater the potential gulf between Americanized children and their Cucurpe kin! Most emigrants try to hang on to the symbols of their Sonoran pasts, the men wearing cowboy boots and hats and perhaps boarding a horse in Tucson, the women continuing to turn out the huge, homemade tortillas of their girlhoods. But their children go to U.S. schools, speak perfect English, and inhabit the same subculture of television programs, video games, and pop music as their peers. They are almost, but not quite, as removed from their grandparents' universe as any other second-generation immigrant group living in urban or suburban America.

The following statistics give some indication of emigration's psychological as well as demographic impact upon Cucurpe society. Nearly 86 percent (215 of 251) of the households surveyed have at least one child. In 56.3 percent of these child-rearing households, one or more offspring live outside the municipio. The total sample population of offspring, including adult children, is 1,202, of whom 38.9 percent (467) have left Cucurpe. Some are attending school in Magdalena. Others are scattered across Sonora and the southwestern

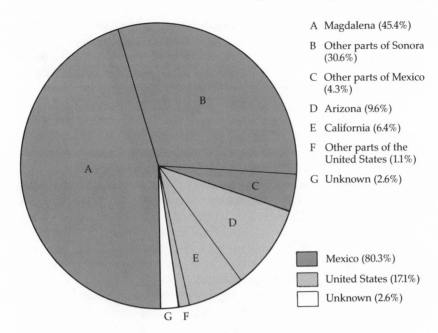

A Magdalena (45.4%)

B Other parts of Sonora (30.6%)

C Other parts of Mexico (4.3%)

D Arizona (9.6%)

E California (6.4%)

F Other parts of the United States (1.1%)

G Unknown (2.6%)

Mexico (80.3%)

United States (17.1%)

Unknown (2.6%)

Figure 2.1. Destinations of Cucurpe Emigrants

United States. In the opinion of their parents, at least 76 percent of these children are never going to return to live in the municipio.

The percentage would undoubtedly be higher if the figures controlled for the ages of the children and the parents themselves. Many households who have not yet lost a son or daughter consist of young couples with children too small to leave home. The mean number of offspring for child-rearing households is 5.6. The mean number of emigrant children per donor household is 3.8. The average couple can, therefore, expect to watch two-thirds of their progeny move away.

Cucurpeños realize that emigration is a necessary fact of life, and this recognition mitigates some of their pain and loss. One woman shook her head with relief when she learned that a son had finally decided to settle permanently in Santa Ana, California, where he had a steady job working in a fiberglass boat factory. Whenever he returned to Cucurpe, she said, all he did was drink. There was no work in the municipio for him, and she feared that he would become just another *borracho* (drunk) if he stayed at home.

Another factor easing such separations is the frequency of contact between the emigrants and their families. At present, about 45 percent of the people who leave Cucurpe move only as far as Magdalena, less than two hours away by car (*see* Figure 2.1). It is easy for such migrants to keep in touch with parents and siblings, since there is constant traffic between the municipio and its nearest commercial center. An additional 30.6 percent of Cucurpe's emigrants have settled in other communities in Sonora. Three-fourths of the migrants, then, remain in the same state. For most of these individuals, a visit back home is less than a day's drive away.

Those who leave Sonora, however, leave Mexico. Arizona (9.6 percent) and California (6.4 percent) rank as the second and third most common destinations, and sizeable communities of Cucurpeños can be found in Tucson, Phoenix, and Santa Ana, where networks of relatives provide financial assistance and emotional support for the newcomers. Temporary emigrants, particularly young men, may wander across the entire western United States, working in fields from the Imperial Valley to eastern Washington. But permanent emigration usually involves moving in with brothers and sisters, aunts and uncles, or cousins and close friends. Few Cucurpeños, in other words, settle in Arizona or California as solitary strangers. The United States may be a foreign country, but relatives provide a familiar emotional geography that buffers emigrants against homesickness or culture shock. Moreover, they can usually return to Cucurpe several times a year, renewing ties of both kin and culture. Thus the journey is gradual rather than abrupt, even if it may last a lifetime.

POPULATION

The long-range consequences of emigration are unclear. As Figure 2.2 points out, Cucurpe's population has been slowly but steadily shrinking since before World War II. The number of inhabitants decreased by 52.2 percent during the 1940s, by 16 percent during the 1950s, by 18.5 percent during the 1960s, and by 10.9 percent between 1970 and 1980. If, in fact, the 1940 census, which reflects the placer-mining boom of the 1930s, is discounted, then Cucurpe has been in demographic decline since 1910.

This decline has not been precipitous. Nonetheless, some fairly subtle changes in the structure of Cucurpe's population may eventually diminish the capacity of Cucurpeños to reproduce themselves. In 1950, for example, the percentage of individuals under 15 years of age was 46.8 percent. By 1981, it had dropped to 40.6 percent. The proportion of women in the child-bearing years of 15–49 had also dwindled from 48.9 percent to 42 percent of all individuals in this age category. If these trends accelerate, fewer children and fewer fecund

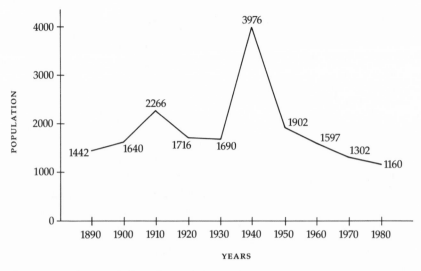

Figure 2.2. Cucurpe's Population, 1890–1980

women may turn Cucurpe into a land of lonely old men like western Ireland or rural Spain (Brody 1973; Brandes 1975).

The present population is a vital one, however, so Cucurpe's twilight may be generations away. As noted earlier, 215 of 251 sample households report at least one child. Total number of offspring ranges from 1 to 18, with a mean of 4.8 for the entire municipio and of 5.6 for child-bearing households themselves. Like other rural Mexicans, Cucurpeños clearly favor large families.

High fertility persists despite the fact that males outnumber females by 55.6 percent (596) to 44.4 percent (475). As Figure 2.3 demonstrates, this imbalance is spread over all of the age brackets except three: 0–4, 75–79, and 85 or older. More to the point, the asymmetry increases as Cucurpeños grow older. Male children comprise 52 percent of the population under fifteen. In the age category of 15–65, on the other hand, 58 percent are men, while males make up 63 percent of all individuals sixty-five years or older. Broad-based like most others in the underdeveloped world, Cucurpe's population pyramid tapers in a rather lopsided fashion to its narrow apex.

Two of the most obvious reasons for the disproportionate number of males are dual residence patterns and differential emigration. Only four households in the municipio are headed by women whose husbands reside elsewhere. Eighteen households, by contrast, consist of married men whose entire families live outside the municipio, while

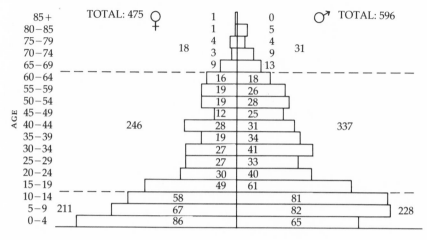

Figure 2.3. Age-Sex Structure of Cucurpe's Population, 1980

six are composed of married men with children whose wives are away. In other words, when couples live apart, the women leave Cucurpe while the men stay behind.

Emigration figures are even more revealing. According to the household survey, 53.2 percent of all emigrant children (248) are female, compared to 46.8 percent male (218). And differential emigration is not just a recent phenomenon. Seventy-four household heads belonging to the comunidad of Cucurpe reported a total of 262 emigrant siblings, 61.8 percent of whom (162) are sisters. For a number of reasons, especially the near absence of wage work for women in Cucurpe, more women than men move away.

Nevertheless, the municipio is not in any immediate danger of being depopulated. Nearly 41 percent of all Cucurpeños are children under fifteen. An additional 54.4 percent fall within the economically active ages of 15–64. Only 49 individuals—4.6 percent of the total— are 65 or older. The structure of Cucurpe's population may be gradually changing, but for the present, it retains the demographic profile of a healthy rather than a declining peasant society.

OCCUPATIONAL STRUCTURE

Regardless of the long-term changes in its population, however, Cucurpe's economy remains overwhelmingly agrarian. The urban world of service and industry may be luring away many of the municipio's sons and daughters, but those who remain are wedded to the land.

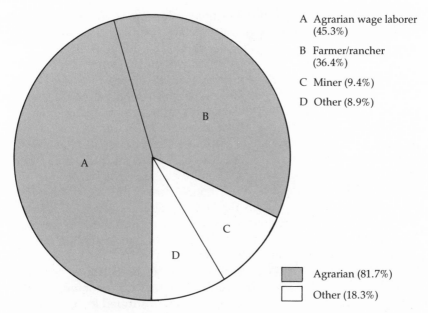

A Agrarian wage laborer
   (45.3%)

B Farmer/rancher
   (36.4%)

C Miner (9.4%)

D Other (8.9%)

Agrarian (81.7%)

Other (18.3%)

Figure 2.4. Cucurpe's Occupational Structure

The structure of Cucurpe's work force reflects this dependence on floodplain and range. Of the 360 individuals who work outside the home, 36.4 percent identify themselves as farmers (*agricultores*) or stockmen (*ganaderos*) (Figure 2.4). These men are largely self-employed, devoting most of their labor to their own fields and animals. About 45 percent of the work force, on the other hand, call themselves or their sons *jornaleros* (wage laborers). At first glance, Cucurpe appears to have a sizeable rural proletariat.

Such a conclusion does not correspond to the daily reality of many of these men's lives. Only 65 of the 163 jornaleros (39.9 percent) are employed full-time, and these are usually employed as cowboys on private ranches. The rest occasionally work for wages, but they also run their own cattle and raise their own crops. Their labeling of themselves as jornaleros simply means that at times they sell their labor to others. They are not proletarians, therefore, in the strict sense of the term because they continue to enjoy access to at least some of the means of production in Cucurpe society.

A good example of this is a tall, gaunt, fifty-five-year-old man named Antonio. Childless throughout their marriage, Antonio and his wife live in a three-room adobe house just north of the Río Saracachi's juncture with the Río Dolores. Along this bend in the river,

Antonio cultivates about three-fifths of a hectare of floodplain land, raising wheat and peas in the winter, corn, beans, and squash in the spring and summer, and alfalfa year-round. He and his wife also own twelve head of cattle, three horses, and two burros. And even though Antonio describes himself as a jornalero, he worked for wages only fifty-six days during 1981, making 200 pesos (roughly U.S. $8) a day. Furthermore, his wage work was highly sporadic—one day in January, four in February, three in March, one in May, four in July, seven in August, four in September, fifteen in October, six in November, and eleven in December. In short, Antonio's brief spurts of wage work are punctuated by long periods when he does nothing but tend to his own affairs—gathering firewood, taking care of his cattle, planting and harvesting his crops. This mixture of wage labor and subsistence ranching and farming characterizes many other jornaleros in the municipio as well, especially those who, like Antonio, belong to one of Cucurpe's three peasant corporate communities.

Even when Antonio works for other men, he performs agrarian tasks. In 1981, for example, he was hired by three different individuals during the course of the year. Some days he substituted for an old man at the communal repairs of the local irrigation system. Other days he watered the crops of a younger man who was also his *compadre*. Toward the end of the year, the president of the comunidad of Cucurpe paid Antonio to weed his temporal with a machete and to scrape off the kernels from his ears of corn. Whatever the job, though, it involved either agriculture or stock raising. Antonio is a farmer and a cowboy whether he works for others or for himself.

Most jornaleros do the same. Although they may occasionally dig trenches, build roads, or lay adobe, most of the time they irrigate other men's fields, take care of their cattle, or harvest their crops. It is safe to say, then, that the professions of agricultor, ganadero, and jornalero are predominantly agrarian in nature. Together these occupations comprise 81.7 percent of the total work force. Crops and cattle, therefore, dominate Cucurpe's economic life.

Mining used to be an important industry in the municipio, supplying jobs for hundreds of miners, woodcutters, and teamsters. By the 1950s, however, the North American companies had moved away, while the *gambucinos* (prospectors) had abandoned their placers for the coastal oases of Sonoran agribusiness. Today miners constitute perhaps 10 to 15 percent of the Cucurpe work force, their numbers constantly ebbing and flowing as new mines are opened and older ones are closed down. Mining may experience a resurgence in the future, but for now its significance pales in comparison to ranching and agriculture.

All other occupations encompass only 8.9 percent of the labor force. Four men and one woman own and operate small grocery stores. The primary school in the pueblo of Cucurpe is staffed by four teachers, and outlying schools employ four others. The municipal government includes an elected president, a full-time secretary, and a chief of police, of which there were three in 1981. Temporary deputies are commissioned when necessary; during fiestas, when public drinking is one of the primary forms of recreation, it is not unusual to see a current deputy arresting the same man who hauled him in during the preceding celebration. In Cucurpe, police work is a part-time job, a revolving door with a bewildering cast of characters who change with each public event. And although a local man does function as *síndico*, or criminal investigator, serious crimes or disturbances of the peace are handled by state or federal *judiciales* (judicial police) stationed in Magdalena.

Cucurpe's remaining bureaucracy, such as it is, consists of three livestock inspectors (*inspectores de ganado; jueces de campo*) who issue transit permits for all livestock shipped out of the municipio and oversee the annual fall roundups (*corridas*). Most years Cucurpe also enjoys the services of a young doctor performing his mandatory year of social service after graduating from medical school. Aside from these few individuals, however, Cucurpe has no professional men or women, no small army of public officials, and no middle-class of merchants or artisans. The state, and especially the federal government, affect Cucurpe life in profound and innumerable ways, but the bureaucrats reside elsewhere, outside the municipio. The local economy is simply not diversified enough to support many people who do not live directly off the land.

PEASANT AGRARIAN SOCIETY IN CUCURPE

The majority of those who do are what the French historian Marc Bloch (1966) terms "agropastoralists." In other words, they depend upon both crops and livestock to survive. Most of their rugged, semi-arid terrain cannot be cultivated, so they run cattle and goats in the uplands. But the scarcity of precipitation and the poor quality of the range often force them to provide their animals with supplementary fodder, or else watch them die. Since most of these peasant rancher-farmers cannot afford to buy feed on a regular basis, they need to be able to grow it themselves. Hence, they depend on milpa and temporal, a dependence that the growing commercialization of the local livestock industry has only intensified.

In the highland areas of the world such as the central Andes, alpine Europe, and the Himalayas, Murra (1972) and others (Netting 1972; Brush 1976; Guillet 1981) have developed the concept of *verticality* to indicate a peasant household's reliance upon a range of resources determined primarily by altitude. Cucurpe's agroecosystem, on the other hand, is not characterized by altitudinal zonation, even though altitude plays an important role in the distribution of natural vegetation. *Horizontality* might better describe the pattern of ecological opportunities and constraints operating throughout arid North America, of which Cucurpe is a part. In this vast region, the availability of water is a much more important variable than elevation because water, not altitude, determines to a far greater degree where people can settle and what they can plant. For much of Cucurpe's largely unmechanized history, then, the subsistence grid has radiated in roughly horizontal rather than vertical lines from the floodplains of the San Miguel watershed. Irrigated fields follow the contours of the floodplains themselves. Temporales spread across pockets of alluvium trapped in the subsidiary drainages twisting away at crude right angles, and rangeland extends from the river valleys to the crests of the surrounding mountains. Most households need to be able to utilize all three of these subsistence niches, or at least the two major ones of floodplain and range. Few survive as either farmers or ranchers alone.

Consequently, the major political and economic problem faced by these peasant households is to ensure their access to both arable and grazing land. They can inherit, purchase, or even clear fields. Securing rangeland is a much more formidable task. It would be hard to make a living as a private rancher on a thousand hectares even though a few of the poorer ones try. But even a thousand hectares are far beyond the reach of most Cucurpeños. Accordingly, over the centuries, they have developed corporate communities—the two comunidades and the one recently created ejido—to control large tracts of grazing land in common and to hold this land in trust generation after generation. Much of Cucurpe's internal political history has been a struggle between comuneros and private ranchers to run their cattle over this rough, thorny, parched terrain.

There is a major contradiction lurking within these corporate communities, however, one which has nothing to do with the classic agrarian battle between peasant and private landowner. In a very real sense, the contradiction is an ecological one, imposed by the natural environment itself. Floodplain fields can be plowed, planted, cultivated, and harvested by individual households. Although neighbors may occasionally be hired to perform certain tasks, agriculture does not require either communal capital or communal labor. Furthermore, land use can be intensified utilizing only household labor. Consequently, it is a household rather than a corporate enterprise. Households prize their agricultural autonomy and bristle at any threats to their independence, whether from the government or one another.

Ranching, of course, is an entirely different matter. Families run their own livestock but they do so on corporate range. Because of this dependence, they recognize that the corporate community has the right to impose certain obligations and constraints on them. They accept the fact that they have to pay dues and attend comunidad meetings in order to maintain the formal organization protecting their access to corporate grazing lands. They also realize that their neighbors have as much right to corporate rangeland, firewood, and wild foods as they do. Grazing land cannot be monopolized the way farmland is.

The nature of these two very different resources creates a sort of ideological schizophrenia among many Cucurpeños. On the one hand, they cherish their economic independence. No one tells them what to grow when. On the other hand, they are committed to the corporate control of certain scarce resources, especially rangeland. Their enemies call them *bolshevikis*. In truth, they are sturdy individualists who join together out of necessity and then grumble about that.

Such a contradiction is neither surprising or necessarily fatal. Like societies everywhere, the modern municipio of Cucurpe is not a finely-tuned, homeostatic organism. Rather, it is an arena for conflict as well as cooperation, a place where small rancher-farmers are trying to survive in a world that often seems to be leaving them behind.[3]

Members of Común de Agua Saguarito/Hornitos repairing one of their irrigation canals along the Río Saracachi.

3. La Tierra No Muere

AGRICULTURE AND WATER CONTROL

It is late August along the San Miguel River—an evening as tangible as adobe and as elusive as the mesquite smoke drifting from an outdoor fire. In a dark, immense night, the stars burn with absolute clarity as the Milky Way—el camino de San Diego—*arches across the desert sky. Inside old* Mojado's *rancho, people have gathered for a* velorio (all-night vigil) *to the* Santo Niño de Atocha. *The little ranch house is crowded with women and children kneeling on the dirt floor, and candles flicker beneath paper flowers. The women rattle off the decades of the rosary, sing a three-note song to the* Santo Niño *in high-pitched voices, and then recite a litany that invokes every manifestation of the Virgin Mary that poets and priests could conceive.*

After the litany is over, the women rest for a moment while the men who are standing in the back of the room drift outside. There is no pisto *that night;* Mojado *is a teetotaler who doesn't like to see his sons drink. But the conversation grows animated anyway as the talk of the men ranges across their favorite topics: cattle, horses, and the land. Geno tells a hilarious story about an old man so drunk on roundup that when his horse trotted under a mesquite, he threw up his arms and pitched backward, knocking himself senseless as he slid down his horse's rump.*

Gradually, however, the jokes and anecdotes dwindle away as the discussion grows more serious. For two weeks, the clouds have built up but no rain has fallen, and the late summer sun is withering the crops. Bean plants beg for water, but the downstream canals are dry. Eleven days ago, the men recall, water users along acequia Saguarito *repaired their ditch and the old wooden flume that carries its water across the Río Dolores. And yet the old man upstream—"el pinche perro viejo" (the fucking old dog), as they call him— is still irrigating while everyone else's fields dry up. "Es muy vivo, el jodido" (He's very crafty, the fucker), everyone agrees, and he irrigates only during the day, refusing to let the water flow down to his neighbors.*

The men then complain that the water judge isn't doing his job. "When there's great necessity, the people ought to irrigate day and night, as the agreement says," Geno observes. "But the people have no conscience," he adds bitterly, smoking his cigarette down to the filter and stubbing it out on the dry, hard-packed ground.

He goes on to say that while water users generally should irrigate by turn, when someone's bean crop needs water, his neighbor upstream should let the water go. "Food crops should be irrigated first," Geno comments. "Alfalfa can survive another three or four days but bean pods will dry up unless they get water."

The other men nod, shaking their heads at human selfishness and greed. "La gente es muy perra," they conclude as the Big Dipper wheels slowly and majestically overhead. Inside the women are still praying but the children have fallen asleep. There are tiny prone bodies everywhere—snuggled under blankets, curled up in the backs of pickups, tucked away in quiet corners of the ranch house itself. Geno resumes his funny stories about men falling off horses, the tranquility of the velorio broken only by the antics of a local drunk nicknamed Chuey Quebrado. Geno asks jokingly if the dog trotting along behind Chuey is his. "Pues, no es mío, Don Geno," Chuey replies. "Pertenece a mí, pero es hijo de una perra." (Well, its not mine, Don Geno. It belongs to me but its a son of a bitch.)

For centuries, Cucurpeños have been holding velorios to supernaturals like the Santo Niño and San Isidro, the patron saint of farmers. They do so because agriculture is the foundation of their economy, and their fields need all the help they can get. Agriculture is a precarious undertaking in Cucurpe, one threatened by a host of environmental hazards, especially flood and drought. Furthermore, there is a chronic shortage of the basic natural resources necessary to farming. Agriculture in the Sonoran Desert requires the beneficent conjunction of arable land and available water, neither of which is abundant in the municipio. It is no wonder, then, that people occasionally seek miraculous as well as material solutions to the problems they confront every day in their fields.

PHYSICAL ENVIRONMENT

The first significant environmental constraint impinging upon Cucurpe farmers is a topographical one: the sheer scarcity of level ground. Agriculture is only practiced in two major microenvironments within the municipio: along the floodplains of the San Miguel drainage or the arroyos of its major side canyons. Just below the juncture of the Dolores and the Saracachi, for example, the floodplain is about 1 km wide from mesa to mesa. Not surprisingly, the largest municipal community—the pueblo of Cucurpe—is located there along with much of the municipio's cultivated land. The Río Dolores also possesses broad stretches of floodplain that support small, scattered agrarian settlements like Milpa Grande, Baisimaco, El Pintor, and El Carrizal. South of Cucurpe, however, the floodplain quickly narrows, widening only at intervals to permit the fields and farmsteads of El Molino, El Tren, El Potrero, and San Javier. And the Dolores' sister tributary, the Saracachi, shelters even fewer agricultural enclaves—El Subichi, Boidolino, and La Calera—until its steep canyon walls suddenly open onto the expansive Agua Fría valley, where Cucurpe's largest hacienda was situated during the early twentieth century.

Such topographical constraints are accentuated and aggravated by climatological ones. According to the published data, mean annual precipitation in the upper and middle portions of the San Miguel watershed ranges from 466.8 millimeters (mm) at Saracachi (930 m in elevation) to 629.1 mm at San Javier (810 m) (Durrenberger and Murrieta 1978; Hastings and Humphrey 1969). The available information is neither extensive nor particularly reliable, however.[1] It is unlikely that Saracachi, 120 m higher than San Javier, receives less rainfall. Nevertheless, it is safe to assume that a rough average of 400–450 mm (15.76–17.73 inches) of precipitation falls on the lower elevations of the municipio where most agriculture takes place. While such amounts insure that Cucurpe's climate is semiarid rather than arid, true dry farming cannot be carried out within the region.[2]

Furthermore, as any geographer and plant ecologist knows, average figures can be remarkably misleading, especially because the standard deviation of mean annual rainfall in the Sonoran Desert often exceeds the mean value itself (Slatyer and Mabbutt 1964). At San Javier, for instance, annual precipitation rose from 311 mm in 1965 to 729 mm in 1966, an increase of more than 100 percent (Hastings and Humphrey 1969). During those same two consecutive years, rainfall in August, the wettest month of the year, varied from 100 mm in 1965 to 314 mm the following year. December precipitation, on the other hand, reached 108 mm in the generally dry year of 1965 while dropping to 8 mm during the abnormally wet one of 1966. These figures strikingly suggest that the annual variability of rainfall exercises a strong influence over Cucurpe's agrarian economy.

Precipitation also varies from season to season but less so than from year to year. In general, the late summer rainy season—July, August, and September—accounts for more than two-thirds of the mean annual rainfall (Figure 3.1). At that time, great roiling pyramids

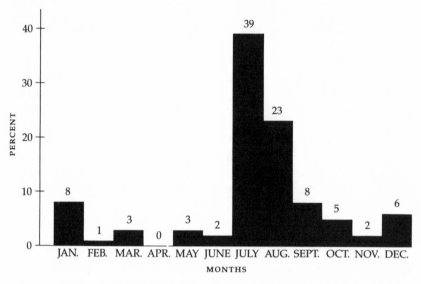

Figure 3.1. Mean Monthly Precipitation in Cucurpe (Percent of Mean Annual Precipitation)

of clouds roll across the sky and often erupt into lightning and driving rain. These convectional thunderstorms are known locally as *las aguas* (the waters).

The driest time of the year, on the other hand, immediately precedes their arrival. During the hot, parched months of April, May, and June, rainfall is negligible—between 4.2 and 7.6 percent of the average total. That quarter of the year is also the most critical in the agricultural cycle—a period when winter and spring crops struggle to ripen while rivers slow to a trickle under clear, cloudless skies. By late summer, in contrast, locally severe flooding often washes away crops and destroys vulnerable sections of the earthen *acequia* (canal) systems. Within a six-month period, then, the climatic pendulum of Cucurpe swings between the twin scourges of arid lands agriculture—flood and drought.

Surprisingly enough, however, truly destructive floods are usually reserved for the winter months. Dramatic though they may be, summer thundershowers are often quite localized. Agua Fría may get drenched while the pueblo of Cucurpe remains bone-dry. But the cyclonic and frontal storms of December and January—*las equipatas*—are the ones that occasionally settle in and rain for days across the entire watershed, or, indeed, across the Sonoran Desert itself. During the winter of 1978–79, for example, sustained and heavy rains generated floods that ravaged the San Miguel valley, gouging arroyos through some fields and sweeping away others. Older farmers recall similar disasters in 1940, 1926, 1914, and as far back as 1905. These are the hydrological events that rearrange local floodplains, scouring large slices of alluvium from one location and depositing them in another. Over the years, Cucurpeño farmers have developed a number of ingenious methods to protect their fields against moderate discharges, but the major floods are acts of God or chance that can only be endured.

Floods are also the only time when the San Miguel, the Dolores, and the Saracachi flow the entire length of their channels. The rest of the time surface water emerges intermittently from small *nacimientos* (springs) seeping from bedrock along the floodplains themselves. These ribbons of water rarely extend more than a few hundred yards before sinking back into the alluvium. Moreover, they hardly ever flow bank to bank, except in the constricted canyons of the Saracachi. In short, the San Miguel and its tributaries are typical intermittent streams of arid North America—shallow stretches of surface water alternating with expanses of river sand.

Unlike many such drainages, however, the upper San Miguel has not suffered serious environmental degradation, largely escaping the most recent cycle of arroyo-cutting that carved twenty- to forty-foot channels through floodplains in the Greater Southwest during the late-nineteenth and early-twentieth centuries (Cooke and Reeves 1976). One of the reasons for its survival are the land-use patterns of the local inhabitants, who have learned how to coexist with their river rather than destroy it (Nabhan and Sheridan 1977; Sheridan and Nabhan 1978). More important is the ubiquitous presence of bedrock at or near the surface of the San Miguel floodplain, which prevents the accumulation of deep deposits of fine alluvium where incision occurs. Lateral cutting rather than downcutting, therefore, is a far more important geomorphological process—one which plays a significant role in the agrarian economy of the watershed.

Despite its floods and droughts, then, the San Miguel survives as a living river—an oasis of exuberant vegetation in a region where many rivers have died. In contrast to the Gila, the Santa Cruz, or the San Pedro of Arizona, for example, the San Miguel has not been devastated by human exploitation of the fragile riparian environment (Cooke and Reeves 1976; Dobyns 1981; Rea 1983). Instead, the Cucurpe floodplains continue to support lush green and yellow fields, living fencerows of willow saplings, massive cottonwoods, and dense bosques of mesquite. These narrow but tenacious bands of green create a vivid contrast with the duns and tans of the surrounding desert uplands. They also constitute the lifelines upon which centuries of human occupation in the San Miguel watershed have hung.

No other resource in Cucurpe is worked as intensively as the irrigated floodplain fields (*milpas*). Milpas are leveled and plowed, planted and harrowed, weeded and harvested two and occasionally three times a year without fallowing. Moreover, they are carefully protected from floods and are nursed through droughts. When the river does manage to breach the battlements of trunk and root provided by the living fencerows of cottonwood and willow planted by Cucurpe farmers (Nabhan and Sheridan 1977), those same farmers patiently haul away the debris by bulldozer or mule and reclaim the soil. One normally taciturn Cucurpeño eloquently expressed the importance of these fields when he said, "I would not sell one ha of my land for 50,000 or even 100,000 pesos. The earth does not die! Never! I had a friend who used to say, 'He who sells his land sells his own mother.'"

Agricultural Cycle

It is not entirely correct to state that there are two distinct agricultural seasons (*temporadas*) a year in Cucurpe because a number of crops like beans or potatoes span portions of both the winter and summer planting cycles. In general, however, Cucurpe cropping patterns are determined by whether or not individual cultigens can withstand the cold of winter or the intense heat of summer. Frost-tolerant Old World grains, broad beans, and vegetables flourish during the cooler months. The ancient American triad of maize, beans, and squash dominate fields from spring to fall. Alfalfa, a perrenial legume, is cultivated year-round, even though growth slows considerably from November through February.

A more detailed analysis of Cucurpe's agricultural cycle can be garnered from the daily records of agrarian activity kept by six municipal households during 1981. As Appendix A notes, these households control from 0.6–9.0 ha of irrigated land. Like most other farming households, they also own livestock. The crops they plant, therefore, reflect both human and animal consumption needs. None of them, with the exception of Household No. 1, sells their produce; none of the household heads can be classified as either a wealthy rancher or a

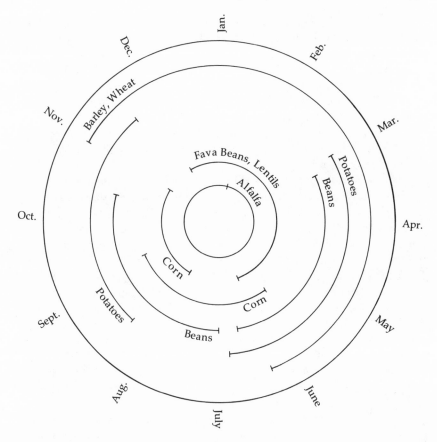

Figure 3.2. Agricultural Cycle in Cucurpe

landless laborer. They are, in short, peasant agropastoralists whose allocation of agricultural resources responds primarily to household rather than market demand.

Barley, the most important winter crop, is planted from the middle of October until early January (Figure 3.2). Wheat is also sown during this period. Both are broadcast by hand, although fields are often plowed and harrowed by tractor. Prior to World War II, wheat was the most common winter crop. Most of the harvest was threshed by horses or mules in circular, hardpacked clearings (*eras*) and winnowed by pitchfork. Then the grain was ground at local water- or steam-powered mills or by backyard *taunas*, small, porous grinding stones turned by horses or burros. Cucurpe households produced most of the wheat they needed to make tortillas, those staples of every

Sonoran meal. By the end of the 1930s, most local mills had shut down, but farmers continued to grind their flour at commercial mills in Magdalena.

Even today, three of the six households in the sample still thresh and winnow small portions of their barley or wheat. Nevertheless, most of Cucurpe's grain crop is cut and baled by tractor for animal feed. Rather than process their own flour, Cucurpe farmers purchase commercial flour in 46 kg (*quintal*) sacks, which cost 200 pesos (about U.S. $8) in 1981. Wheat and barley are now raised primarily to feed livestock, not people.

The reason for this major shift in cropping patterns vividly demonstrates how international economic developments have affected daily life in this isolated municipio. Prior to World War II, a steer brought about ten dollars in the regional livestock market. Cucurpeños ran a lot of cattle, but they also consumed more of the animals themselves. In 1980, on the other hand, a male feeder calf weighing 120 kilos sold for an average price of 3,500–4,000 pesos (U.S. $140–160). Consequently, Cucurpe has become completely integrated into the international livestock industry during the last forty years, exporting feeder calves that are fattened on U.S. ranges (*see* chapter 4). Moreover, the enormous postwar expansion of commercial wheat farming, especially in oases of agribusiness like the Yaqui valley, has rendered local food grain cropping and milling obsolete. It is simply more economical today for a Cucurpeño farmer to fatten his animals rather than his family on homegrown grains.

Similar shifts from food to forage crops have characterized many other areas of the Mexican countryside during the postwar period (Yates 1981; DeWalt 1985). Not surprisingly, this shift has had repercussions which extend far beyond what farmers plant in their fields. In Sonora, for example, river valleys like the San Miguel are lined with the ruins of adobe flour mills that represented the nodal points of once-thriving local economies. Older Cucurpeños, especially those whose parents were prosperous, often wax eloquent about the good old days when the mill wheels turned and local artisans produced everything from saddles to soap. Memories, of course, are selective, utilizing the past as a political weapon in the present. But many rural areas like Cucurpe did support more people and more local industry two generations ago than now. The technological progress of the postwar period has not been uniform, even in a dynamic state like Sonora. Instead, the postwar boom has tended to truncate or destroy the diversity of many local economies by turning them into dependent components of a much larger regional system. Cucurpeños rarely eat their own wheat anymore. And Americans eat most of their calves.

These changes did not come quickly or easily in the municipio. Many people found it hard to break old habits of self-sufficiency and surrender themselves to market exchange. Nonetheless, pragmatists that they are, the Cucurpeños eventually made the transition. The president of the Cucurpe comunidad in 1981—a man who left Cucurpe as a young boy and made his fortune in the construction industry before returning home—recalls encountering a local farmer ten or fifteen years earlier who was cutting wheat by hand in his field. It was a drought year and many cattle were starving, including the farmer's own animals. The president asked the man why he didn't save his cattle by turning them into the milpa. The farmer replied that his family needed the flour for tortillas. "Listen," the president said, "You could buy your family the 20–30 *quintales* of flour you'll harvest from this field with the sale of one calf." The farmer did not immediately respond, but a few days later the president noticed the farmer's cattle in the milpa eating his wheat.

Because of the rise in cattle prices, varieties of wheat (*trigo barbón*) bred to produce good flour have been displaced by barley, alfalfa, and other strains of wheat (*trigo flor*) better suited for forage. Barley (*cebada pelona*) in particular has become the most cultivated winter crop, with alfalfa a close second. Barley is considered better fodder than wheat. As one farmer said, "It is more commercial, nearly as good as alfalfa." Furthermore, it is more drought-resistant than the other forage crops. Alfalfa, a notoriously thirsty plant, needs to be irrigated at least every two weeks in Cucurpe's semiarid climate. Wheat requires supplementary water at least once a month. Barley, on the other hand, can survive with only two irrigations (*riegos*) during its four- to five-month growing season if winter rains are relatively abundant. Since irrigation water is a painfully scarce resource in Cucurpe, especially in late spring when the grains mature, barley's hardiness makes it the most attractive fodder crop in the municipio.

Nevertheless, alfalfa is almost as popular, and its acreage would undoubtedly surpass barley's if farmers had more water. One of alfalfa's major advantages is its status as a perennial; a single planting will produce five to seven cuttings a year for three to five years. Its disadvantages include a heavy demand for water and its toxicity during certain stages of growth. Local farmers lose cattle every year to alfalfa bloat, which may afflict the animals if they eat the legume green or after a frost. Recently, the government has been promoting the cultivation of rye grass, and a few agriculturalists have begun to plant it in the region.

Despite the clearly recognized strengths and weaknesses of certain crops, however, seed availability often determines what a particular farmer sows in his fields. In 1981, for example, one man was forced to plant *trigo barbón*—a variety of wheat poorly suited for forage because its long grain spikes (*espigas*) irritate the throats of livestock—because he could find no barley or *trigo flor* seed in Magdalena.

Although grains dominate Cucurpe's winter fields, a number of other crops are also cultivated during the cooler months. Many households grow Old World broad beans, especially lentils (*lentejas*) and fava beans (*habas*). Other common winter vegetables include onions (*cebolla*), garlic (*ajo*), and peas (*alverjones*).

By spring, Cucurpe farmers are ready to begin raising some of the staples of the human diet. In the first or second week of March, the eyes of potatoes (*papas*) which have been cut and dried with lime or ash are carefully planted by hand in rows (*surcos*). A week or two later, pinto beans (*frijoles*) are sown, usually in rows in the same field. Nearly every household with irrigated land plants one or more varieties of pinto beans (*garapata, azufrado,* etc.), and a surprising number cultivate potatoes. The first bean crop is harvested three months later in mid-June. Potatoes with a slightly longer growing season are gathered at the same time. Some households also plant summer squash during the spring.

The summer season itself begins in late May after the winter grains have been harvested. A number of farmers attempt to grow two crops of corn, planting the first in late May. Depending upon the variety, green corn is ready in 60–90 days and mature ears in 90–120 days. Whether or not a farmer plants an early corn crop is determined in large measure by the availability of water. April, May, and June are the driest months of the year, and many farmers simply do not want to gamble that there will be enough flow in the communal acequias to meet their needs. Consequently they wait for the onset of the summer thundershowers before sowing their corn.

The appearance of the summer rains also influences the time when the second crop of beans and potatoes is planted. Farmers replant beans from early July until early August and resow potatoes the first or second week in August. Winter squash is generally in the ground by mid-July. Beans are then harvested in mid-October, potatoes in early November, and corn, depending on whether it is picked green or mature, from October through early December. The first two crops, of course, are consumed by humans. Corn, on the other hand, is eaten by both people and animals, particularly the pigs which many households fatten in their backyards.

Agricultural Technology

Despite how intensively they cultivate their milpas, Cucurpeños follow no regular pattern of crop rotation. Sorghum and milomaize (*sorgo, milomaíz, ceterita*) are recognized as plants that exhaust the soil, but they are usually confined to *temporales* rather than irrigated fields. Alfalfa and fava beans, on the other hand, are believed to enrich the ground. According to one prominent Cucurpe farmer, "With these two seeds the soil is improved very much. With these two seeds you don't need fertilizers." Nonetheless, such nitrogen-fixing legumes are not necessarily grown in fields where the earth has been depleted by other cultigens. Instead, crop succession is determined more by the compatibility of the growing seasons, the availability of seeds, and, to a lesser extent, regional market demand. If a field is double-cropped, corn almost always follows a winter grain like wheat or barley, while successive plantings of beans and potatoes are sown in the same plots. The neatness of peasant European cropping patterns has not been replicated by the subsistence farmers of the San Miguel.

Neither do these farmers renew the fertility of their soil by applying chemical fertilizers. Out of a sample of 150 households in the municipio who control arable land, only 5 (3.3 percent) stated that they use commercial fertilizers. Many farmers pasture livestock in the stubble (*rastrojo*) of their fields, so cow and horse manure undoubtedly enrich the soil to some degree. But livestock manuring is not practiced in a systematic fashion as it is in other areas of Mexico such as the Tarahumara country, where Indian agriculturalists pen their goats and sheep in movable corrals each night to ensure their entire milpa gets fertilized. At first glance, then, it seems remarkable that Cucurpeños are able to crop and doublecrop their milpas year after year without fallowing.

Once again, however, the key to agricultural success lies in their creative give-and-take with the San Miguel River. Like all Sonoran Desert drainages, the San Miguel experiences periodic flooding—floods, which, because of the sparse vegetation of the surrounding watershed, carry abundant sediment loads. After heavy rains, particles of soil and nutrient-rich detritus like leaves and twigs are washed into the San Miguel and its tributaries. This residue is then carried

Living fencerows along the Río San Miguel: newly planted willow saplings (foreground); mature fencerow with brush weave (background).

downriver by the floods. Known locally as *limo del río* (mud from the river) or *abono del río* (fertilizer from the river), these flood-born sediments serve as the major source of soil replenishment in the municipio.

Nevertheless, the process is not a passive one. Cucurpeños first must break the force of the muddy floodwaters, which they call *agua puerca* (piggish or dirty water), before the sediment can precipitate onto their milpas. Their solution to this problem is as simple as it is ingenious: the propagation of living fencerows of cottonwoods and willows which slow the floodwaters down and cause the *agua puerca* to flow gently across their fields (Nabhan and Sheridan 1977). These fencerows are called *cercos de tejido* (woven fences) or *cercos de rama* (branch fences), and they consist of nothing more than riparian vegetation available right at hand. During the winter months, farmers prune branches from nearby cottonwood and willow trees. These saplings are then planted in trenches in the floodplain 1–3 m from the edges of their fields. After the saplings take root and grow, brush from common riparian shrubs such as mesquite, seep willow (*batamote*), and burrobush (*jecote*) is woven tightly between the trunks. By the time flooding begins in July or August, these fencerows are usually stout enough to resist all but the strongest discharges.

According to local farmers, the *cercos de rama* perform three major functions. First, their trunks and roots protect fields from the erosive action of most floods. Secondly, they trap floodwater sediment between the fencerows and the fields themselves, thereby adding long strips of nutrient-rich soil to the milpas. Finally, they curb the force of the floodwaters, compelling the *agua puerca* to spread across the fields and renew the soil. One Cucurpe farmer described the process by saying, "The trees and woven branches accept the floodwater and make it tame." Another stated that by employing the fencerows, "You can make the river flow where you wish."

Unfortunately, not all floods can be tamed. The living fencerows are able to handle moderate discharges and make them work *for* rather than *against* the farmers. Major floods, on the other hand, rip through or behind the fencerows and devastate fields. Two such episodes have occurred in the last ten years, the first in December 1978–January 1979, the second in early October 1983. Many Cucurpe households lost portions of their fields, and a few unlucky families watched helplessly while entire milpas washed away. As one Cucurpe farmer said, "Here the river brings the soil and carries it away."

Nonetheless, most years the *cercos de tejido* protect, extend, and enrich floodplain fields. Erosion control and the renewal of soil fertility in Cucurpe are, therefore, carried out with nothing more than axes, shovels, and an intimate knowledge of riparian vegetation. At present, the antiquity of the living fencerows is unknown, although they may date from the colonial or perhaps even the pre-Columbian period. Some local farmers, in fact, attribute the *cercos* to the famous Jesuit missionary Eusebio Francisco Kino, who often assumes the dimensions of a mythical culture hero in northern Sonora. Regardless of their origins, the fencerows testify to the ingenuity and self-sufficiency of local farmers, who have managed to live in peaceful coexistence with their river rather than damming or destroying it.

Many other agricultural methods practiced in the municipio also reflect Cucurpe's traditional agrarian heritage, a combination of Iberian and Native American crops and techniques adapted to the San Miguel watershed. Grains such as wheat or barley are still threshed in circular *eras* which have been cleared of vegetation, watered down, and hardened by pounding the soil with large wooden rammers (*pisones*). A tall wooden pole is then erected in the middle of the circle, and after grainheads have been piled there, four to six horses or mules

Threshing wheat on an *era* in the middle of a field at El Caporachi north of Cucurpe.

are hitched to the pole and driven around until the grain has been knocked loose by their hooves. As old as the Old Testament, this Near Eastern method of threshing occasionally receives a modern twist when Cucurpeños use pickup trucks rather than horses to separate the grain.

Beans are threshed and winnowed by hand as well. Other agricultural tasks, in contrast, are now being carried out by tractors, of which there were ten in the municipio in 1981. Although some farmers still harvest their wheat or barley with hand-sickles (*hoz*), others cut and bale winter grains, alfalfa, and even maize stalks by machine. Of the 135 households reporting their methods of cultivation, 101 of them— 75 percent of the total—employed a tractor at some point in the 1980 or 1981 agricultural cycles. During peak harvest times such as late April through early June, these tractors are so much in demand that desperate farmers often contract them to bale their grain at night.

In summary, then, most farmers in the municipio utilize all three sources of energy—machine, animal, and human—to perform the necessary agricultural tasks. Fields are generally plowed and disked by tractor and cultivated by horse or mule. Forage crops are usually baled, but beans, corn, squash, lentils, favas, and potatoes are harvested by hand. Of the 135 households in the sample mentioned above, 54 percent (73) of the total employed both tractors and *bestias* (draft animals) to work their fields. By contrast, only 21 percent (28) relied solely upon tractors, while 25 percent (34) continued to depend exclusively on the labor of animals or their own hands. Machinery is utilized when feasible, but the small scale of Cucurpe agriculture simply has not allowed or demanded a total reliance upon mechanization.

Water Control

Like other aspects of Cucurpe's agricultural technology, water control reflects the municipio's mixture of the modern and the traditional. Of the 105 households who control irrigated fields, 97 (92 percent) rely at least in part upon the surface water of the San Miguel drainage. This water is channeled onto their fields through an intricate web of earthen canals call acequias. The remaining 8 percent of the farmers get their irrigation water from pump-powered wells, nearly all of which are located on the floodplains themselves. At present, major acequias are regulated by traditional water-users' associations known as *comunes de agua*, while wells are completely controlled by private individuals. Since these pumps and acequias usually tap the same aquifers, however, the potential for conflict between the two methods of water control remains great.

In 1980–81, there were at least eighteen different acequias snaking along the floodplains of the San Miguel and its tributaries. Twelve of these canals serve only a handful of farmers and are not subject to formal control. Six acequias, on the other hand, are important enough to be under the jurisdiction of organized water users' associations, of which there are three in the municipio. The Común de Agua El Pintor/Cañada Ancha encompasses the irrigation district running from El Pintor to Cañada Baisimaco along the Río Dolores. Común de Agua Saguarito/Hornitos controls irrigation water from Buenavista at the junction of the Dolores and the Saracachi to Los Alisos south of the pueblo of Cucurpe. The third association—Común de Agua El Molino/Cerro Blanco—exercises jurisdiction over surface water from Cerro Blanco to El Molino along the San Miguel below Cucurpe. All three of these associations control two major acequias each, one on either side of the floodplain itself.

Although all three of these associations are presently within the boundaries of the reorganized Comunidad of Cucurpe, water control is not a function performed by the corporate community. Rather, the comunes de agua act as autonomous organizations responsible only to their members and the president of the municipio. In January, members of each organization meet to elect a water judge (*juez de agua*; *comisionado de agua*) and his substitute (*suplente*). At this time, the local regulations governing each común are reiterated and particular problems facing the association discussed.

No one knows exactly how old these particular associations are. One document from the fragmentary municipal archives notes the presence of fourteen landowners utilizing the waters of Acequia Saguarito in 1937, but the canals and their respective comunes undoubtedly date from a much earlier period. Similar systems were introduced by the Spaniards throughout the arid and semiarid New World (Simmons 1972; Hutchins 1928; Meyer 1984). These organizations have probably been an integral part of the Cucurpe body politic since colonial times.

The acequias themselves are relatively simple affairs. Wherever a permanent spring (*nacimiento*) flows out of the river sand, crude diversion weirs (*represas*) of sand, wood, and brush channel the water into earthen canals approximately 0.5–2 m wide and 1–1.5 m deep. These acequias then wind along the floodplain for up to 5 km, their banks stabilized by riparian vegetation such as burrobush (*Hymenoclea monogyra*), seep willow (*Baccharis salicifolia*), desert broom (*Baccharis sarathroides*), and tree tobacco (*Nicotiana glauca*). In areas where the floodplains narrow, the canals either hug canyon walls, where they are occasionally protected by living fencerows, or bore through rock outcrops in tunnels chiseled or dynamited years before. Masonry sections (*tramos*) of the acequias even cling to the cliffs themselves along particularly constricted stretches of the floodplain.

As mentioned earlier, each común is responsible for two major canals, one on the east bank of the river and one on the west. Water users on both sides of the floodplain join together in one association because the acequias usually share the same intake areas (*tomas de agua*). Furthermore, in times of drought, there is often not enough water in the river to fill both canals. During these critical periods, flow is channeled from one acequia to the other for a specified number of days to enable irrigation to take place on both sides of the river.

Because irrigation water is frequently in such short supply, the job of *juez de agua* assumes considerable importance. The water judge makes sure that water users along both acequias under his jurisdiction irrigate according to their proper turns (*por turno*). Upstream water users always precede downstream ones unless special temporary arrangements are made. The juez de agua also organizes and supervises

A brush-and-sand weir diverting water from the Río Saracachi into Acequía Saguarito upriver from the pueblo of Cucurpe.

the work parties that clean and repair the canals. During times of the year when flow is decreasing, this official decides whether turnos need to be limited, or whether water is to be transferred from one acequia to the other. When water is scarce, the *comisionado* is supposed to institute round-the-clock irrigation (*por día y noche*) and prevent irrigators from sleeping on the job or letting water escape from their fields. As the 1981 juez de agua for común de agua Saguarito-Hornitos said, "The water judge needs to exercise great vigilance. One cannot leave the water alone."

Despite all the traditional customs and regulations surrounding these comunes, however, they are not smoothly running institutions. On the contrary, they are wracked by minor but persistent conflict among water users and threatened by a host of environmental hazards. The simple but inescapable problem the comunes face is the scarcity of water; there is simply not enough surface flow to meet the demands of every water user belonging to the associations. Moreover, the physical systems themselves are vulnerable to a number of perturbations, particularly the floods which wash out the represas and sections of the acequias themselves at least several times a year. At times, these canal systems resemble Rube Goldberg creations with their patchwork modifications and repairs.

A more detailed examination of the largest water users' association—Común de Agua Saguarito-Hornitos—brings some of these conflicts and constraints into sharper focus. Saguarito-Hornitos is composed of 36 water users who control land along its canals. Twenty-one members irrigate from Acequia Saguarito on the west bank of the Río San Miguel, while fifteen draw their water from Acequia Hornitos on the east bank. During the general cleanings (*limpiezas generales*) of the acequias which take place in February and August, each water user must send a fixed number of workers (*jornaleros*) corresponding to the amount of land he or she irrigates. The same system also applies when the canals must be periodically maintained and repaired throughout the year. The number of workers is determined by the traditional *hijuela* system. According to custom, an hijuela consists of twelve *tareas*, or roughly two-and-one-half ha of land.[3] For each hijuela, a water user must contribute a day's work (*jornal*), either going himself or paying someone else to work for him. The correlation between the number of hijuelas and the amount of acreage irrigated is not precise. For example, one Cucurpeño complained that he has to provide one jornal for his five tareas (approximately one ha), while his brothers only contribute one for the nine tareas they each possess. Despite these inconsistencies, however, the system manages to function most of the time.

Nevertheless, it demands considerable expenditures in both labor and time. Water users or their jornaleros worked on the acequias at least twenty-seven different days during 1981, cleaning, repairing, and rebuilding the canals and diversion weirs. The total number of man-days, of course, was much higher, because many tasks required work forces of ten to twenty men or more. Not surprisingly, the peak period of labor occurred during the late summer rainy season when flooding was most frequent. During August 1981 alone, work parties labored on the irrigation network eleven different days, or more than one-third of the month.

Much of this labor is expended because of the ramshackle nature of the system itself. There are no permanent dams or reservoirs along the San Miguel, no way to impound water when flow is abundant in order to ration it out when the river begins to dry up. During most winters and after the summer rains, more than enough water courses down the drainage to meet the needs of the farmers along its banks. By April of most years, however, the flow begins to decrease; permanent

Wooden flume carrying the water of Acequía Saguarito across the bed of the Río Dolores.

nacimientos slow to a trickle and many springs completely disappear. To compensate, Cucurpe farmers are forced to adopt a number of survival tactics in order to stretch the remaining surface water as far as possible. They extend their intake canals further up the river to increase the amount of water diverted into their acequias. They hack away riparian vegetation along the canal banks to reduce transpiration loss, and they scrape off (*deslamar*) the algae which clogs the acequias themselves, choking off flow. Time and again they repair the leaky wooden flume (*canoa*) that spans the Río Dolores and carries water to the Saguarito water users opposite the pueblo of Cucurpe. Finally, after every flood, they rebuild the sand-and-brush diversion weirs and the sections of acequias destroyed by the floodwaters. If the represas were permanent, if the canals were concrete, if the flume were replaced with an underground siphon, many of these tasks could be eliminated. But the water users have neither the money or the organization to accomplish such modifications of their irrigation system's infrastructure.

What they have is a system that clearly does not meet their needs.

Every year, especially in the summer, a handful of farmers lose entire harvests or suffer greatly reduced yields. They do so because the acequia flow has either been disrupted by floods or is insufficient to irrigate their crops at critical periods in the growth cycle. One such period is late May, when beans planted in March are beginning to flower. Without water every six to eight days, the beans will not set or the pods themselves will wither. As one farmer noted, "The sun is very intense. It burns the entire plant including the pods. With such an intense sun the bushes break open and the pods are baked."

Another risky time of year is late summer, when the convectional thundershowers rage across the sky and send flash floods surging down the drainages. Nearly all these floods sweep away the diversion weirs and vulnerable stretches of the acequias themselves. Water users may repair the damage only to suffer the same consequences a week later. Some years many of them simply give up the battle and let their summer fields lie fallow. And since they have no crops planted in their own milpas, they feel little incentive to repair the system so that the fields of their neighbors can be irrigated. At least one household lost its late-summer corn crop in 1980 because Acequia Hornitos was washed out in July and not repaired until September.

As might be expected, these natural slings and arrows cause considerable conflict among the water users themselves. As the days grow hotter and plants demand more water, the water in the river diminishes. Farmers begin to curse the weather and each other and claw for every extra hour of irrigation they can beg, borrow, or steal. During these critical periods, the juez de agua is besieged with requests for extensions or special favors. One farmer wants the tail-end of an irrigation turn (*la cola de agua*) to water his beans. Another needs several extra hours to finish irrigating his alfalfa. Occasionally, farmers even sneak out to the acequias at night to breach the canals with their shovels and illegally divert water onto their fields. On two occasions in 1981, the water judge caught the culprits and reported them to the municipal president, who ordered them to compensate the water user whose turn they stole. But others were not apprehended, stepping beyond the bounds of law and custom to irrigate their crops. Punishment is not always forthcoming. Neighborliness is not always strong enough to overcome individual household needs.

The dwindling water supply may also pit water users along one canal against those along another in the same común. By mid-April of 1981, flow along the Río Saracachi had subsided to such an extent that the water judge was forced to divert all water into one acequia and then another for eight- and eventually five-day periods. By May tempers were flaring. The Hornitos water users demanded that the water be shifted to their acequia. The Saguarito water users pleaded with the comisionado to allow them just a little more flow. As one Saguarito farmer said, "The others are in a big hurry. They don't want to let us have the water five or six hours more. But now is the critical time for beans because they're already in flower. If you don't irrigate them now, you'll lose your harvest."

The juez de agua, of course, is caught in the middle, damned by one side or another no matter what he does. In return for carrying out his duties and enduring the abuse of his neighbors, the water judge receives 75 kilos of wheat flour or its monetary equivalent for every hijuela a water user owes the system. Despite this incentive, however, the office is not particularly sought after by members of the comunes. The 1980 water judge, in fact, vowed never to accept the position (*cargo*) again. "I'm very busy," he said. "Besides, the *comuneros* are very devious. They all want their water rights but they don't comply with their obligations. They're coyotes."

The same man went on to say that what the farmers really need is a pump-powered well to provide groundwater for irrigation when surface water runs short. Most other water users would have agreed with his assessment. The acequia systems allow Cucurpe agriculturalists to survive, but sometimes that margin grows pretty thin. Moreover, the supply of surface water is too limited and the network of canals too vulnerable to enable farmers to intensify or expand agricultural production. Maize, the staple of Native American horticulturalists for thousands of years, occasionally fails during the late summer months because the acequia system has temporarily broken down. Other potentially lucrative crops such as chile and onions rarely can be grown on a commercial scale because they require more water than most farmers are allocated. The same man who expressed the need for groundwater complained in August 1981 that he and others were losing their crops because they did not have the water to irrigate them. "It takes away your desire to work," he said. He then talked about the beautiful chile and corn crops some of his friends were raising on land they sharecropped north of the pueblo of Cucurpe. There, however, the sharecroppers had access to a pump-powered well and could irrigate their fields on a regular basis. "How it makes me jealous to see those milpas!" the man exclaimed.

Pumps are seen as the only viable alternative to an antiquated system of water control that prevents any real agricultural progress in the municipio. One of the major goals of the Cucurpe comunidad is to secure government financial and technical assistance for the drilling of wells and the purchase of necessary machinery (*see* chapter 9). In meetings and on street corners, men constantly debate the merits of deep, perforated wells versus shallow, hand-dug wells that seldom reach depths of more than 40–50 feet. Cucurpeños argue about where the wells should be placed. They even dream about sinking wells in the floodplain and then pumping the water in tubes up and over the surrounding mesas to irrigate the fertile side canyons of the San Miguel watershed. In short, like farmers all over arid North America, they hunger for a technological fix.

Pump-powered wells are not a recent innovation in Cucurpe. One individual stated that the first well was dug at Milpa Grande along the Río Dolores in 1939–40. The well failed and was abandoned in 1943. But several other wealthy farmers, including the man's father, soon drilled perforated wells at Cañada Ancha and Milpa Grande—wells still in operation today. In the entire municipio, there are at least twenty-five irrigation wells, most of them located in the floodplain of the San Miguel drainage itself. Nineteen of these wells are open and relatively shallow; water is brought to the surface by centrifuge pumps. These wells are known locally as *pozos de luz*. A few of the wealthier farmers, on the other hand, have drilled perforated wells that utilize turbine pumps. In some areas such as Cañada Ancha, agriculturalists with considerable experience flatly state that perforated wells are the only ones that will work. They claim that the alluvium is so fine it simply clogs up (*ensolver*) the pozos de luz.

In other areas, however, pozos de luz are the only ones capable of supplying water. During the late 1970s, the federal government spent hundreds of thousands of pesos to sink deep, perforated wells in the three major side canyons of the upper San Miguel watersheds—Cañadas Cuervo, Baisimaco, and Ancha. After drilling as deep as 500 feet and installing turbine pumps that were supposed to deliver 10–12 inches of water in diameter, government technicians, to the great dismay of everyone involved, found that only about 2 inches of flow trickled from the pipes. Designed to open up several hundred ha of land for cultivation, the wells turned out to be monumental failures, suitable only for the filling of cattle tanks. In Cañada Ancha the technicians even abandoned their drilling rig to the vandalism of both people and time. The massive apparatus stands in mute testimony to expensive technological failure.

An official of the Secretaría de Agricultura y Recursos Hidráulicos (SARH) in Magdalena said in an interview that Cucurpe is "one of the most privileged areas of Sonora" because recharge of groundwater aquifers was so much greater than discharge. He also noted that most of the water is located near the surface of the floodplain or its side canyons. In his opinion, the perforated wells were simply drilled too deep and missed these alluvial aquifers. He said that various government agencies were going to help the Cucurpeños install pozos de luz in order to intensify and expand agricultural production.

The official also discussed how groundwater pumping would be regulated in the future. At present, all wells have to be registered with SARH. If a farmer wishes to drill a new well, he has to obtain SARH's permission, which is often a complicated and expensive undertaking. Once a well is installed, however, the amount of water pumped from it is not controlled or taxed. As long as he can afford the fuel, a farmer can keep his pump running constantly if he so chooses. He can also sell water to his less fortunate neighbors. At critical times in the growing season, in fact, many farmers are forced to purchase flow from the handful of well-owners with large and dependable pumps. These owners were charging seventy pesos (U.S. $2.80) an hour for water in 1981.

The SARH official recognized the logical inconsistency of such a dual system of water control. On the one hand, surface flow along the San Miguel and its tributaries is strictly regulated by the traditional comunes de agua. Groundwater, on the other hand, is considered a private resource. Since most wells are shallow, they tap the same saturated alluvium that feeds the springs upon which the comunes depend. Nonetheless, the water users' associations enjoy absolutely no jurisdiction over these wells.

All this may one day change. The official said that SARH will probably not authorize any new wells in Cucurpe unless they benefit a number of water users rather than just one. Furthermore, there are rumors that well-owners may be forced to pay for the water they pump. Although no one believes that wells in such a marginal area as Cucurpe are likely to be metered, the government may institute some form of a water tax based upon the amount of irrigable acreage a well-owner possesses.

Without a doubt, groundwater is the most important unknown factor in Cucurpe's agrarian equation. Its exploitation and distribution in large measure will determine the future of agriculture in the municipio. If the government places it within the reach and jurisdiction of the comunes de agua or the corporate communities, then Cucurpe's peasant agropastoralists may survive and even flourish. But if the resource remains in private hands, the days of the comunes—and of the farmers who depend on them—may well be numbered.

In the meantime, Cucurpeños do the best they can with sticks and shovels and sand. They continue to plant their fencerows and repair their acequias. Some of them scrounge and save to buy small pumps for their own shallow wells so they can keep their beans from withering in June or their corn from burning up in late August. The battle is endless and full of frustration. One man purchased a four horsepower pump in Tucson for 7,000 pesos (U.S. $280) and then paid a 3,000-peso bribe (U.S. $120) to smuggle it across the border. After installing it, he found it did not work in his well, so he immediately began to search for another pump. Other, less determined farmers make do with the acequia flow, gambling that the rains will fall at the right times so that they will be able to glean at least a modest harvest from their milpas. Traditional technologies of water control possess great and enduring strengths, enabling farmers in Cucurpe to have survived for centuries. But they also have painful limitations—the limitations of low yields or lost harvests, of backbreaking labor and petty conflict over the one resource no farmer in the Sonoran Desert can do without.

TEMPORALES

Temporal or rainfall-dependent agriculture is also practiced in the San Miguel watershed, particularly in the major side canyons of the drainage. Necessary soil moisture comes from precipitation rather than from any permanent source of water. Nevertheless, temporal farming does not necessarily imply the absence of waterworks. In fact, very few temporales rely entirely upon direct rainfall alone.

Many Cucurpe farmers employ what Ressler (1966) terms the channeled floodwater technique. In other words, they dig wide, shallow ditches from normally dry arroyos to the temporales themselves. When rain falls, runoff collects in the arroyos and flows into the ditches and onto the fields. At least one Cucurpeño has introduced an elaboration into this system by throwing a crude earthen dam (*tapón*) across a small arroyo so that runoff is diverted into the ditch leading to his temporal in Cañada del Cuervo. Other farmers construct brush weirs to intercept arroyo flow. The owner of Hacienda El Pintor even practices a form of *bolsa* agriculture, sowing crops in a large, excavated depression which retains moisture (Dobyns 1951). All of these modifications of the natural environment are designed to increase the amount of water available to temporales without resorting to outright irrigation.

Because they rely entirely upon rainfall, however, temporales are even riskier ventures than the milpas themselves. Rainfall-dependent agriculture is aptly described as "a battle" (*una lucha*) by many farmers in the municipio because their temporal crops are completely at the mercy not only of the amount but also the timing of precipitation. Heavy rains in July, for example, may be followed by six weeks of dry weather—enough time for young corn and squash plants to wilt in the fields. Just such a situation occurred in Cucurpe in 1981. One man, in fact, lost both his winter and summer temporal crops that year. His barley rotted in the fields because late spring rains thoroughly dampened the cut fodder before it could be baled. His corn and *ceterita* (a variety of sorghum), on the other hand, withered in the hot, dry August weather. Too much water or not enough, the results were the same: the loss of a harvest.

Most years farmers sow corn, sorghum, squash, melons, and occasionally beans soon after the onset of the summer rains in late June or July. If the winter rains are abundant, Cucurpeños may also plant wheat or barley. Many farmers did so in 1981 following heavy rains in early January. Fields are usually plowed by tractors or draft animals and then the seeds are planted in the damp soil. Winter grains are broadcast, while summer crops are usually sown in rows (*surcos*). The fields are then disked or harrowed to cover the seeds so they will not be devoured by birds.

Once seeds are in the ground, however, temporales receive considerably less attention than milpas. Due to the vagaries of precipitation in the Sonoran Desert, rainfall-dependent agriculture simply does not merit the labor devoted to irrigated fields. Temporales are rarely cultivated; weeds like amaranth (*bledo; Amaranthus palmeri*) and Johnson grass grow interspersed with corn, squash, and sorghum. Furthermore, the domesticated plants themselves are often intercropped. In many fields, the broad, mottled leaves of squash (*calabasas*) spread in the shade beneath dark green stalks of maize. And since the ultimate success of the temporales depends more upon regional climatic patterns than upon human effort, most farmers simply place the seeds in the soil and hope for the best.

Unfortunately, no long-term record of temporal harvests has been kept in Cucurpe, so it is not possible to precisely evaluate their contribution to the agrarian economy. Yields certainly do not match those of the milpas. Some years, farmers are lucky to get their seed back. The year 1981 was definitely a poor one. As one Cucurpeño noted in August, "The plants are pleading for rain," pleas which fell on deaf ears that season. Nonetheless, the often meager harvests are usually worth the minimum amount of labor the farmers invest. Even if the crops are too sparse to be baled for fodder or threshed for seed, at least they provide "good pasture for the animals." In a region where natural forage all but disappears at certain times of the year, "good pasture" is a precious commodity indeed.

AGRICULTURAL LABOR

Even though agricultural modernization has not yet overwhelmed Cucurpe, mechanization has reduced the amount of human labor necessary to cultivate municipal fields. A 1.5 ha plot of wheat which used to take two men three days to harvest with hand-sickles (*hoz*) can now be cut and baled by machinery in several hours. Plowing with horses or mules also consumes considerably more time than employing a tractor. Roughly 75 percent of Cucurpe's farmers, therefore, pay high prices to rent tractors and their operators to prepare fields for planting and to harvest crops. In December 1980, for example, it cost 1,050 pesos (U.S. $42.00) to plow, disk, and harrow a one ha field. During the same period, tractor-owners charged 20 pesos a bale (U.S. $0.80) to cut forage selling for 60–70 pesos per bale (U.S. $2.40–2.80). In other words, one-third of the total harvest wound up in the hands of tractor-owners.

Despite an increasing dependence upon machinery, however, the Cucurpe agrarian economy still relies heavily upon human and animal labor. As noted earlier in the chapter, many agricultural tasks continue to be performed either by hand or by draft animals. Most of Cucurpe's fields are simply too small to permit the efficient mechanization of all activities.

Perhaps the most important decision Cucurpe households must make during the course of an agrarian cycle is the allocation of labor among the three sectors of the agropastoralist economy: milpa, temporal, and livestock. In order to better understand the distribution of labor at the household level, it is again necessary to consult the daily records of agrarian activities recorded by six Cucurpe families. Careful analysis of these records reveals many of the economic and ecological opportunities and constraints operating upon municipal rancher-farmers.

As might be expected from such a small sample, there is a tremendous amount of variation in the allotment of labor among the six households. Moreover, it must be reiterated that the sample is not representative of the municipio in any strict statistical sense (*see* Appendix A). These necessary caveats notwithstanding, several general trends emerge quite clearly from the daily records. Irrigated agriculture demands from 50–70 percent of a household's labor. On the average, a household devotes 110 man-days to each hectare of irrigated land it controls. Temporal farming, by contrast, receives only 3–15 percent of a household's work time; Cucurpeños expend a mean of 9.9 man-days on a corresponding hectare of temporal land. Because the temporales have no guaranteed water supply, they simply do not warrant the care lavished upon floodplain milpas.

Livestock raising, the most remunerative of Cucurpe's agrarian activities, consumes only 12–30 percent of the household labor pie. These figures translate into a ratio that neatly encapsulates the paradoxes of Cucurpe's peasant agrarian economy. Even though most of their cash incomes derives from cattle sales, Cucurpeños devote three times as much labor to their milpas as their animals. At first glance, this seems like a glaringly inefficient allotment of labor. But as chapter 4 makes clear, the ratio accurately reflects the demands of stock raising on a corporate and degraded range. When a household's cattle graze communal pastures, it has little or no incentive to improve its herd through either selective breeding or range management. Such practices would only benefit that household if most of its neighbors using the same range adopted similar procedures. Within Cucurpe's corporate communities, such levels of cooperation are rarely achieved (*see* chapters 8 and 9). About the only effective way a household can protect its cattle from drought and add valuable kilos to their rangy frames is to cultivate fodder crops on its milpas and temporales. Consequently, much of the labor invested in agriculture becomes an indirect but vitally important investment in stock raising as well.

DISTRIBUTION OF ARABLE LAND

Distribution of arable land in the municipio is not quite as skewed as the distribution of livestock (*see* Chapter 4). Within the sample of 242 households who actually reside in the municipio, no domestic unit controlled more than 52 ha of irrigated milpa or 45 ha of rainfall-dependent temporal. Even among the nonresident elite, holdings remain small. The largest single owner of irrigated land in Cucurpe, a wealthy businessman who possesses mines and other enterprises throughout northern Sonora, cultivates only 70 ha of milpa within the municipio itself. There is just not enough high-quality arable land in Cucurpe to attract the agribusinessmen. Farms, therefore, have not been consolidated as much as they have been in other areas of north-

Table 3.1. Distribution of Arable Land Among Resident Households in
Cucurpe

Amount (ha)	Households	Percent Households	Amount Land	Percent Land
Irrigated Land (Milpas)				
0	141	58.3	0	0
5 or less	85	35.1	179.4	43.6
6–10	11	4.5	87.2	21.2
more than 10	5	2.1	145.0	35.2
TOTAL	242	100.0	411.6 ha	100.0
Nonirrigated Land (Temporales)				
0	134	55.4	0	0
5 or less	87	35.9	173.4	36.6
6–10	13	5.4	93.0	19.6
more than 10	8	3.3	208.0	43.8
TOTAL	242	100.0	474.4 ha	100.0

western Mexico. Because of its agricultural marginality, the municipio
continues to shelter a fairly large class of subsistence farmers, a situation characterizing other peripheral areas of Mexico as well (Kearney
1980; Janvry and Garramón 1977; Esteva 1980).

Nevertheless, the distribution of farmland still manifests significant inequality. Among resident households in the municipio, 58.3
percent (141 households) control no irrigated land whatsoever (Table
3.1). Only 5 resident domestic units cultivate more than 10 ha of milpa.
These same 5 households occupy 35.2 percent (145 ha) of all irrigated
farmland controlled by Cucurpe residents. The remaining 39.6 percent
(96 households) divide 266.6 ha among themselves. The average
amount of irrigated land for the total resident sample is 1.7 ha with a
standard deviation of 4.9. The mean for only those 101 households
that control land is 4.1 ha. This mean drops to 2.8 ha when the 5
households mentioned above are removed from the sample.

Nonresident households own at least 222.4 ha of irrigated land
within the municipio, or 34.9 percent of the 636 ha in cultivation.
Only 8 of 32 households in the sample possess milpas, an average of
27.8 ha, considerably more land than the resident households themselves. If their total landholdings are combined with the land of the 5
resident households controlling more than 10 hectares, these 13
households occupy 57.8 percent (367.4 ha) of the total irrigated acreage
in Cucurpe.

The distribution of temporal land closely approximates that of
milpas among resident households (Table 3.1). One hundred and

thirty-four of these households (55.4 percent) control no rainfall-dependent fields. Eight households, on the other hand, cultivate more than 10 hectares for a total of 208 ha, or 43.8 percent of the temporal acreage occupied by Cucurpeños themselves. The average amount of temporal land for all 242 resident households is 1.96 ha with a standard deviation of 5.1. The mean rises to 4.4 if only landholding households are included in the sample.

One significant difference exists between the distribution of milpa and temporal, however, and that is the amount of rainfall-dependent land held by nonresidents. Only 4 of 32 nonresident households bother to cultivate temporales at all. Together these households sow only 31.6 ha, a mere 6.2 percent of the total amount of rainfall-dependent arable (506 ha) in the municipio. Members of the nonresident elite clearly feel little need to invest their labor in such a low-yield venture as temporal agriculture.

The reasons for this difference in distribution are not difficult to determine. First of all, 8 of the 32 nonresident households in the sample own irrigated farmland within the municipio on which they raise fodder for their livestock. A number of these families also own fields in surrounding municipios, especially in the Magdalena area. These milpas provide them with the supplementary forage they need. Secondly, many members of the nonresident elite pasture their livestock on much better range than municipal residents and therefore require less supplementary fodder to begin with. Thirdly, nonresident households rarely feel compelled to engage in subsistence agriculture, and so they can dispense with the spotty harvests of corn, beans, squash, and winter grains which the rainfall-dependent fields produce. Perhaps more than any other measure, the distribution of temporal land reveals the relatively low value placed on this particular resource within the Cucurpe agrarian economy.

AGRICULTURAL LAND TENURE

At this point in the narrative, it is necessary to make a point that is reiterated at much greater length farther on: the distribution of land is not equivalent to the distribution of land tenure within the municipio. Households may control a certain amount of irrigated, rainfall-dependent, or even pasture land without actually owning that land. Landholding and landownership, particularly within the three peasant corporate communities, are two very different factors in the Cucurpe agrarian equation.

As the following chapters demonstrate, land tenure is the most volatile element in the politics of Cucurpe resource control. Even within the corporate communities themselves, members are bitterly divided over the question of land ownership, especially of the culti-vated fields. According to federal agrarian reform law, all land within a comunidad or ejido, arable or nonarable, belongs to the corporation. Many comuneros, on the other hand, refuse to concede that the fields their families have farmed for generations are owned by the com-unidad and not by them. To complicate matters even further, several households which refuse to join the corporate communities still retain control over farmland within corporate boundaries, a situation which has generated a number of lengthy lawsuits and has brought the conflicting parties to the brink of violence on several occasions.

Arable lands, especially the milpas, are tended with care and defended with an ardor reserved for no other municipal resource. Milpas are considered part of a man's patrimony to his children as well as a hedge against disease and disaster. Both milpa and temporales form an integral part of a household's total wealth. In modern Mexico with its exploding population, arable land, even tiny plots of one or two hectares, often mean the difference between survival and flight— between living the way your parents did or gambling on an uncertain future in urban Mexico or the United States. People undoubtedly have been fighting over farmland in Cucurpe since prehistoric times. The battle rages today and is unlikely to come to an end for many years.

A brief analysis of land tenure in the municipio, therefore, helps to reveal where many of the battle lines are drawn. As Table 3.2 indi-cates, the three peasant corporations nominally control 40.1 percent (255.1 ha) of irrigated land and 68.5 percent (346.4 ha) of rainfall-dependent land within the municipio. Nearly 60 percent of the milpas and 31.5 percent of the temporales, by contrast, belong to households outside the corporate communities. Despite this imbalance, however, 68.6 percent of the resident population (719 of 1,048 individuals in the sample) are affiliated with the peasant corporations. In other words, nearly 70 percent of all people in the municipio make their living, in whole or in part, on less than 40 percent of Cucurpe's irrigated land. The inequality and inadequacy of such a distribution have profound demographic, economic, and political repercussions which will be discussed in succeeding chapters.

At the household level itself, the land is held under a variety of tenure arrangements, the most common of which is either outright ownership or entrenched usufruct. Nearly 88 percent of the house-holds farming temporal land and more than 90 percent cultivating irrigated land exercise such direct control over those milpas and tem-

Table 3.2. Tenure of Arable Land in Cucurpe

Status	Irrigated	Nonirrigated	Households	Municipal Population
Corporate	(ha)	(ha)		
Cucurpe	208.9 (32.8%)	269.3 (53.2%)	108 (39.4%)	493 (47.0%)
San Javier	45.9 (7.2)	58.1 (11.5)	34 (12.4)	131 (12.5)
6 de Enero	0.3 (0.1)	19.0 (3.8)	19 (6.9)	95 (9.1)
SUBTOTAL	255.1 (40.1%)	346.4 (68.5%)	161 (58.7%)	719 (68.6%)
Private				
Resident	158.5 (24.9%)	128.0 (25.3%)	81 (29.6%)	329 (31.4%)
Non-Res	222.4 (35.0)	31.6 (6.2)	32 (11.7)	— —
SUBTOTAL	380.9 (59.9%)	159.6 (31.5%)	113 (41.3%)	329 (31.4%)
TOTAL	636.0 ha	506.0 ha	274	1,048

porales. Only three households belonging to the corporate communities and only two private households rented all or part of the milpas they cultivated in 1980. Renting in any of its manifestations, including sharecropping, is of negligible importance within the municipio as a whole.

This characteristic of Cucurpe land tenure greatly influences the politics of resource control within the municipio. Most households engaged in agriculture farm land which they regard as their own. They decide what to plant and when. They determine whether the harvest is to be consumed within the household or sold. In the eyes of the law, the land may not belong to them. They may not be able to sell, rent, or otherwise alienate the land without the permission of the corporate community holding that land in trust. Nonetheless, the difference between what the law says and what the people believe is often immense. As chapters 8 and 9 make clear, many comuneros do not accept the restrictions imposed upon them by the federal government. The concept of the personal ownership of arable land is deeply ingrained, even among members of the corporate communities themselves. Government attempts to change or challenge that abiding belief have only increased the amount of conflict and dissension within the peasant corporations. The resolution of these conflicts may very well determine the future success of these organizations and the shape of Cucurpe's agrarian economy in the years to come.

Roundup on the Comunidad of Cucurpe.

4. El Ganado Le Da la Vida

LIVESTOCK RAISING

It is late October and the annual roundups have begun. Today the juez de campo *meets a small group of cowboys at Huero's* temporal, *and they ride into the mountains west of Cucurpe to gather the cattle there. The cowboys separate and work the ridges, driving the scattered animals out of the brush and down into the arroyos toward Huero's corral. The country is steep and rugged—choked with mesquite on the south-facing slopes and with oak on the north. One old cow refuses to descend, hiding in every brush thicket she can find.* "Hija de tu chingada madre, jodida, cabrona," *the cowboys repeat over and over until their epithets become a kind of litany to bovine defiance and the open range.*

At a saddle along the summit, the riders come together again. The crest of the mountains forms the western boundary of the comunidad; *east is a private ranch owned by one of the most powerful families in Sonora. The contrast between the two ranges is striking—high clumps of grass on the private side of the fence, the cover close-cropped and nearly denuded on the* comunidad *side. But the country is magnificent—a high oak basin studded with* sotol. *As the cowboys wheel their horses around and push the cattle down the drainage, they flush four whitetail deer who bound out of the brush in front of them, their rumps flashing in the sun.*

By late morning, a small herd has been collected. The cattle trail behind one another, bunching up in the flats, stringing out along the ridges. Occasionally, one of the animals veers suddenly to make its escape. When it does, the cowboys chase after it, galloping through the mesquite, forcing their horses up rocky slopes, their mounts lunging and scrambling for hoof holds in the loose stones. Nearly every one of these men has sustained at least one major injury on horseback; dented foreheads or sets of plastic front teeth testify to accidents suffered and survived. But the morning is uneventful. The cowboys ride the flanks of the herd, smoking, prodding, cursing the gaunt, dusty cattle with good-natured contempt.

Most of the cattle file into the little corral by early afternoon. There they jostle for position, haunches splattered with liquid green cowshit. The corral is a kaleidoscope of dust and color and moving forms—barsinos *(dark, speckled browns)*, hueros *(whites)*, amarillos *(yellow browns)*, colorados *(reddish browns)*, prietos *(blacks)*, and canelas *(whites flecked with brown) mounting and butting and ramming into one another as more and more animals are driven into the mesquite enclosure. The cattle are all* ganado corrido—*intermixtures of every major breed in the region from Herefords to zebus. No selective breeding there, just survival of the toughest and the rangiest.*

As soon the last recalcitrant beast has been forced through the gate, the cowboys break for lunch, resting in the shade of Huero's one-room rock hut as he lights a fire to brew coffee and roast fresh goat meat. After the meal, they smoke and talk about the cattle and play joke after joke on old José, who is trying to take a nap. One of his nephews even cinches José's saddle on backwards. José grins at the boy and calls him a male whore. Then he stretches out in his jacket and chaps and falls asleep in the warm, late-October sun.

Cucurpe exports two basic commodities—cattle and people. While the people may occasionally send remittances back to their families, the sale of cattle is the municipio's true economic lifeblood. As the inspector for the first of Cucurpe's three livestock zones said, "Stock raising's the only way to make a living here. There's nothing else." Cattle plug this isolated little section of Sonora into an international web of buyers and sellers, of government regulations and the fluctuations of an unstable market. Cucurpeños exchange their animals for the bounty of the outside world—beer, flour, coffee, sugar, clothes, medicine, pickup trucks, and propane stoves. In the process, they become increasingly dependent upon economic decisions and political policies made, never by them, on both sides of the international border.

THE PHYSICAL ENVIRONMENT

Physiographically, Cucurpe falls within the basin and range province of southwestern North America, its broad, dissected valleys broken by a series of mountain ranges whose crests occasionally reach 2,000–2,500 m in elevation. Even in the valleys, however, the terrain is often rugged, consisting of hills, bluffs, bajadas, and a few small mesas slashed by numerous arroyos. As noted earlier, only about 1,142 ha of land are presently being cultivated in Cucurpe. The rest of the municipio—roughly 188,000 ha—can be utilized only as grazing land (*agostadero*) or for non-agrarian activities such as mining.

Stock raising itself is difficult across such a rough and semiarid landscape. According to Shreve and Wiggins (1964), the Sonoran Desert encompasses most of the municipio, the area east of the San Miguel River being classified as a narrow southern tongue of the Arizona Uplands subregion, the area west of the river as part of the Plains of Sonora. In other words, most of Cucurpe is desert country with desert vegetation and a desert climate. But such broad categories fail to convey the vegetational diversity of the region or the range of micro-environments that influence the Cucurpe livestock industry. The municipio, in fact, embraces at least five major vegetation types determined by altitude, slope exposure, and edaphic conditions. These vegetation types are the environmental variables most critical to ranchers. Consequently, their distribution directly affects the number of livestock different areas of the municipio can support.

The most restricted vegetation type is the pine-oak woodland, which is found only on the peaks of the higher mountain ranges like the Sierra San Antonio northeast of the Agua Fría valley. In general, pine-oak woodland occurs between altitudes of 1,800 and 2,400 m and is dominated by the intermingling of both pines (*Pinus engelmanni, P. leiophylla*) and oaks (*Quercus hypoleucoides, Q. viminea, Q. arizonica*, etc.). While this vegetation type is often associated with good grazing conditions, it is of little importance to Cucurpe because of its limited acreage.

Oak woodland, on the other hand, is more widespread. Known locally as *encinal*, this vegetation type is found at elevations of 1,300–1,800 m and frequently assumes a savannalike appearance well-suited to stock raising. Characteristic species include Arizona oak (*Q. arizonica*), Mexican blue oak (*Q. oblongifolia*), and the economically important Emory oak (*Q. emoryi*), whose acorn (*bellota*) is gathered for commercial sale. Associated species of economic value are lechuguilla (*Agave palmeri*), the century plant distilled into bootleg mescal, and sideoats grama (*Bouteloua curtipendula*), an important range grass. Many of the municipio's largest and finest private ranches, in fact, consist largely of oak woodland, which supports more animal units than vegetation types occurring at lower elevations. Moreover, oak woodland largely covers Ejido 6 de Enero as well, one of the reasons why the ejido has been the focus of conflict between campesinos and private ranchers since the 1960s.

Intergrading with oak woodland at lower altitudes is mesquite grassland, or *mesquital*. As the name suggests, this vegetation type is dominated by mesquite (*Prosopis juliflora*), which grows widely spaced in the uplands and in dense forests (*bosques*) along the watercourses.

Just south of the hacienda of Agua Fría, one of the largest bosques in the region extends for miles along a branch of the Río Saracachi, its mesquite pods helping to fatten the cattle of private ranchers there. In addition, various economically important grasses grow in association with mesquite, including beard grass (*Andropogon* sp.), three-awn (*Aristida* sp.), and various types of grama (*Bouteloua* sp.). Consequently, mesquite grassland is one of the most important vegetation types in Cucurpe. Along with oak woodland, it sustains much of the region's livestock. Not surprisingly, it is largely in private hands as well.

Below the mesquite grassland on the interfluves bordering the San Miguel River lies the desert scrub. This is the vegetation type surrounding most major human settlements in the municipio. Moreover, desert scrub covers much of the terrain within the comunidades of Cucurpe and San Javier. Characterized by microphyllous trees like mesquite, palo verde (*Cercidium* sp.), and various species of *Acacia*, and by numerous species of cacti including saguaro (*Carnegiea gigantea*) and organ pipe (*pitahaya*; *Stenocereus thurberi*), desert scrub also contains a number of important forbs and grasses. But this extensive vegetation type is not as rich in such species as either oak woodland or mesquite grassland, and much of its floor supports very little grass cover at all, a consequence of overgrazing as well as aridity. The desert scrub does, on the other hand, supply seasonally abundant ephemerals that are particularly important for livestock on corporate ranges. During drought years, in fact, ephemerals may be the only fodder available to cattle across these denuded uplands.

The fifth major vegetation type—riparian woodland—is located only along the San Miguel and its major tributaries. Utilized more for agriculture than for stock raising, this vegetation type is composed of winter-deciduous trees like sycamore (*Platanus racemosa*), Arizona elder (*Alnus oblongifolia*), Arizona ash (*Fraxinus arizonica*), walnut (*Juglans major*), cottonwood (*Populus fremontii*), and willow (*Salix goodingii*). These trees form cool and leafy canopies along much of the San Miguel floodplain whether they occur naturally or are humanly propagated as living fencerows. They also shelter a number of shrubs and herbs that serve as food for both people and animals. More importantly, the fields carved out of the riparian woodland furnish the fodder crops that allow livestock to survive when natural forage fails.

Prior to the Spanish conquest, Cucurpe's rugged stretches of desert and mountain provided the region's human inhabitants with little more than game and wild plant foods. Then the Spaniards introduced domesticated Old World animals, and suddenly natural grasses and forbs could be converted into meat, hides, tallow, and the animal power to pull a plow or haul a load of wood. Cattle, goats, and horses soon roamed from floodplain to mountain, greatly intensifying the exploitation of nonarable terrain. These animals also allowed the local economy to diversify and expand. Ranching quickly became a way of life as well as an economic endeavor among Cucurpe's Indian and mestizo inhabitants, shaping every aspect of their culture from diet to world view.

The introduction of livestock also initiated a remarkable symbiosis between agriculture and animal husbandry, one that grows stronger with each passing year. No one knows the condition of Cucurpe's range before the Spaniards drove their herds of cattle into the area in the mid-seventeenth century. Most likely, there were more forbs and grasses for animals to feed upon, even in the desert scrub, and those early herds undoubtedly multiplied in the San Miguel watershed. After more than three centuries of overgrazing, however, the range has become so degraded that most ranchers have to provide their cattle with supplementary fodder at certain times of the year. Cattle may provide Cucurpeños with most of their cash income, but unless stock raisers can grow their own forage, they have to spend substantial portions of that income to buy feed. As one farmer said, "Here the cattle give you your livelihood. But without a milpa you can't raise cattle."

Arable land, of course, is severely limited. At best, local farmers produce enough fodder to carry their animals through critical periods of drought; livestock cannot be pastured year-round in the fields. And since rainfall is often extremely localized, especially during the summer months, poor range conditions are aggravated by spotty precipitation patterns. Consequently, cattle require large areas upon which to forage for wild grasses and shrubs. In other words, livestock raising in a semiarid region like Cucurpe is a land-extensive rather than a land-intensive activity, one that demands considerable amounts of agostadero. Scientific range management can improve the land/animal ratio to a certain extent, but the vagaries of rain and the harsh nature of the terrain impose implacable constraints on the number of livestock even the best of ranchers can run.

Nevertheless, there are often sharp contrasts in the quality of private and corporate ranges that affect the condition of their cattle as well. Some of the private ranchers conserve and improve their rangeland and practice modern techniques of livestock breeding. Many comuneros and ejidatarios, on the other hand, simply allow their animals to shift for themselves. Within a half hour's drive, it is possible to see fat herefords grazing knee-high grass in the Agua Fría valley and skinny *corrientes* (mixed breeds) munching on cardboard scavenged from garbage dumps outside the pueblo of Cucurpe. Differences in land tenure influence the practice of animal husbandry far more than they do agriculture in the municipio, perpetuating the economic differences that so profoundly shape Cucurpe's politics of resource control.

CORPORATE GRAZING LANDS

The Comunidad of Cucurpe, the largest and most powerful corporate community in the region, enjoys title to 21,050 ha of municipal land. Comunidad San Javier exercises jurisdiction over 9,867 ha, while Ejido 6 de Enero holds 8,000 ha in trust. Together these three peasant corporations control 38,917 ha, approximately 21 percent of Cucurpe's terrain. Although many private ranchers complain that Mexico's agrarian policies are "communistic," it is clear that most of the municipio's land remains in private hands.

Nearly all the land that is corporate consists of broken, sparsely vegetated agostadero. As Table 4.1 makes clear, only 1.5 percent of the corporate land is presently being cultivated, even though the percentage of corporate arable land is higher than the percentage of arable land in the municipio as a whole. Comuneros and ejidatarios, there-

Table 4.1. Total Amount of Arable and Nonarable Land in Cucurpe

Status	Irrigated	Nonirrigated	Total Arable	Nonarable	TOTAL
Corporate					
Cucurpe	209 ha	269	478	20,572	21,050
	1.0 %	1.3	2.3	97.7	
San Javier	46 ha	58	104	9,763	9,867
	0.5 %	0.6	1.1	98.9	
6 de Enero	0 ha	19	19	7,981	8,000
		0.2	0.2	99.8	
SUBTOTAL	255 ha	346	601	38,316	38,917
	0.6 %	0.9	1.5	98.5	
Private	381 ha	160	541	149,543	150,084
	0.3 %	0.1	0.4	99.6	
TOTAL	636 ha	506	1,142	187,859	189,001
	0.3 %	0.3	0.6	99.4	

fore, are stockmen and cowboys as much as they are farmers or day laborers.

Ranching heritage runs deep in Cucurpe. Whenever men gather—on the trail, in town, while drinking together under the shade of a cottonwood on a hot summer afternoon—their conversation invariably turns to cattle, horses, or the condition of the range. Many of them call their cows by name and know the habits and quirks of their own animals as intimately as they know their neighbors. Cucurpeños may spend twice as much time working in their milpas, but stock raising and horsemanship capture their imaginations in ways agriculture never can.[1] As soon as they can walk, little boys are fashioning makeshift lariats (*reatas*) to rope dogs, cats, and one another as they learn the skills of adulthood through play. And when they are old enough to sit a saddle, they perform simple chores under the watchful eyes of their fathers or older brothers—chores such as herding nursing cows and their calves between milpa and milking corral when cheese is being made during the fall. By the time they are teenagers, then, most Cucurpe males are expert cowboys, chasing rangy corrientes across the broken terrain. In the process, they acquire a thorough knowledge not only of horses and cattle, but of the surrounding rangeland as well.

Despite this knowledge, however, members of the corporate communities have seriously degraded their environment, largely through overgrazing. Cattle dominate the landscape, even when they cannot be seen. Cattle trails meander everywhere, leaving trampled vegetation and hard-packed soil in their wake. Most hillsides have been cut into a series of narrow terraces by centuries of hooves, and saddles along ridges are often hollowed and denuded by the dusty wallows of resting cows. Only the steepest crests and the most precipitous canyon walls escape the plodding search for forage. And where cattle cannot scramble, goats often can.

Because of overgrazing, grasses have disappeared from many areas within the two comunidades. About the only ground cover left are the herbaceous ephemerals that appear in spring or late summer following the Sonoran Desert's two rainy seasons (Shreve and Wiggins 1964). Summer ephemerals are usually abundant because of the reliability of *las aguas*. Winter ephemerals, on the other hand, fluctuate in response to the whims of the winter rains. In 1981, for example, heavy storms in January, February, and March carpeted patches of the desert scrub with ephemerals by April or early May. A year later, those same areas lay barren as Cucurpeños worried that many of their cattle would die.

Table 4.2. Total Number of Livestock on Cucurpe Ranges

Status	Cattle	Horses/Mules	Burros	Goats
Corporate				
Cucurpe	3,120*	740*	194*	759*
San Javier	2,056†	274†	30†	89*
6 de Enero	378†	75*	42*	260*
SUBTOTAL	5,554	1,089	266	1,108
Private	22,198†	647†	15†	68†
TOTAL	27,752	1,736	281	1,176

*From author's questionnaires.
†From municipal livestock censuses (1981).

Winter ephemeral production is especially critical to corporate stockmen because its arrival coincides with the onset of the driest time of the year—a time when surface water is scarce and winter forage crops have not yet been harvested. As the Cucurpeños say, the winter rains are *"puros billetes"* ("pure money") because they insure the survival of their livestock during late spring. If the rains fail, however, cows do not calve and some animals starve. Meanwhile, a household's money drains away into the pockets of those few farmers who have extra bales of barley or alfalfa to sell.

During such lean times when ephemerals are not available, cattle are forced to browse shrubs and trees. Cucurpeño stockmen also rely upon a number of other strategies to help their cattle survive. After they harvest their crops, for example, they turn their cattle into the stubble (*rastrojo*) to glean whatever is left. Pregnant cows, or those nursing calves, may also be corralled and fed to keep up their strength or to stimulate milk production in order to make cheese. If times are particularly hard, stockmen may singe the thorns off pads of prickly pear and chop them up for their cattle. But the poor conditions of the range and the scarcity of fodder occasionally make the cows of the comuneros look like bony ghosts of the animals grazing on private ranges.

Rangeland in the two comunidades is particularly poor, reflecting a long history of overgrazing. In 1980–81, the Comunidad of Cucurpe supported at least 3,120 head of cattle, 740 horses or mules, 194 burros, and 759 goats on its 21,050 ha (*see* Table 4.2). The actual figures were probably higher, since the annual livestock censuses underenumerate animal totals and my survey data represent a 90–95 percent sample of stockmen utilizing comunidad terrain (*see* Appendix A). Of course, not all of these cattle represent a complete animal unit, which is

Table 4.3. Estimated Land/Animal Unit Ratios on
Cucurpe Ranges

Status	Animal Units	Acreage	Ratio
Corporate			
Cucurpe	3,438	21,050 ha	6.12
San Javier	1,909	9,867	5.17
6 de Enero	425	8,000	18.82
SUBTOTAL	5,772	38,917	6.74
Private	17,473	150,084	8.59
TOTAL	23,245	189,001 ha	8.13

generally considered to be a 1,000-pound cow, or a cow with calf. According to the 1981 livestock census, in fact, 22.6 percent of the total number of cattle were unweaned calves. Many others were young cows or steers which had not yet reached their full weight. Nevertheless, if only 75 percent of the total number of cattle are calculated as animal units, then the Comunidad of Cucurpe maintained 2,340 animal units of cattle alone in 1980–81. Considering horses and mules as 1.25 animal units, burros as 0.5, and goats as 0.1, an additional 1,098 animal units can be added for a total of 3,438 animal units as a whole. This means that there are only 6.12 ha per animal unit within the Comunidad of Cucurpe's boundaries, a staggeringly low land/animal ratio for such semi-arid terrain (Table 4.3).

The Comunidad of San Javier is in even worse shape. Stockmen there run at least 2,056 head of cattle, 274 horses or mules, 30 burros, and 89 goats for a total of 1,909 animal units. These figures yield a woefully inadequate land/animal ratio of 5.17 for the comunidad's 9,867 ha (Table 4.3).

The comunidades of Cucurpe and San Javier are located in the southern portions of the municipio where both elevation and precipitation are low. Vegetation is primarily desert scrub intergrading with a few fingers of mesquite grassland to the north and east. Only along the northern slopes of the higher mountains do patches of oak woodland occur, and this vegetation type is extremely limited. Moreover, large stretches of the Comunidad of Cucurpe consist of outcrops of rhyolitic tuff, locally known as *cantera*. Such white, chalky wastelands support very little forage. Even under virgin conditions, then, the landscape could never support so many animals without degradation.

As it is, more than three centuries of livestock have taken a serious toll. Although no comprehensive survey of the range has yet been conducted, one official in the Department of Agrarian Reform estimated that at least 26 ha are needed to maintain an animal unit at Cucurpe or San Javier. If such is the case, the optimal number of animal units for the Comunidad of Cucurpe would be 810 rather than 3,438, while San Javier should be supporting no more than 380 animal units instead of 1,909. Consequently, these two corporate communities may be running from four to five times as many animal units as their ranges can sustain.

Ejido 6 de Enero is in a much better position, at least for now. Prior to 1976, when a presidential resolution created the ejido, the land belonged to a number of private ranchers. By 1980–81, therefore, the ejidatarios had only been in possession of their 8,000 ha for five years. Furthermore, because they are among the poorest residents of the municipio, they had not had a chance to build up their herds. As a result, the ejido maintained a livestock population of approximately 378 head of cattle, 75 horses and mules, 42 burros, and 260 goats, or roughly 425 animal units. That gave the ejido a land/animal ratio of 18.82 in 1980–81, far higher than those of the other two corporate communities and even of many private ranches (Table 4.3). And since much of the ejido is oak woodland or mesquite grassland with areas of fairly abundant grass cover, 6 de Enero's livestock population is within the carrying capacity of its range, at least for now.

Despite the dangerously low land/animal ratios, however, Cucurpe's corporate communities do little to control the number of livestock on their ranges. Considerable variation in livestock ownership exists among members, and the Agrarian Reform regulation limiting comuneros to fifty head of cattle apiece is not enforced. In a sample of 103 households belonging to the Comunidad of Cucurpe, for example, 20 households owned no cattle whatsoever. Eighteen households, on the other hand, ran more than 50 on the communal range. Mean number of cattle was 26.2 with a standard deviation of 27.6, a sure sign that neither economic equality nor economic regulation characterized Cucurpe's largest comunidad.

Interestingly enough, 14 households which did not belong to the comunidad also grazed their stock on corporate land. Together these 14 households controlled 398 head of cattle, nearly 13 percent of the total, while 3 owned more than 50 head, ranking them among the wealthiest households making a living off the communal range. Despite the fact that defense of the corporate grazing lands was the reason most comuneros fought to win official recognition from the federal government, the regulation of livestock is not yet a function of the reconstituted corporate community (*see* chapters 8 and 9).

The distribution of cattle among the members of Comunidad San Javier is even more skewed. Within a sample of 34 households, 8 owned no cattle while 12 possessed more than 50. Mean number of cattle was much higher than Cucurpe—53.6 with a standard deviation of 73.8—but most of that difference was accounted for by the large livestock owners. At Cucurpe, comuneros with 50 head of cattle or more owned 61.6 percent of all cattle within the comunidad. At San Javier, the figure was 87.5 percent. Only one nonmember grazed his livestock on San Javier land, but San Javier is clearly dominated by a minority of comuneros far wealthier than their fellow members.

The distribution of livestock in the Ejido 6 de Enero is not quite as variable. Five of 19 sample households owned no cattle while only 1 possessed more than 50. Mean number of cattle was 14.1 with a standard deviation of 17.7. It must be reiterated, however, that 6 de Enero is an entirely new corporate community which is still in the process of being colonized. Many ejidatarios continue to reside out-side the municipio while most living on ejido land occupy ocotillo *jacales* rather than more permanent adobe houses. In contrast to Cu-curpe or San Javier, which have been in existence since the colonial period, 6 de Enero is an infant organization with very few full-time stockmen as members. As tensions between ejidatarios and private ranchers subside, exploitation of ejido resources will undoubtedly intensify. That intensification may, in turn, lead to greater economic inequality among ejidatarios as well.

For a number of historic reasons, it is evident from this discussion that neither the two comunidades nor the ejido effectively regulate livestock on corporate lands. First of all, the three organizations are relatively new institutions, at least in their present incarnations. Even though grazing lands have been corporate in Cucurpe and San Javier for several hundred years, these corporate communities were not formally organized until 1976, when the president of Mexico "recon-firmed" their existence as legal, resource-controlling entities under the jurisdiction of the Department of Agrarian Reform. Prior to reconfir-mation, however, local households simply turned their livestock loose on traditional corporate land. None of the comuneros in either Cu-curpe or San Javier can ever remember comunidad officials with the power to limit livestock. Here again, household autonomy took prece-dence over corporate needs.

Secondly, Cucurpe in many respects continues to be influenced by its frontier past. The traditional comunidades never developed mecha-nisms to regulate livestock among their members because there was not much reason to do so until World War II. Before the introduction of barbed wire, all range in the region was open, so cattle were free to move over larger expanses of land. More to the point, the corrientes were not valuable enough to exercise much control over until the expansion of the livestock industry during the 1940s. Cattle were raised as much for household consumption as for cash sale. If they starved or fell prey to the "long ropes" of neighboring ranchers, not much was lost. Because of these frontier conditions, long-term ecological and demographic constraints were neither strong enough nor constant enough to stimulate the comunidades to challenge household autonomy and restrict the number of livestock on corporate ranges.

Finally, and perhaps most importantly, most stockmen in the region reject overgrazing as a causal factor in the degradation of their land. According to them, declining rainfall is responsible for the denuded quality of the once flourishing agostadero. The period of abundance did not come to an end until, as one Cucurpeño said, "the droughts began about 1943."

Unfortunately, the corporate control of grazing lands, at least in Cucurpe, does not encourage conservation. Even if local households perceived overgrazing as a problem, they would have little or no incentive to correct the situation. Families voluntarily choosing to reduce the number of animals they run on corporate ranges would probably see their neighbors decide to run more. Improving a resource which is not controlled at the household level simply requires more consensus or coercion than either of Cucurpe's two comunidades can muster at the present time. Although the situation is not yet terminal, the "tragedy of the commons" remains a distinct possibility for the municipio's corporate communities (Hardin 1968).

Corporate control of grazing land also does not stimulate other aspects of range or livestock management. Selective breeding, for example, is nearly impossible. Where cattle roam at will and the range is not divided into specific pastures, stockmen cannot determine which bulls impregnate their cows. One man's purebred Charolais may mount a neighbor's animals while someone else's corriente bull may sire the Charolais owner's calves. Because of the open range, comunidad cattle are mixtures of just about every breed known to northern Mexico. These corrientes may be wonderful to look at but they do not necessarily represent the optimum beef-producing animal for the regional export market.

The basic problem is a political one, revolving around the levels at which most decisions of resource control are made. Even though members of the comunidades depend upon the corporate grazing lands, the allocation of basic resources such as arable land and labor takes place almost entirely within the households themselves. Individual comuneros and their families determine what to plant in their fields and how many livestock to turn loose on comunidad agostadero. Any attempt to limit such decision-making is considered a threat to the autonomy of local households, one of the ideological pillars of Cucurpe society.

Along with the tenure of arable land, the regulation of livestock is a critical economic domain where the gap between local perception and federal law is immense. According to Article 138 of the Federal Law of Agrarian Reform, comunidades and ejidos are required to determine in their general assemblies the maximum number of livestock that members are allowed to pasture on corporate range. If a member owns more animals than the determination allows, that member must pay a tax for each animal exceeding the legal limit. Despite Article 138, however, none of Cucurpe's corporate communities have attempted to enforce any such determination. Livestock regulation is extremely difficult to institute, especially if local stockmen are accustomed to doing what they please. Neither the two comunidades nor the ejido has the experience, the fortitude, or the moral authority to compel their members to cut back on their herds.

Under such circumstances, outside authorities often intervene as the U.S. government did among the Navajo Indians during the 1930s. The various government agencies overseeing the administration of Cucurpe's corporate communities, on the other hand, have not yet made an effort to institute livestock reduction programs. In 1980–81, officials from both the Department of Agrarian Reform (SRA) and the Department of Agriculture and Water Resources (SARH) said in private that such programs may be carried out in the future. But the very idea was never even broached in official meetings of the two comunidades during the same two years. When and if livestock reduction does take place, however, governmental coercion will probably be required. Like the Navajos, the Cucurpeños are unlikely to give up their animals without a fight.

PRIVATE GRAZING LANDS

Approximately 79.4 percent of the municipio of Cucurpe is controlled by private ranchers. On these roughly 150,000 ha, stockmen run at least 22,198 head of cattle, 647 horses or mules, 15 burros, and 68 goats (Table 4.2). These livestock totals represent 17,473 animal units, giving the private range an overall land/animal ratio of 8.59 (Table 4.3). While one animal unit per nine ha is still far too low for Cucurpe's semiarid landscape, it is better than the ratios for either of the two comunidades.

Most of the private ranges are also in better shape than the corporate ones, with the aforementioned exception of Ejido 6 de Enero. The private ranches generally lie at higher elevations, often in mesquite grassland or oak woodland, with better ground cover and more reliable precipitation. Since a number of these ranches, especially those on the northeastern edges of the municipio, can support an animal unit on as little as sixteen hectares without degradation, overgrazing is not as acute as it is on corporate land.

In contrast to the comuneros, most of the owners of the private ranches live outside the municipio in cities like Magdalena, Hermosillo, Nogales, or Agua Prieta. Not surprisingly, some members of this nonresident group are wealthy individuals with business interests in other areas of Sonora as well. One man, for example, owns mining enterprises throughout the state and maintains a condominium in Tucson along with a luxurious home in Hermosillo. Other private ranchers, on the other hand, run fewer cattle than some comuneros. It was impossible to interview all individuals with holdings in the municipio, but fourteen private stockmen were contacted and information was gathered on ranches encompassing 58,494 ha—approximately 39 percent of Cucurpe's private range. The 1981 livestock censuses provide additional data on the number of animals private ranchers own. Both sources of information reveal that considerable variation in terms of both land and livestock exists within the private sector.

The sizes of Cucurpe's private ranches range from 230 to 17,500 ha, with most running between 2,000–5,000 ha. Nevertheless, it is difficult to determine the average size of a private ranch because many of the holdings belong to a number of owners running cattle on the same range. Complicating the situation even further is the fact that nearly one-fifth of all private land in the municipio (29,248 ha) is divided into two large sections of open range (*tierra mancomunada*) where many different co-owners (*condueños; coproprietarios*) pasture their livestock. None of these co-owners controls enough grazing land to fence his or her share off and operate a commercially viable private ranch. Consequently, the condueños, like members of the corporate communities, are forced to pool their individual holdings and maintain an open range. The result is a group of private stockmen running the gamut from diversified entrepreneur to hardworking rancher to absentee heir.

Table 4.4. Distribution of Cattle Among Private Ranchers in Cucurpe

Cattle Owned	Cattle Owners	Percent		Total Cattle	Percent	
1–99	45	45.9	(45.9)	2,012	9.1	(9.1)
100–199	20	20.4	(66.3)	2,749	12.4	(21.5)
200–299	11	11.2	(77.5)	2,587	11.7	(33.2)
300–399	3	3.1	(80.6)	961	4.3	(37.5)
400–499	3	3.1	(83.7)	1,379	6.2	(43.7)
500–599	3	3.1	(86.8)	1,695	7.6	(51.3)
600–699	4	4.0	(90.8)	2,567	11.6	(62.9)
700–799	0	0	(90.8)	0	0	(62.9)
800–899	0	0	(90.8)	0	0	(62.9)
900–999	1	1.0	(91.8)	956	4.3	(67.2)
1,000+	8	8.2	(100.0)	7,292	32.8	(100.0)
TOTAL	98	100.0		22,198	100.0	

According to the 1981 livestock census, at least ninety-two different individuals own cattle on private ranges in Cucurpe. The real figure is undoubtedly higher since at least one ranch with six co-owners was not included in the census. If a revised total of ninety-eight is utilized, then, private stockmen own an average of 227 head of cattle with a standard deviation of nearly 386. In other words, even though private ranchers in general possess considerably more livestock than comuneros, the variation in livestock ownership among the private sector is immense.

Table 4.4 details just how skewed this distribution really is. Eight individuals—four of whom are brothers who jointly run their cattle on land rented from the heirs of the Agua Fría hacienda—possess 1,000 or more animals apiece. Together they own 32.8 percent of all private livestock in Cucurpe. Forty-five private stockmen, on the other hand, run fewer than 100 head of cattle apiece. Fewer than one-fourth of the private ranchers control about three-fourths of the private herd.

Much of this variation stems from the fact that many ranches are owned by families, not individuals. Although one or two family members may oversee the actual operation of the ranch, parents and siblings may also run cattle on the land under their own individual brands. A ranch in the northwestern corner of the municipio exemplifies this common practice. The ranch belongs to a widow and her six children—three sons and three daughters. One son administers the ranch but all seven family members possess their own animals. Such absentee owners may rarely set foot on their ranches or work their animals themselves. Nevertheless, the cattle bear their brands, and presumably these individuals share in the profits when the cattle are sold.

Considerable differences also exist in the land/animal ratios on private holdings. One of the most progressive ranchers in the municipio—a mining entrepreneur who considers his ranch little more than "a hobby"—owns 5,000 ha of grazing land divided into ten separate pastures (*potreros*). He keeps his bulls in one potrero while running only productive cows on the other nine sections, each of which is rested a year in rotation. To insure that no barren animals remain on his range, he hires a veterinarian to palpate his cows to determine if they are pregnant. Nonpregnant cows (*vacas horras*) are immediately sold. The pregnant ones stay on the ranch, where they give birth. As soon as their calves are old enough to be weaned, however, the calves are trucked to his seventy hectares of irrigated farmland along the Río Dolores, where they are fattened on rye grass before being marketed. In 1981, this man's herd included 250 productive cows and his ranch—most of it mesquite grassland or oak woodland—enjoyed a land/animal ratio of 15.4.

A few other ranches boast land/animal ratios even higher than the one cited above. Some private operations, on the other hand, run nearly as many animal units as the two comunidades. Interestingly enough, the private holdings with the heaviest concentrations of animals are the two areas of open range—the *predios* (properties) of Torreón and San Bruno, both of which are located in the northern part of the municipio. These figures strongly suggest that open range makes it more difficult to regulate livestock or to practice sound range management regardless of the type of tenure which prevails.

The largest of these holdings—the predio of Torreón—consists of 19,248 ha bordering the Comunidad of Cucurpe. The property originated as a land grant awarded to Francisco Javier Gil Robles in 1793. On November 25, 1964, 171 years later, Mexican president Adolfo López Mateos granted joint title (*título de propiedad mancomunada*) to forty condueños, many of whom were descendants of the original grantee.[2] Although each co-owner was given a specified amount of land ranging from 197 to 850 hectares, no fences were erected to separate these relatively small portions of grazing land from each other. Instead, the condueños of Predio Torreón decided to keep the range open rather than carve it up.

In 1981, the livestock census revealed that seventeen of these co-owners were still pasturing their animals on Torreón land. Livestock numbers varied considerably from condueño to condueño. The largest stockman ran nearly 1,000 cattle and horses on the open range. At least two others, by contrast, possessed fewer than 50 head. Mean number of cattle was 189, larger than the averages for both comunidades but certainly not an indication of great ranching wealth. Together, these seventeen co-owners ran 3,209 cattle and 158 horses and mules, or approximately 2,604 animal units. These totals gave the Predio of Torreón a land/animal ratio of 7.39, which fell below the average figure of 8.59 for private range and was only 1.27 ha higher than that of the Comunidad of Cucurpe at 6.12.

Even more revealing is the land/anmial ratio of the Predio of San Bruno in the northeastern corner of the municipio. Like Torreón, San Bruno probably dates from the late colonial period, even though precise documentation concerning its origins has not yet been found. In contrast to Torreón, however, San Bruno has not been able to preserve all of its original territory, which consisted of approximately 18,000 ha. In 1976, the twenty or so condueños pasturing their animals on San Bruno land lost 8,000 ha to the newly created Ejido 6 de Enero. This loss culminated a long and bitter struggle between private ranchers and campesinos in the area, one which still occasionally flares into physical confrontation and violence.

According to the 1981 livestock census, the co-owners of San Bruno were running 3,091 cattle and 100 horses and mules on the predio's open range for a total of roughly 2,443 animal units. If ejido land is excluded, the 10,000 ha that remained in private hands were supporting an extremely low land/animal ratio of 4.09, 4.5 ha below the average for private range as a whole and 2.03 units lower than that of the Cucurpe comunidad. At least some of these animals were still grazing ejido agostadero, so the land/animal ratio for San Bruno was probably higher than the official figures indicate. Nevertheless, the land/animal ratios for both Torreón and San Bruno are significantly lower than those on ranches owned by an individual or a single family.

To emphasize this point, let us consider another statistic. If the acreage and total animal units of these two predios are subtracted from the private holdings as a whole, the remaining 120,836 ha support 12,426 animal units, yielding a land/animal ratio of 9.72. The combined land/animal ratio of Torreón and San Bruno, on the other hand, is 5.79, 3.93 ha lower. Regardless of tenure, then, open range is more heavily grazed than strictly private agostadero.

Fragmentary data for San Bruno and Torreón also indicate that other aspects of range management are more difficult to carry out as well. The distribution of livestock among various co-owners on these predios suggests that livestock numbers are not regulated by any formal mechanisms of control. Even though the wealthiest condueño received only a 500 ha portion of Torreón in 1964, for example, this individual still runs nearly 1,000 animals on the open range. Consequently, there seems to be no correspondence between livestock ownership and the amount of land a condueño legally controls.

As in the comunidades, the only real checks on livestock numbers appear to be either natural or economic rather than legal. In other words, condueños pasture as many animals on the open range as they can afford. Cultivated fields and floodplain pastures along the Río Dolores in both San Bruno and Torreón are fenced and exploited exclusively by individual owners. Those who possess large milpas or temporales are able to raise considerably more forage than those who do not. As a result, their cattle survive the inevitable periods of drought in greater numbers than those of their less fortunate co-owners. They tend, therefore, to dominate more of the open range than their individual patrimonies warrant.

The social organization of production at Torreón and San Bruno resembles the corporate communities on another level as well. Condueños may band together when they perceive a threat to their common interests such as the reconfirmation of a traditional comunidad or the creation of a new ejido. They do not appear to exercise much corporate control over range management, however, a factor which in the long run influences their economic well-being as significantly as agrarian reform or expropriation. Again, the major economic decisions affecting the ecology of these predios are made at the household rather than the corporate level. There, as in the corporate communities, household autonomy overwhelms sound ranching practices. The result is growing economic inequality and a steadily deteriorating range.

LIVESTOCK MARKETING

Environmental degradation notwithstanding, stock raising continues to be Cucurpe's most important industry. Moreover, ranching, that symbol of frontier freedom, ironically insures Cucurpe's dependence upon the outside world. Like small ranchers throughout northern Mexico, Cucurpeños find themselves at the bottom of an international economic hierarchy. Cucurpe stockmen run the cow-calf operations that take such a toll on semi-arid rangelands. Their feeder calves then pass through as many as three different layers of livestock brokers before the animals are purchased by U.S. buyers. If a single image could capture Cucurpe's place in the modern world-system, it would be a truckload of frightened, bellowing calves bouncing along the dirt road that leads from the municipio to Magdalena, Nogales, and the feedlots of the southwestern United States.

Needless to say, cattle dominate Cucurpe's range. As Table 4.2 shows, households belonging to the three corporate communities own slightly more than twice as many cows as they do horses, burros, or goats. Among private ranchers, the ratio of cattle to other forms of livestock is much higher, more than thirty to one. Cattle are the primary cash product of the Cucurpeños, and most of them are utilized for breeding stock or exported. The majority of the municipio's goats, on the other hand, are consumed locally. Men on a drinking spree often jump in a pickup and rattle from one *rancho* to another looking for a young goat to buy and butcher. These goats cost 600–900 pesos (U.S. $24–36) in 1981, so a household or a group of friends occasionally can afford to purchase one for family gatherings or a particularly memorable drunk. Cattle, by contrast, are worth ten times as much (6,000–8,000 pesos; U.S. $240–320), a price which few Cucurpeños can justify on a regular basis.

Most Cucurpe beef, therefore, winds up on somebody else's table, usually in the United States. Municipal stockmen sell their cattle to two distinct markets, one domestic, the other foreign. The U.S. market is by far the more important and more lucrative of the two. Brokers from the United States want calves of 150 kilos or less to pasture on U.S. ranges for quick and substantial weight gains. Mexican slaughterhouses, on the other hand, purchase barren cows or those too old to calve. Despite sporadic attempts by the Mexican government to increase internal beef consumption by limiting the export of cattle to foreign markets, most of the young and tender animals cross the border while the tough and rangy old bulls and cows remain behind.

A few figures demonstrate just how vital the U.S. market is to the Cucurpe economy. More than 50 percent of the livestock sold by comuneros and about 74 percent of the number of animals marketed by private ranchers consist of feeder calves. When U.S. demand slackens or the Mexican government reduces exports, cattle prices drop and the Cucurpeños have less money in their pockets to buy the outside goods they need. As a result, the permeability of the international border is a condition directly affecting household economy as well as household demography.

The fluctuations of the international livestock market also impinge upon all Cucurpeño stockmen regardless of size. No private rancher, no matter how large, completely escapes the political and economic manipulations of the livestock brokers or the politicians. One private cattleman cynically explained how a handful of powerful ranching families with friends in high places cornered the feeder calf market—*la becerrada*, as he called it—by regulating export and demand along the border. For example, he said that there was little or no U.S. market for Mexican calves until February 1980, even though most Mexican stockmen needed to sell their animals in November or December 1979. As a consequence, all but the largest ranchers were forced to sell cheap or to borrow money from the banks at exorbitant rates.

Nevertheless, significant differences exist in the marketing strategies pursued by private and peasant stockmen. Among the comuneros, for example, female calves (*becerras*) constituted only 3.6 percent of the total number of livestock sold. Most such calves served as replacement stock for barren cows or those too old to calve. Among private stockmen, by contrast, becerras made up 26.1 percent of all cattle sales. Private herds generally graze better forage and receive better care. Consequently, mortality is lower, calving percentages are higher, and fewer cows need to be replaced.

Private ranchers also exercise more control over when and to whom they sell their animals. In 1980, comuneros were receiving approximately 28–32 pesos (U.S. $1.12–1.28) per kilo for their calves. Private ranchers, on the other hand, generally sold their calves for 32–41 pesos (U.S. $1.28–1.64) per kilo, an increase of 16–36 cents per kilo or roughly 22–50 dollars per animal. Comuneros usually sell to itinerant buyers who purchase small truckloads of calves in the late fall when prices are lowest. Private ranchers often transport their calves out of the municipio in large stock trucks and send them directly to brokers along the border. Furthermore, they are able to sell later in the year or in early spring after prices have risen. Greater control over the market, therefore, translates into significant increases in profits as well.

Regardless of tenure, livestock sales account for the lion's share of most household incomes whether those households be corporate or private. Within a 75 percent random sample of all resident households belonging to the Comunidad of Cucurpe, a mean of 71.8 percent of the income derived from the sale of household products—animals, agricultural produce, handicrafts, cheese, or bootleg mescal—came from livestock. Nearly 40 percent of these domestic units reaped their entire revenue from this source, while only 23 percent received less than 50 percent of their income from livestock sales.

Of course, such figures do not reflect the total income of Cucurpe households. Wage labor also brings in some cash, even if the cash flow is sporadic. Nonetheless, it is safe to say that livestock sales are the most important source of revenue for most municipal households. Cattle sales allow Cucurpeños to purchase clothing, medical care, luxury items, and even basic food staples such as flour, sugar, lard, and coffee. When the demand for beef declines, municipal incomes suffer. Cattle prices are the barometers of both prosperity and dependence in this isolated little corner of the Sonoran Desert.

Reliance upon the livestock market also makes access to grazing land an even more critical variable than it was earlier in Cucurpe's history. It is not surprising, then, that Cucurpe households fight to maintain control of this resource in the courts and corridors of government bureaucracies. And when legal methods fail, rifles are loaded and fences cut to prevent such access from being denied. As the following chapters point out, the control of rangeland is the one issue which clearly and concisely polarizes Cucurpeños into two bitterly divided classes. Consequently, the struggle for grazing land provides the strongest hinge upon which the politics of Cucurpe resource control revolve.

A mescalero bottling *lechuguilla* for transport back to Cucurpe.

5. *Mineros y Mescaleros*

NONAGRARIAN ECONOMIC ACTIVITIES

*It is a surprisingly cool morning for early April, the clouds just breaking up
from a storm that blew through the night before. The ground around the still
(tren) is damp, and the fire burning beneath the* olla *warms us as well as the
fermented agave inside the fifty-gallon drum. "Falo" places a tin cup below the
spigot at the bottom of an old car radiator cooled by water in another drum.
Then he siphons off a little of* la cola, *the tail-end of the run. We sip it slowly,
passing the cup back and forth in a ritual as old as distillation in the Sonoran
Desert.*

The liquor is smooth and flavorful, not as strong as the cabeza, *or first
part of the run, but still definitely alcoholic. Usually, the cabeza and cola are
mixed and allowed to age in glass bottles, but this time Falo decides the entire
batch has to be run through again. Yesterday the wind from the storm whipped
the fire around so the batch didn't distill at a constant rate.* "El mescal es
muy delicada," *he says.* "Muy celosa, muy limpia," *talking as if the liquor
were a person who had to be placated and pleased. He goes on to point out that
the apparatus must be immaculate; the flame must burn evenly; no sugar can
be added to the agave while it ferments. Otherwise the product is second-rate,
and Falo takes great pride in his craft.*

*Although Falo is a comunero with a few head of cattle and a small plot of
land, he makes most of his living as a* vinatero *or* mescalero, *carefully plying
his trade away from strangers' eyes. Falo, after all, is a moonshiner, and what
he does is against the law. He peers carefully between the juniper trees hiding
his still as a couple of cowboys from a nearby ranch ride up. They rein in their
horses and dismount for a taste of the liquor and a few moments of conversation
with Falo. But the cowboys would never say anything to anyone with a badge.
Falo is their friend, their neighbor, their supplier. And they may make moonshine themselves when times grow lean.*

*After they ride away, Falo slowly and carefully prepares the second run.
He keeps the fire low and steady, telling me about the brother of a friend of his
who was blown up when his still exploded. For men like Falo who know what*

they're doing, however, the profits make the risks worthwhile. This run of more than one hundred cabezas will yield about fifteen gallons of pisto, which Falo will transport back to Cucurpe in a gas tank scavenged from an old pickup. At 500 pesos a gallon, his return on ten to twelve days' work will be 7,500 pesos, or roughly 300 dollars. Wage work, on the other hand, pays about 8 dollars a day.

But Falo is a mescalero *for more reasons than money. Pouring himself a cup of coffee while we drink the last of the cola, he reminisces about the years he spent driving a truck in Magdalena. He used to love crowds and noise and movies, which he called his "illusion." Now, on the other hand, a day or two in the city just gives him a headache. Still a young man, gaunt and unshaven, Falo is unmarried; he prefers the solitary life of the mescalero. "You don't have to buy firewood or water or light, like you do in town," he says. "Besides, if you need meat, you can kill a deer. A much more tranquil life," he concludes. Above us, the midmorning sun—*la covija de los pobres *(the blanket of the poor people)—drives away the last of the clouds as moisture quickly evaporates from the wet desert earth.*

Cucurpe's economy is overwhelmingly agrarian. As chapter 3 points out, more than 80 percent of the total work force are farmers, ranchers, cowboys, or agricultural laborers. Many of the remaining 18 percent engage in at least some agriculture or stock raising in addition to their nonagrarian activities. In a region as underdeveloped as Cucurpe, it is hard to escape working the land.

Nevertheless, a number of people do pursue livelihoods that have nothing to do with raising crops or running cattle. Three major occupations dominate this nonagrarian sector: mining, quarrying, and moonshining. Since the resources upon which these occupations depend are not necessarily controlled in the same fashion as arable or grazing land, their exploitation merits some attention.

MINING

Mining has run like a broken thread through Cucurpe's history ever since the colonial period. During the late eighteenth century, the *real* of Saracachi was a mining district of considerable importance in Sonora. An even more impressive expansion of the mining industry occurred during the regime of Porfirio Díaz, when North American capital developed sophisticated operations at Cerro Prieto, Tucabe, and Klondyke. Later, during the worldwide Great Depression, Franklin Roosevelt's raising of the price of gold from twenty to thirty-five dollars an ounce stimulated a veritable placer mining boom in the municipio. As gold became more valuable while the prices of other commodities dropped, *gambucinos* (prospectors) flocked to Cucurpe from all over Mexico to search for the elusive grains of this precious metal. The evanescent little boomtown of El Mesquite, between Cucurpe and Magdalena, boasted a population of several thousand people at that time.

Today all that is left of the settlement is a checkerboard pattern of abandoned placers bordering the Cucurpe-Magdalena road. By the mid-1940s, the boom was over and the placer-mining communities of La Higuera, Las Panochas, El Batamote, El Pozo, and El Mesquite soon became little more than honeycombed ruins. Even the largest operations like the Sonoran Consolidated Mining Company at Cerro Prieto packed up what they could salvage and moved away. Work at mines like Klondyke, Tucabe, La Calera, and Mercedes ground to a halt. Tunnels fell into disrepair, machinery rusted, and the adobe homes of the miners weathered into unobtrusive mounds. At La Brisca, angry ranchers even called in federal soldiers to drive the restless gambucinos from their grazing lands. The municipal cabecera of Cucurpe, described by one old Cucurpeño as a "very happy and prosperous town in the 1930s," soon lapsed back into agrarian lethargy. Modern irrigated agriculture along Sonora's coastal plains replaced mining as the industry of expansion. An entrepreneur with both mines and ranches in Cucurpe said, "All the gold miners emigrated to those agricultural fields. Cucurpe's mining tradition was lost. Now there are no more miners left."

His elegy for Cucurpe's mining industry was premature. Mining no longer enjoys the importance it did during the first half of the century, but it still lures a small number of men with its gold and silver. At present there are probably forty to fifty men making a living as miners in the municipio. Since most of the mines are little more than pick-and-shovel operations, the number of miners fluctuates considerably from month to month. Employment is rarely permanent. Men may work in a mine for several months and then drift on to other jobs.

According to Mexico's constitution of 1917, subsurface mineral deposits belong to the nation. Individuals may acquire mineral rights to certain sections of land, but the right to do so is essentially a concession granted by the government. Permanent title to such deposits can never be obtained. Nonetheless, claims may be filed on surface land belonging to someone else. Most of the active mines today, in fact, are located on private ranches in the central and eastern portions of the municipio. As noted above, this disjunction in resource control caused problems at least once in the past. During the 1930s and early 1940s, gambucinos excavated shallow placer deposits near La Brisca along the upper Río Saracachi. So many prospectors swarmed to this area that a school and four stores were opened to serve them. But local ranchers soon perceived the mining community of La Brisca as a threat to their grazing lands and pressured the government to drive the miners away. In such fashion, the government was forced to take sides in a dispute over resources to which both miners and ranchers may have had legitimate claims.

Large mining operations were too powerful to be closed down. Besides, local ranchers themselves often owned substantial interests in the mines. The owner of Agua Fría, for example, entered into partnership with a group of U.S. businessmen to develop Mina Klondyke in the mountains east of his hacienda. Even those ranchers who did not own mines profited from their presence through increased sales of beef and cheese. Mining and stock raising, therefore, must have grown in symbiosis with one another, creating a regional economy that supported more people than the municipal economy today.

Modern mines, on the other hand, demand very little goods or labor. Individual operations in 1980–81 employed no more than two to eleven men, many of whom came from Magdalena, not Cucurpe. Although some new shafts and tunnels were being dug, progress proceeded slowly, following the rhythms of picks and shovels rather than sophisticated machinery. Forty years ago, electricity powered carts hauling ore out of mines like Tucabe. Today miners hoist the buckets of ore by pulley or carry them out of the tunnels themselves. At several mines, workers pick through the tailings of older operations instead of searching for new veins of ore. Not surprisingly, yields are low, averaging six to nine grams of gold and seventy-five grams of silver per ton.

The biggest impediment to the development of Cucurpe's mining industry, however, is transportation, not technology. During the 1930s, at least eight ore-grinding mills in the municipio shuddered and hummed. At present, ore can only be processed in Cananea, Sonora, or Douglas, Arizona, several hundred kilometers from Cucurpe. Local miners must haul their raw chunks of ore by dump truck to Magdalena, where it is loaded onto freight cars. Such a process is both expensive and time-consuming. To make matters worse, the plants near the border are already operating at full capacity and have to assign quotas to individual mine-owners. One local miner can only ship 120 metric tons a month to the Cananea plant. Since he can extract that much ore in fifteen to twenty days employing six to eight men, his mines never produce at full capacity. Like many others, he believes that Cucurpe could experience another florescence of the mining industry if processing facilities were expanded and located closer to the municipio.

QUARRYING

Cucurpe's mining industry is devoted entirely to gold and silver. There is another type of mineral deposit, however, that attracts attention in the municipio, and that is volcanic tuff. North and east of the pueblo of Cucurpe, large outcrops and ridges of this soft, easily worked material ripple across the landscape in porous waves. Known locally as *cantera*, tuff has been utilized as a building material in the region for centuries. Cucurpe's unfinished adobe mission rises on cantera blocks, while the town's fountain gracefully curves skyward in cantera swirls. Local artisans even carve beautiful *ollas* out of the material for local and regional sale. When the governor of Sonora visited Cucurpe in 1981, the community presented him with a cantera replica of the mission as a symbol of the municipio's future as well as its past.

At that time, cantera was supposed to play an important role in that future by diversifying Cucurpe's economy and providing jobs for young men and women who otherwise would move away. Cantera had been quarried on a commercial scale in the past. During the early 1970s, for example, a company in Santa Anna, Sonora, fashioned the material into small tiles. The company folded because of "administrative deficiencies," but in 1977, the federal Department of Planning and the Budget (*Secretaría de Programación y Presupuesto*) decided to finance construction of a cantera-processing plant in Cucurpe itself.[1] Moreover, the government planned to place the plant under the jurisdiction of the Comunidad of Cucurpe as part of Plan PIDER, a nationwide program of rural development sponsored by President López-Portillo's administration. *Canteras de Cucurpe*, as the phantom enterprise came to be called, was trumpeted as a solution to too many emigrants and too few jobs.

Like so many development efforts, however, *Canteras de Cucurpe* was both poorly conceived and improperly executed. First of all, it took several years to construct the plant, which was not completed until mid-1981. Then the comuneros had to wait more than a year for the plant's stone-cutting machinery to be delivered and installed.

Numerous trips by comunidad officials to Hermosillo and Mexico City failed to speed up the process, and many comuneros concluded that government officials somewhere along the line were profiting from the delay by raking off interest from bank accounts created for the project. Once the machinery did arrive, the generator, manufactured by a Brazilian affiliate of General Electric, proved to be too complicated for Cucurpe's diesel-powered electric plant. That caused yet another delay while the comuneros waited for technicians to return and modify the machine.

By then, many comuneros agreed with one of their members who called *Canteras de Cucurpe* a *"coyotada."* Like many other people in North America, the Cucurpeños use the coyote as a metaphor for trickery and deception. In this case, their cynical assessment was close to the truth. By 1982, the plant had begun to operate part-time, employing twenty-two individuals—all of them comuneros or sons of comuneros. Six men quarried the cantera which was transported by truck back to the plant (*laminadora*). There, another six individuals cut the rough-hewn blocks into tiles of various sizes. The remaining employees worked as drivers, watchmen, administrators, and office help. The president of the comunidad himself was responsible for marketing the finished product. At last it seemed that the Cucurpeños were going to see some return on the government's ambitious development plan.

But new problems soon surfaced to disrupt the scheme. After producing hundreds of tiles, the comuneros discovered that their dimensions were slightly askew. The saws had not been installed properly and were failing to cut perfect squares or rectangles. Before the defect was corrected, the plant had to close down for nearly a month. At that point, the plant's chief of operations—a comunero and local businessman—confided that the machinery was not new; it had only been repainted to look that way. Once again, corruption or poor planning hampered the nascent industry.

Three years later, the plant was rusting away, abandoned because the Cucurpeños discovered that their market for cantera had evaporated, if, indeed, it had ever existed. Not a single consignment of the material had been sold. Aside from a few months of wages, no member of the comunidad had made any money from a project that had cost the Mexican government millions of pesos. Located on the mesa above the town of Cucurpe next to the mission ruins, *Canteras de Cucurpe* stands as a skeletal reminder of cupidity and incompetence, another example of federal mismanagement and development gone awry.

WOODCUTTING AND WILD-PLANT GATHERING

Despite its failure, the quarrying enterprise represented a fascinating new direction in corporate resource control. According the the Federal Law of Agrarian Reform (1981:35), ejidos and comunidades enjoy communal jurisdiction over "pasture, forests and woodlands" as well as arable land and water. The agrarian code says nothing about mineral resources. The bounty of the *subsuelo* (subsurface) belongs to the nation and is apportioned under a system entirely different from surface resources. In the case of *Canteras de Cucurpe*, though, the government appeared to be classifying Cucurpe's cantera deposits in the same category as natural forage, firewood, and wild plants.

Both federal law and local custom entitle members of comunidades and ejidos to share in such corporate resources. Comuneros and ejidatarios, therefore, gather firewood (*leña*) to fuel their wood stoves, cut mesquite, acacia, and oak posts to build their fences, excavate clay deposits to make adobe bricks, and harvest a wide variety of wild plants for culinary and medicinal purposes. Most of these activities are carried out at the household level for domestic consumption rather than for commercial sale.

Woodcutting is perhaps the most important of these activities. Nearly every household within the three corporate communities depends upon wood stoves to cook and to heat their homes. Consequently, there is a tremendous demand for firewood, which is filled entirely by local resources. Cucurpeños in general do not cut down living trees. Instead, they usually remove dead limbs and branches in order to preserve their resource base. Nevertheless, good firewood is getting harder to find near centers of population, and households often have to travel five to ten kilometers by wagon or pickup to gather the firewood they need. Furthermore, woodcutting is selective; most people prefer mesquite—"*la leña del hombre*" (a man's firewood)—to *tesota* (*Acacia occidentalis*) or *palo chino* (*Pithecellobium mexicanum*). As a result, woodcutters must journey farther to obtain mesquite in substantial quantities, so expenditures of both time and money increase.

Wild-food gathering, on the other hand, receives relatively little attention in Cucurpe. In late June, households occasionally knock down the fruit of the saguaro cactus (*Carnegiea gigantea*) with long poles in order to boil it down and make sweets (*dulces*). During July, some families may even travel to the uplands to harvest the acorns (*bellotas*) of Emory oaks (*Quercus emoryi*, also known as *bellota*). In August and September, the tiny green berries of the wild chile plant

(*Capsicum annuum* var. *minimum*; *chiltepín*) are gleaned so that they can be bottled in vinegar, as a particularly fiery spice. A month or two later, the mature red fruits of *chiltepines* are collected for use as a dry condiment. Cucurpeños also gather the sweet berries of desert hackberry (*Celtis pallida*; *garambullo*) as well as various species of wild greens (*quelites*) including *bledo* (*Amaranthus palmeri*; pigweed), *berro* (*Rorippa* sp.; watercress), *verdolaga* (*Portulaca oleracea*), *rapaca* (*Rumex* sp.), and *mostasa* (*Brassica* or *Sisymbrium*; wild mustard). In the past, residents of the municipio also picked mesquite pods in order to make *péchita*, or mesquite flour, which was baked or mixed with water to provide a sweet drink similar to wheat or corn *pinole*. But times have changed and many of the old desert ways are being abandoned as commercial foods become more available.

At present, the only two wild plant foods harvested on a commercial scale in Cucurpe are *bellotas* and *chiltepines*, and even they are of minor economic importance. This contrasts with other areas of Sonora where acorn- and especially wild chile-gathering contribute substantial amounts of cash to household coffers (Nabhan 1985). Nonetheless, wild plants do add variety and nutrition to the Cucurpe diet, providing significant food reserves when times are lean. One old man, remembering such times, called wild greens "*la carne de los pobres*" (the meat of the poor people) and said that farmers often granted their poorer neighbors the rights to glean greens from their stubble.

MESCAL-MAKING

One wild plant continues to be of economic importance, however, and that is *lechuguilla* (*Agave palmeri*). In a region as isolated as Cucurpe, recreational facilities are few and far between, so most men break the monotony of agrarian life by indulging in a favorite Sonoran pastime—binge drinking. Weekend evenings are punctuated by the shouts and screams of inebriated men on horseback galloping up and down the San Miguel riverbed. And whenever Cucurpe hosts one of its many dances, importing electric *conjuntos* (bands) from Magdalena to play *norteño* music or *cumbias*, it is not unusual to see a man waltzing an imaginary partner across the floor while his friends cheer him on with piercing *gritos*. Binge drinking is an accepted form of male recreation, and few people frown when a hard-working family man or even a school principal winds up in the municipal jail (*bote*) after a particularly boisterous drunk. During fiestas like *Semana Santa*, in fact, the streets of Cucurpe are crowded with scores of mounted men and boys passing bottles back and forth as their horses rear or jostle or merely wait patiently for their masters to settle down or fall to the ground.

Nowadays, men are as likely to *echar una chevy o un Tecatito* (knock back a beer or a Tecate) as they are to consume hard liquor. But the spirit of preference—and of tradition—remains lechuguilla, the bootleg mescal distilled from the local century plant. Men drink the smooth but potent *pisto* from Coca-Cola bottles during festive occasions, and nearly every household keeps a gallon or so of the liquor on hand for cold mornings or stomach aches or for visits from friends and neighbors. Like its more famous cousin *bacanora*, which is distilled from *Agave pacifica*, a species of century plant not found in the municipio, lechuguilla is as much a part of rural life as horseracing or poaching deer. And like those other two activities, its illegality is an inconvenience Cucurpeños usually ignore.

Most municipal residents, in fact, are quite proud of their bootleg liquor. Even the dour Jesuit Ignacio Pfefferkorn, missionary at Cucurpe during the early 1760s, admitted a liking for the local mescal. In his famous *Description of Sonora*, he wrote:

> Pleasant spirits are distilled from the root. These excell the best so-called Rossoli and, besides strengthening the stomach, stimulate the appetite and are very good for the digestion. Hence, in Sonora, where wine is hardly known and water is usually unhealthful, this drink can be considered a real healing remedy if it is used moderately and only according to the needs of health (Treutlein 1949:60–61).

Of course, moderation was as elusive in Pfefferkorn's day as it is in our own. After praising its medicinal qualities, the Jesuit went on to decry the abuses of mescal among Sonoran Indians:

> The Indians formerly had no knowledge of other kinds of liquor. However, through intercourse with the Spaniard they learned about spirits, which met with their approbation, and they now consider this injurious beverage far superior to their own. There are even some Opatas and Eudebes who have learned from the Spaniards how to distill spirits, but fortunately the Sonoran's circumstances do not allow him to make frequent use of this knowledge. The preparation of spirits calls for ability, apparatus, knowledge, and trouble, and therefore it is an occupation not suited to the Sonoran. For the same reason there are few Spaniards who engage in its preparation. How much mischief would result if the making of spirits were more common! This wild people has an insatiable desire for strong liquors. They drink as long as they can, and they are able to drink until they fall to earth just like blocks, completely void of reason and out of their heads. When the spirits heat their blood and have gone to their heads, there follow altercations, fights, blood-spilling, murder and death, and even the most horrible revolts.

Pfefferkorn's rather apocalyptic view of mescal exaggerated its dangers. Altercations do indeed break out in Cucurpe, but the results are usually drunken fistfights rather than "blood-spilling, murder and death." Young cowboys may swing at one another during a dance as their friends crowd around. They may even jump on their horses and race through town, lassoing each other out of the backs of pickups or galloping out onto the riverbed in the dark to avoid arrest by the local police. But such outbursts of anger or high spirits rarely end in tragedy. The worst alcohol-related incident in 1981, in fact, occurred one evening when a comunero accidentally shot himself through the fleshy part of the knee while drinking lechuguilla around a friend's kitchen table. Violence, drunken or otherwise, hardly ever escalates beyond a brawl.

Such relative peacefulness reigns despite the fact that mescal has apparently become more common than it was during Pfefferkorn's era. Moonshining is one of rural Sonora's most important underground industries, a shadow economy that provides work and revenue for hundreds, perhaps even thousands of men across the state. During the late 1950s, anthropologist Roger Owen (1959) estimated that thirteen of fifty-nine households in the village of Meresichic south of Cucurpe made and sold mescal. More than two decades later, at least twenty-four men in the municipio of Cucurpe distilled lechuguilla. And while a handful of these individuals produced only enough pisto for their personal consumption, the rest sold their liquor to their neighbors on a fairly regular basis.

In the process, many of them even today reap modest profits. Mescaleros or *vinateros* harvest agaves from October to June; during the summer rainy season, the water content of the plants is so high that it is usually not worth the effort to distill lechuguilla at that time. Throughout the rest of the year, however, an average run demands ten to fifteen days of intermittent labor and yields fifteen to twenty gallons of *vino*. In 1981, a gallon of lechuguilla was selling for 500 pesos (U.S. $32). If a mescalero completes only one run a month eight months a year, he can pocket 2,000–3,000 dollars.

Moonshining can be a hazardous occupation, especially if the mescaleros are inexperienced. If, for example, the flames beneath the still leap too high, the alcohol may ignite and blow both still and mescalero to kingdom come. And even though vigilance is not great, vinateros must be careful not to attract the attention of state or federal *judiciales*. One man hides his *culebra* ("snake"; copper coil) in a dense stand of catclaw acacia outside his ranch house. Another keeps to the back country when gathering agave. *"No quiero barullo"* (I don't want trouble), he explained with a shrug when questioned about his caution.

Despite these occasional dangers, however, mescal-making is an attractive occupation because it requires so little capital. All a vinatero needs is a string of burros, some fifty-gallon drums, a copper coil or an old car radiator, and some aluminum tubing. Everything else can be scavenged from the surrounding countryside, including a thorough knowledge of mescal-making.

The process is a relatively simple one. First, a mescalero gathers the century plants by prying them loose from the hard, stony soil with an iron bar (*jimando las cabezas con una vara*). Then the sharp leaves protecting the agave's caudex (*cabeza*; "head") are hacked off with a machete or long knife. When several burro-loads of agave have been accumulated in this fashion, the mescalero drives the animals to his still, which is usually hidden in a side canyon or behind a thick stand of trees near a *rancho*. There the agave hearts are roasted from twenty-four to forty-eight hours in a rock-lined pit called an *horno*, or oven.

Once the agaves have been baked, the mescalero places the caudices between the stout, forked trunk of a mesquite (*horquilla*) embedded in the ground. The agaves are then shredded with an ax and thrown into three or four fifty-gallon drums (*tambos*) where they are allowed to ferment. The first day they ferment dry. The second day, however, the pieces of agave are covered with water for five to ten more days until a good mescalero no longer hears the fermentation process taking place. It is during this stage that sugar may be added to speed the process along, even though most vinateros swear they never do so themselves. Sugar increases the yield as much as fourfold, but the resulting mescal doesn't taste as good or last as long. Furthermore, it inflicts painful hangovers on its more enthusiastic consumers. Most mescaleros, therefore, claim that their pisto is sugar-free.

After fermentation, the distillation process begins. The agave along with the liquid inside the tambos is transferred to the *olla* (pot), another drum resting over an open fire. As the liquid is heated it turns into vapor that passes through an aluminum tube (*arco*) into the *enfriador*, a second tambo filled with cold water. Within the enfriador, the vapor condenses as it moves down through the *culebra*, a copper coil or car radiator that has, one trusts, been thoroughly scoured and cleaned. The resulting liquid, called the *resaque*, is then poured into the olla and distilled a second time to give it more flavor and force. Once the first part of the run—the *cabeza* or head—has been mixed with the

A still (*tren*) in the mountains west of Cucurpe: the vapor of fermented agave passes from the *olla* (left) through the *arco* into the *enfriador* (right), where a car radiator surrounded by water cools it into liquid.

less alcoholic *cola*, or tail-end, the finished product is ready to be transported back to town in glass bottles or gas tanks torn from old cars.

Mescal-making constitutes an important economic safety net in a region characterized by underemployment and an inequitable distribution of agrarian resources like land and livestock. When times are hard, men make more lechuguilla. When other jobs are available, mescal production declines. Demand, on the other hand, never seems to be a problem in the equation. No matter how much lechuguilla is distilled, there are always enough pesos to pay for it and enough thirsty people to drink it down.

The basic resource itself is not so elastic. At least fourteen to twenty agave caudices are required to produce one gallon of lechuguilla, and it appears that plants are becoming harder to find in the municipio even though agaves enjoy remarkable powers of propagation. One vinatero said that lechuguilla is "very scarce within the comunidad," so he and others have to travel to private ranches to gather the plants they need. There they generally ask permission from the ranch's cowboys, who usually grant such requests in return for a gallon or so of the final product.

Within comunidad boundaries, then, agaves apparently have been overexploited. Nonetheless, lechuguilla is treated—in practice if not in law—just like other corporate resources, such as firewood or the edible products of wild plants. Any member of the corporate community is free to collect agave caudices as long as he avoids the clutches of state or federal police. The comunidad, not surprisingly, does nothing to regulate the mescal industry. Legally, of course, all it could do is suppress it, since making pisto is against the law. But no self-respecting comunidad official or municipal authority would ever venture such a campaign. Lechuguilla, after all, is a municipal treasure, serving as a powerful social currency in the isolated area. It makes friends of strangers, cements the already existing bonds between neighbors and relatives, and provides a much-needed release from the everyday world of crops and cattle. *La vida Cucurpeña* would be inconceivable without it.[2]

A comunero with his prize bull.

6. Ganaderos y Comuneros

ECONOMIC INEQUALITY
AND THE ORGANIZATION OF
RESOURCE CONTROL

We eat dinner by kerosene light in the ranch house southeast of Cucurpe, surrounded by the rough comforts of a largely masculine environment: wide canvas cots, coffee brewing on the wood stove, a gallon of lechuguilla resting on the kitchen table. The big dark room is as much storage area as living quarters, filled with feed sacks and saddles and tools. Women and children occasionally visit, but the ranch is home only to the young cowboy working for the rancher, who has just driven in from Magdalena in his short-bed Chevy pickup.

The rancher is dressed in a gray felt cowboy hat and leather boots. He is a bluff, hearty man, cynical and Sonorense to the core. He, his father, and his two brothers own 3,000 ha of a wide, mesquite-lined valley between Cucurpe and Agua Fría. There they run 400 head of cattle and raise a small herd of horses renowned for their speed in local match races. None of the four live on the ranch, however. The rancher is a cattle-buyer operating out of Magdalena, where his father, the patriarch of the clan, has retired. One of his brothers works in the pecan orchards of Continental, Arizona, south of Tucson. The family belongs to that diffuse network of absentee landowners who control nearly four-fifths of the Cucurpe municipio.

But the family came from Cucurpe originally, and there it made its modest fortune, largely, old-timers say, by rounding up and branding calves dropped by other men's cows. In the old days, abigeato *(cattle-rustling) was relatively common, and a number of local ranching families got their start skimming the surplus off Cucurpe's open range. It was a part of the region's frontier heritage, like moonshining or Apache raids. Sly old men still wink and accuse each other of eating the other's beef. And when the governor of Sonora arrived to dedicate Cucurpe's* cantera *plant, one group of poor comuneros even dubbed themselves the "comevacas" (cattle-eaters) and posed for pictures across from ranchers hoisting the banner of the local stockmen's association. In an area as rugged and isolated as Cucurpe, no one knows how many animals fall prey to hungry neighbors' knives.*

Nowadays, money is made in the cattle business by controlling the market, not by stealing the dumb, lumbering beasts themselves. Swinging his boots onto the table, the rancher leans back in his chair and downs a shot of lechuguilla before explaining how the economics of Sonoran ranching really work. Among all but the largest stock raisers, he says, calves pass through as many as "three hands" between the producer and U.S. buyers. But the official guías, or bills of sale, are rarely changed, in order to avoid paying sales taxes. In the process, la becerrada, as the calf market is called, becomes concentrated in fewer and fewer hands. Most stockmen need to sell their animals in November or December. For the past three years, though, U.S. brokers haven't purchased calves until February. As a result, Sonoran ranchers either sell cheap or have to borrow money from the banks at exorbitant rates until they can move their calves.

When asked why there was such a delay, the rancher shrugged and speculated that collusion existed between big U.S. and Mexican buyers to keep prices down. He talked about how a handful of men, including the brother of the governor, control la becerrada in Sonora. Small ranchers like himself, by contrast, feel trapped—squeezed between the wealthy power brokers on the one hand and the forces of agrarian reform on the other. "La pequeña propiedad va a desaparecer" (Small ownership is going to disappear), he argued, claiming that the government was implementing "comunismo, socialismo." Yet at the same time, he noted, latifundismo continues to flourish as large landowners hold parcels in other people's names. He picked up the bottle of lechuguilla and shook it, watching the cloves and fruit rinds which give it flavor swirl around at the bottom. According to agrarian reform law, private ranches could turn out to be as large as the number of hectares needed to raise 500 cows—at least 5,000 ha in semi-arid Sonora. Nonetheless, ranches of 3,000, 1,500, and even 500 ha were being expropriated by the government and handed over to ejidatarios. "La ley vale verga" (The law's not worth cock), the rancher laughed, shaking his head at how easily regulations were twisted or circumvented in rural Mexico.

The phrases varied from person to person, but time and again other Cucurpeños expressed the same sentiment. "Hay mucha trinquete aquí en México" (There's great prevarication here in Mexico), one man said. Another proclaimed, "Desgraciadamente, México no es democracia. Los billetes tienen potencia. Los billetes son los que mandan" (Disgracefully, Mexico is not a democracy. Money has power. Money controls everything). In other words, everyone is out for himself, and the government is as corrupt as it is incompetent. Such attitudes reflect deep and abiding dissatisfaction with the present system, counterbalanced only by a profound skepticism about human *nature itself.* "Así anda el mundo" *(That's the way the world works), the rancher shrugged. Then he poured us another shot while the dull yellow glow of the lantern flickered against the soot-covered walls.*

The previous three chapters have focused on particular resources and how they are exploited, allocated, and controlled. Now it is time to discuss how wealth in general is distributed at the household level.

Having done so, it will be possible to explore the crucial relationships between economic status and the organization of resource control. One of the central hypotheses of this analysis is that wealth differences, based primarily on differential access to the basic means of production, largely determine agrarian politics in the municipio. In order to test this hypothesis, however, it is necessary to examine the range of household economic status within as well as between the major groups competing for Cucurpe's scarce resources. These groups fight internal battles as well as external ones. Only by understanding economic differences at every level can the fundamental conflicts of Cucurpe society be discerned.

WEALTH VS. INCOME

Before proceeding, it is necessary to explain why wealth, not income, was chosen as the focus of this analysis. The first reason is methodological: while wage labor is important in the municipio, it is extremely difficult to determine accurate income levels for most households because so few Cucurpeños enjoy steady wage work (*trabajo corrido*). For example, only 65 of 242 resident household heads (26.9 percent) reported that they worked full-time for an employer. Most of these individuals were employed as cowboys on private ranches, receiving wages of 4,000–6,000 pesos a month (U.S. $160–240).

The majority of Cucurpeños, on the other hand, remain on the periphery of the wage labor market. Eighty-two household heads (33.9 percent) stated that they were self-employed. Thirty household heads (12.4 percent) characterized themselves as self-employed with only occasional wage work. Thirty-four individuals (14 percent) claimed they were not steadily employed, either within the household economy or outside it. In other words, 60 percent of the municipal household heads draw most of their income from the sale of household products or from wage work that is sporadic at best. And because few of these households keep detailed records of their income, monthly and yearly estimates were difficult to elicit. When asked how much they made, time and again household heads shrugged and gave the standard Cucurpeño response to unanswerable questions: *"Pues, sabe?"* (Well, who knows?).

An even more important reason to concentrate on wealth rather than income has to do with the nature of Cucurpe's economy. In contrast to urban societies with their large classes of merchants, professionals, and administrators, economic status in Cucurpe is tied much more directly to control over the basic means of production, especially land and livestock. Households with more of these resources generally earn more income. Furthermore, most households meet at least some of their subsistence needs by growing their own food. Consequently, even if it could be accurately assessed, monetary income would be an inadequate measure of prosperity.

THE DISTRIBUTION OF TOTAL WEALTH AMONG
RESIDENT CUCURPE HOUSEHOLDS

In order to determine household economic status, an index of total wealth was compiled. This index reflects household ownership or usufruct control of three resources fundamental to Cucurpe's agrarian economy: 1) land, including milpa, temporal, and agostadero; 2) livestock, including cattle, horses, mules, goats, and pigs; and 3) machinery, including cars, pickups, cattle trucks, and tractors. Each one of these resources was weighted according to its approximate value in pesos, and then all were combined to yield an index of total wealth for the 242 resident households in the municipio. The actual index of a household represents 1/1000 of the 1980–81 peso value of its estate. The mean index of total wealth for the sample—301.5—indicates that the average value of a household estate in Cucurpe is 301,500 pesos (U.S. $12,060). (*See* Appendix B for a more detailed explanation of the index.)

Figure 6.1 shows the distribution of total wealth with the households divided into deciles. Forty-four households (18.2 percent) have indices of total wealth equal to zero. In other words, nearly one-fifth of all Cucurpe families possess no land, livestock, or machinery. The wealthiest resident household, on the other hand, has an index of 4,884, controlling an estate worth approximately 4,884,000 pesos, or nearly 200,000 dollars. The top 10 percent of the domestic units possess nearly 53 percent of the sample's total wealth; the two lowest deciles control hardly any wealth whatsoever. The bottom *half* of the

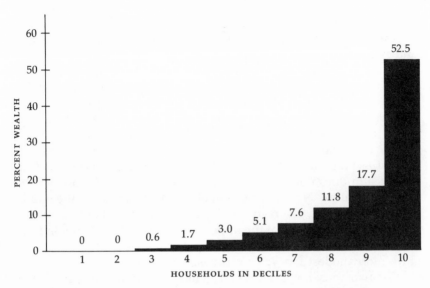

Figure 6.1. Percentage of Total Wealth Among Cucurpe Households

sample, in fact, holds only 5 percent of the wealth in question. By no stretch of the imagination can Cucurpe be considered an economically egalitarian society.

The consideration of a few actual Cucurpe households will help to flesh out these statistics and make them understandable in human terms. Let's take, for example, the two households whose indexes of total wealth (295) fall closest to the mean of 301.5. The first consists of two unmarried brothers, both older than fifty, who belong to the Comunidad of Cucurpe. Together the brothers have usufruct rights to 2 ha of irrigated land and 7 ha of temporal within the comunidad. They also run forty head of cattle and six horses. Neither owns any machinery, so their index of wealth in land and livestock equals their index of total wealth: the equivalent of 200,000 pesos (U.S. $8,000) worth of cattle, 30,000 pesos (U.S. $1,200) of horses, 30,000 pesos (U.S. $1,200) of irrigated land, and 35,000 pesos (U.S. $1,400) of temporal. Combined, these resources give the brothers a total estate worth approximately 295,000 pesos (U.S. $11,800).

The second household in many respects resembles the first. The household is composed of three adults—a sixty-year-old rancher and his wife and their unmarried, slightly retarded thirty-two-year-old son. The head of the household is a member of Comunidad San Javier, and at present, all of his wealth comes from livestock in the form of fifty head of cattle and nine horses and mules. He used to control several hectares of milpa along the San Miguel, but floods carried that land away.

These two cases suggest that an "average" Cucurpe household controls an estate worth about U.S. $12,000, and that most of its wealth is tied up in land or livestock, especially cattle. And since both cases belong to comunidades and run their livestock on comunidad range, it is clear that Cucurpe's "middle-class" of small rancher-farmers could not exist without access to corporate grazing lands.

At this point, however, it must be stressed that the mean index of total wealth does not represent the economic reality of most households in Cucurpe. Nearly 72 percent of all domestic units in the municipio fall below this "average," which has been inflated by a relatively few wealthy households at the upper end of the scale. A better indication of economic status is the median index of total wealth, which is a much more modest 120 (120,000 pesos; U.S. $4,800).

The two households with such an index constitute something of a watershed in the Cucurpe agrarian economy, since seventy households are poorer and seventy households are richer than they are. Both households consist of single individuals, one a married man, aged fifty-six, whose family resides in Magdalena, the other a bachelor aged thirty. Both belong to the Comunidad of Cucurpe. The married man farms 1 ha of irrigated land along the Río Saracachi and runs eighteen cows, one horse, and two mules on comunidad range. The bachelor controls 2 ha of milpa and owns ten head of cattle and eight horses and mules. Because their meager amounts of land and livestock do not provide an adequate living, these men are forced to supplement their income in time-honored ways. The younger works steadily for a local mine-owner. The older makes mescal. Such a mixed subsistence strategy, which includes stock raising, farming, wage work, and bootlegging, best reflects the struggle for survival characterizing Cucurpe life.

Part of that struggle, as we have already seen, stems from the underdeveloped nature of Cucurpe's agrarian economy. Nonetheless, the marginal economic status of many households is also based upon a highly inequitable allocation of scarce and necessary resources, as the distribution of wealth in deciles makes clear. Another measure of inequality reinforces this conclusion in an even more telling fashion. In order to compare Cucurpe with other societies across the world, a Gini coefficient for total wealth was calculated; despite its drawbacks as a measure of inequality, the Gini was chosen because of its widespread use among social scientists (Davis 1977; Galt 1980; McGuire and

Netting 1982). The result was a Gini of .687, considerably higher than most other agrarian societies for which similar measures have been computed. Cucurpe's resident population manifests a greater degree of economic inequality than agrarian communities in Switzerland, Italy, India, the Philippines, Jordan, and other regions of Mexico. Interestingly enough, only the Iberian peninsula and Sicily rank higher.[1]

THE DISTRIBUTION OF LIVESTOCK
AMONG CUCURPE HOUSEHOLDS

It must be reiterated, however, that measures of inequality based upon resident households alone seriously underestimate the inequitable distribution of wealth within the municipio. They do so because they fail to include Cucurpe's absentee landowners—the private ranchers who own nearly four-fifths of the municipio's land and livestock. Only by incorporating this absentee elite can the true picture of economic inequality in Cucurpe emerge.

Because these absentee landowners are scattered across Sonora, it was not possible to interview all of them. As a result, another source of information was utilized: the annual livestock censuses compiled for Cucurpe's three livestock zones. In 1981, these censuses listed the number of cattle, horses, mules, and goats owned by 202 individuals ranging from comuneros to private ranchers regardless of residence. These censuses can be employed to generate an index of wealth in livestock encompassing all levels of economic status in Cucurpe except for those households that own no livestock whatsoever.

Obviously, such an index is not as complete as the index of total wealth. First of all, it does not include important resources such as land and machinery. Secondly, there are a number of methodological problems with the livestock censuses themselves, particularly under-enumeration (*see* Appendix A). Nevertheless, these censuses do allow both resident and nonresident livestock owners to be compared. Moreover, livestock are the most important source of wealth in the municipio. Sixty percent of all resident households derive at least 50 percent of their total wealth from livestock, while 14 percent depend upon their animals for all their assets. In short, livestock ownership is the single best measure of economic status in Cucurpe.

To determine the index of wealth in livestock, animals were weighted according to their approximate value in pesos (*see* Appendix B). Like the index of total wealth, the index of wealth in livestock

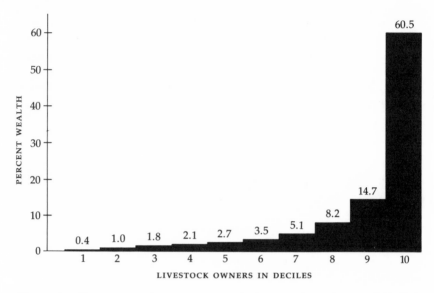

Figure 6.2. Percentage of Wealth in Livestock Among Cucurpe Livestock Owners

represents 1/1000 of the value of the livestock in 1980–81 pesos. Not surprisingly, the resulting mean—663.3—is more than twice as high as the average amount of total wealth (301.5) among resident households. The livestock index, after all, includes the absentee elite. Like the distribution of total wealth, wealth in livestock is extremely skewed. Its Gini coefficient of .693 compares quite closely with the Gini of .687 for total wealth. Breaking the sample into deciles reveals that the upper 10 percent of all livestock owners control 60.5 percent of all range animals in Cucurpe. The lower five deciles, on the other hand, own less than 10 percent (Figure 6.2). Even among stockmen, Cucurpe's major form of wealth remains concentrated in relatively few hands.

Once again, though, the analysis needs to be carried one step further. According to my survey of Cucurpe households, fifty-nine domestic units own no livestock at all. A revised index of wealth in livestock incorporating these fifty-nine households yields an even higher Gini of .735, the top decile holding 62.4 percent of the municipio's wealth in livestock, the lower 50 percent owning less than 5 percent (Figure 6.3). This Gini, in fact, represents the best available approximation of economic inequality in Cucurpe.

Yet not even the revised index of wealth in livestock captures the total range of economic status among households making a living in the municipio. Many private ranchers, it must be remembered, own

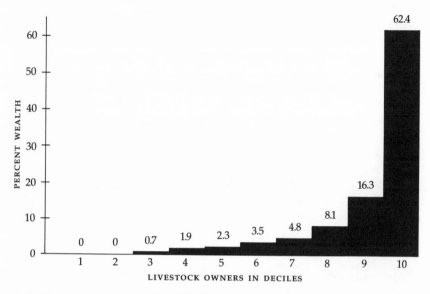

Figure 6.3. Percentage of Wealth in Livestock Incorporating Households with No Livestock

land, livestock, mines, and other business enterprises outside Cu-curpe. Both the index of total wealth and the index of wealth in livestock, on the other hand, reflect only assets and capital located in Cucurpe itself. And since these same ranchers often bring the force of their external wealth and influence to bear on municipal matters, the total wealth of the absentee elite plays a very important role in munici-pal politics. The statistics presented above, then, represent conserva-tive estimates of the economic distance among households competing for Cucurpe's scarce resources.

ECONOMIC INEQUALITY AND THE
ORGANIZATION OF RESOURCE CONTROL

Individual households rarely compete for resources such as farmland or rangeland on their own, however. Rather, they join together in formal or informal groups to pursue common goals such as the protec-tion of corporate grazing lands or the preservation of private property. Currently, the two comunidades and one ejido represent the interests of peasant rancher-farmers in Cucurpe. Private ranchers, by contrast, possess no single overarching organization, even though they do dominate the local stockmen's association (*asociación ganadera de Cu-curpe*). Nonetheless, wealthy ranchers are able to manipulate government programs and policies through such associations, as well as through their family connections and their individual contacts with various government officials. The politics of resource control in Cucurpe is a complex, often murky process that takes place in Magdalena, Hermosillo, and Mexico City as often as it does in the municipio itself.

This process is rendered even more complicated by the fact that none of the four major groups noted above is characterized by economic homogeneity. On the contrary, significant differences in economic status exist within as well as between these factions. Only by examining the range of such differences can we begin to understand why these groups behave as they do, and where the true epicenters and fault lines of Cucurpe political power lie.

The Comunidad of Cucurpe

Indexes of total wealth among households belonging to the Comunidad of Cucurpe run from zero to 1048, indicating that some households possess no land, livestock, or machinery, while one household has an estate worth 1,048,000 pesos (U.S. $41,920). The average household index is 259.9 (259,900 pesos; U.S. $10,396), but nearly 60 percent of the 103 households in the sample fall below the mean. The highest decile controls about one-third of the comunidad's total wealth (Figure 6.4). The lowest decile possesses a miniscule 0.2 percent. In other

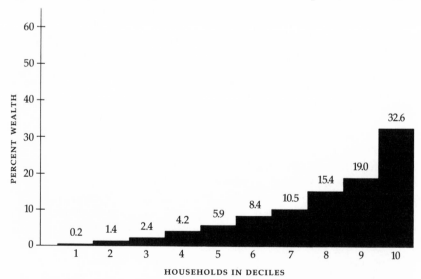

Figure 6.4. Percentage of Total Wealth Among Households in the Comunidad of Cucurpe

words, Cucurpe's largest and most powerful peasant corporate com-munity encompasses considerable differences in economic status.

Nonetheless, the level of inequality within the comunidad is sig-nificantly lower than that of the municipio as a whole. The com-unidad's index of total wealth yields a Gini coefficient of .492, com-pared to .687 for the entire municipio. Similar levels of inequality characterized the peasant closed corporate community of Törbel in the Swiss alps (McGuire and Netting 1982). As chapters 8 and 9 demon-strate, the Comunidad of Cucurpe is riven by economic and political cleavages, yet it still manages to take effective political action by mobi-lizing the majority of its members who share certain basic economic concerns.

The Comunidad of San Javier

Differences of economic status within the Comunidad of San Jav-ier, on the other hand, are more pronounced. Individual household indexes of total wealth range from zero to 2,466, indicating a much broader gap between poor and prosperous families. The highest decile owns nearly 50 percent of the comunidad's total wealth (Figure 6.5). The lowest possesses no wealth whatsoever. With a Gini coefficient of .607, San Javier's level of inequality approaches that of the municipio as a whole.

Much of this disparity arises from the presence of a handful of

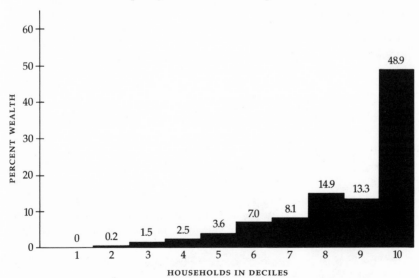

Figure 6.5. Percentage of Total Wealth Among Households in Comunidad San Javier

comuneros who are as wealthy as many private ranchers. Even though San Javier's mean index of total wealth is 419.6 (419,600 pesos; U.S. $16,784), at least 60 percent of the households' wealth is less. Three families, on the other hand, have indexes of total wealth higher than that of any household in the much larger Comunidad of Cucurpe. All three of these domestic units run more than one hundred cattle on comunidad range, with two owning nearly three hundred animals apiece. Not surprisingly, the interests of these wealthy comuneros often conflict with those of their less well-to-do brethren, a point that will be dealt with at greater length in the following chapter.

The Ejido 6 de Enero

The smallest and poorest corporate community in Cucurpe is also the youngest—Ejido 6 de Enero. Household indexes range from zero to 468.6, and the mean stands at only 139.2 (139,200 pesos; U.S. $5,568), much lower than either Cucurpe or San Javier. With a Gini coefficient of .514, Ejido 6 de Enero falls between the two comunidades, but the sample size of nineteen households is so small that such comparisons must be treated cautiously. About the only firm conclusion that can be drawn is that 6 de Enero is a poverty-stricken enclave of people who are just beginning to make the transition from landless proletarians to landed peasants.

Other Municipal Residents

Residents of the municipio who do not belong to the three corporate communities are difficult to categorize. Above all, they are not formally organized. On the contrary, they fall into at least three different groups with different levels of wealth and different class interests. Consequently, their impact upon the local politics of resource control is diffuse at best, expressing itself in roundabout ways if, indeed, it is expressed at all.

Most of the households in this residual category consist of *jornaleros* and their families, individuals who work as cowboys or miners for the absentee elite. Many of these people have drifted into Cucurpe from other places in Sonora or northern Mexico, so they rarely have long-standing ties of either kinship or residence in the municipio. Whenever political controversies erupt, most of them either support their *patrones* or stay out of the fray.

The second identifiable group are the few *profesionistas* residing in Cucurpe. In 1981, this group included the principal of Cucurpe's grade school, the handful of teachers whom he supervised, and a young doctor completing his mandatory year of social service after graduating from medical school. The principal and one of the women teachers have married into families belonging to the Comunidad of Cucurpe and have put down roots in the municipio. The rest, on the other hand, planned to leave Cucurpe as soon as less isolated posts became available. Occasionally, these professionals take an active role in local politics. In 1985, for example, the school principal was chosen as the Comunidad of Cucurpe's candidate for municipal president until the state organization of the *Partido Revolucionario Institucional* (PRI) in Hermosillo imposed someone else.[2] Usually, however, the doctors, teachers, and government technicians who spend a year or two in Cucurpe remain detached and ironic observers of the local scene.

Finally, there are the private ranchers who actually live in the municipio itself. These individuals generally own less land or fewer cattle than members of the absentee elite; in a sample of eighteen households, the average number of cattle was only fifty while the average size of a ranch was just under 400 ha. Nevertheless, these resident stockmen still run more animals than most comuneros and take an active interest in municipal politics. On most issues of resource control, they side with the absentee elite since both share a common interest in avoiding expropriation and limiting the growth of the corporate communities.

Because they are so disparate, households in this residual category exhibit the widest range of economic status. Their indexes of total wealth run from zero to 4,884, with a Gini coefficient of .838. The upper decile controls an overwhelming 70 percent of the total wealth. The lower five deciles hold less than 0.1 percent. These structural characteristics suggest what Cucurpe would be like if the corporate communities were removed from the municipio: a society of private ranchers and their employees, with a few professionals thrown in to service their needs. Such a society would have no local focus. Rather, Cucurpe would be little more than a hinterland of Sonora's cities, a collection of cattle ranches whose owners lived someplace else.

The Absentee Elite

Even today, the wealth of the private ranchers who reside in the municipio is paltry compared to that of the absentee elite. Only three local private stockmen run 100 head of cattle or more. The most prosperous individual, in fact, grazes a herd of 150 cattle on 2,000 ha of agostadero. Two members of Comunidad San Javier own more animals than he owns.

In contrast, sixteen ranchers living outside Cucurpe run 500 head of cattle or more, while eight possess herds of at least 1,000 animals. But as chapter 4 suggests, even the absentee elite are characterized by great economic diversity. Many individuals listed in the livestock censuses are family members who take little or no part in the operation of family spreads. Others control diversified business empires throughout northern Mexico. Based both on the livestock censuses and on the limited number of interviews with the absentee elite, it is clear that private ranches in Cucurpe range from modest household operations to large enterprises managed almost entirely by employees.

Private Ranchers in General

No matter where they reside or how many cattle they run, private ranchers are the wealthiest, most powerful group in Cucurpe. Their average number of cattle—227—is far higher than the number of animals owned by all but the wealthiest comuneros (see Table 4.4). Moreover, a Gini coefficient of .562 reveals that there is less disparity in economic status among private stockmen than among municipal residents in general. They may live in different cities, and their dependence upon Cucurpe resources may vary, but private ranchers still share certain basic concerns that unite them on major issues of resource control.

WEALTH AND THE ORGANIZATION OF RESOURCE CONTROL

Clearly, differences of economic status exist within the different groups involved in the politics of resource control. As the next three chapters demonstrate, such differences explain why conflicts among members of these organizations are often so bitter and so prolonged. Nonetheless, the magnitude of economic inequality within groups remains dwarfed by the inequitable distribution of resources in the municipio as a whole. Divided as they are, these groups continue to function as meaningful political factions in the municipal arena.

A brief and final look at the distribution of wealth on the household level reveals just where the members of these groups fit into the general economic hierarchy. Sixty-two percent of the families belonging to the Comunidad of Cucurpe and nearly 68 percent of those in Comunidad San Javier rank in the upper five deciles of total wealth among municipal residents. Only 42 percent of the members of Ejido 6 de Enero, on the other hand, can be so classified. Within the munici-

Table 6.1. Distribution of Livestock Owners in Cucurpe

		According to Their Wealth in Livestock			
Decile	Cucurpe	San Javier	6 de Enero	Private	Unknown
1	8	1	0	0	9
2	11	4	0	1	4
3	8	9	0	3	3
4	5	2	2	5	6
5	6	1	1	4	8
6	6	6	1	3	3
7	7	3	1	9	1
8	8	5	0	11	1
9	1	2	0	17	0
10	0	1	0	21	0
TOTAL	60	34	5	74	35
Wealth in Livestock	9,746	10,565	1,045	108,350	4,739
Percent	7.2	7.9	0.8	80.6	3.5

pio, members of the two oldest corporate communities are relatively prosperous, at least by local standards.

But such numbers tell only part of the story. Again, it is necessary to turn to the index of wealth in livestock to get a more accurate picture of the relationship between household economic status and the organization of resource control. The two comunidades and one ejido possess only 16 percent of the municipio's wealth on the hoof. Private ranchers own nearly 81 percent. When the sample is broken into deciles, only one comunero from Cucurpe and three from San Javier make it into the top two deciles, while seventeen private ranchers are found in the ninth decile and twenty-one in the tenth (Table 6.1).

By any measure of economic status, then, private ranchers dominate the municipal economy far in excess of their actual numbers. Economic dominance, in turn, makes them formidable enemies of Cucurpe's three peasant corporate communities. But the statistics presented above only outline the economic and political structure of Cucurpe society. In a sense, these differences of economic status are little more than a latent matrix for political action. They only become important when they are perceived and acted upon—in short, when they become part of the ideology of resource control.

A jacal made from ocotillo and cartón, housing a family belonging to Ejido 6 de Enero.

7. Capitalistas y Bolshevikis

THE IDEOLOGY OF RESOURCE CONTROL

It seems like a cattlemen's spring picnic at first—a warm, clear day in early April, cottonwoods rustling, the San Miguel flowing past beds of watercress and budding willows. The members of Comunidad San Javier are gathering today to carry out a new census of their organization under the guidance of the Department of Agrarian Reform. They arrive on horseback or in pickups, cadging cigarettes, bitching good-naturedly about having to go to a meeting on a morning like this.

Because the weather is so pleasant, the officials from Magdalena set up their table in a field shaded by tall trees bordering a shallow acequia. No place in the world seems as green as a spring floodplain in the desert. The cottonwoods have leafed out, the fresh tendrils of mesquite are slowly uncurling, and the sturdy young corn shoots are pushing through the moist alluvial soil. A good day to roast a goat and drink beer with your friends, or to stand barefoot in the mud and watch irrigation water slowly spread across your milpa. On a day like today, land is tangible, not some abstraction coded in a book of laws.

For the first hour or so, the meeting proceeds as peacefully as the morning itself. After explaining the procedures to be followed, the officials call the comuneros forward one by one to record their ages, the composition of their households, and how many livestock they own. Only about half the original members of the comunidad as it was constituted in 1976 are present at this junta extraordinaria. *The others have either died or left the municipio. Occasionally, someone registers for a missing comunero. Other times the people at the meeting agree that the person has emigrated for good and his name is stricken from the list.*

There are plenty of men waiting to fill these vacancies, however, sons of comuneros or individuals living in Magdalena who wish to be recognized as legal members of the comunidad. The most vocal person at the meeting, in fact, is an aggressive young man who was born in San Javier, but who had not been included in the original census. As the junta progresses, it is clear that he is the leader of a faction of comuneros and would-be comuneros who are determined to seize control of the organization and shape it to their own ends.[1]

One of their immediate goals is to force other comuneros to attend regular meetings and to pay their dues, many of which are deeply in arrears. At first glance, these demands seem eminently reasonable: juntas ordinarias are held just once a month and dues are only 25 pesos. But the real issue is not dues or fines; it is the nature of the comunidad itself. The young activist and his followers, known as bolshevikis, want a corporate community that follows the letter of the agrarian reform laws. Their enemies, on the other hand, want tradition, not law.

Trouble begins when the government officials call the name of an old comunero who also owns a small ranch bordering San Javier. As the man approaches the table, the leader of the bolshevikis accuses him of a long list of misdeeds—of not attending meetings or paying his dues, of instigating a lawsuit against the comunidad itself. The last charge refers to a battle over a piece of land included within San Javier boundaries. The old man claims it belongs to his family. The bolshevikis disagree, arguing that the comunidad boundaries were established by four different surveys. The parcel also contains an aguaje, or water hole, which the old rancher has fenced off from other comuneros' cattle. The leader of the bolshevikis states that the old man wants to enjoy all the rights of a comunero without fulfilling any of the obligations. He then asks four other comuneros whether the man should be expelled. All four agree that under the circumstances, expulsion is justified.

As tensions mount in the soft spring air, the government representatives attempt to defuse the situation by offering a compromise. They ask the old man to allow his fellow members to water their livestock at the water hole in question. Many comuneros seem to feel that this is a reasonable solution to the problem, but the taciturn old cattleman disagrees. After listening quietly to the discussion, he mutters, "I'm not going to leave the land." He then reiterates his claim to the parcel, stating that he has "titles and papers." Neither side gives an inch. As a result, the new census does not contain the old man's name.

Shortly thereafter, another old rancher draws the bolshevikis' ire. Again, their leader accuses him of not coming to meetings or paying his dues. He responds that he's tired of showing up for juntas that never take place. Then he demands to know what right the younger man has to challenge him—a lifelong comunero—when the young man doesn't even belong to the comunidad. And when pressed about the several thousand pesos in back dues and fines that he owes, the tough, weathered old rancher explodes. "No voy a pagar ni cinco centavos, ni verga!" (I'm not going to pay five cents or cock!), he spits. Not surprisingly, he doesn't sign up for the census either.

The meeting ends in an angry standoff, both sides muttering threats and insults against the other. Caught in the middle, the government officials do *their best to minimize the hostility, but they are clearly distressed by the proceedings. Like most other bureaucrats, they want consensus, not conflict. And even though the purpose of the census is to determine who has access to comunidad resources, they have no intention of forcing anyone off the land, at least not now.*

Inconclusive as it is, however, the junta sheds stark light on the potentially fatal cleavages within the comunidad. On the one hand are a group of stubborn old cattlemen who want to be left alone to run as many cattle as they like on corporate land. On the other hand are the bolshevikis who want change—more land, more jobs, the redistribution as well as the protection of corporate resources. It is a case of tradition versus law, of custom versus a code of regulations written in Mexico City. Neighbor pitted against neighbor with a bitterness only people who have known one another all their lives can feel.

The previous chapter presented only external or so-called "etic" measures of economic inequality in Cucurpe. It is a sociological truism, however, that people's behavior is conditioned by their perception of reality, not reality itself. Marx, among others, recognized this basic social phenomenon when he discussed differences between "classes in themselves" and "classes for themselves." Individuals may share similar relations to the productive forces, but they only become a self-conscious class when they grow into an awareness of their common interests and act upon them. It is not enough to talk about the economic structure of a society or about the different strata composing that society's economic hierarchy. Those segments only become meaningful when people mobilize in response to perceived opportunities or threats. It becomes critical, therefore, to understand how Cucurpeños place themselves in their economic universe, and how that process of classification influences their participation in the politics of resource control.

LOCAL MODELS OF ECONOMIC INEQUALITY

In order to elicit Cucurpeño models of economic inequality, eleven heads of households were asked to group the names of individuals making a living in the municipio according to their economic status (*según su nivel de vida*). This ranking technique was pioneered by the sociologist August Hollingshead (1949), and has been employed by a number of anthropologists during the last two decades (Silverman 1966; DeWalt 1979; McGuire and Netting 1982). All but one of the eleven individuals who performed the time-consuming task lived in the municipio, and all but one were men of property who controlled both land and livestock. Representing neither the very rich nor the very poor, they came from the municipio's middle strata of peasant rancher-farmers, chosen because of their knowledge of municipal affairs and their willingness to devote several hours to the ranking process itself. (*See* Appendix A for a more complete description of the methodology employed.)

The ranking was conducted in the individuals' own homes, where they were given 164 names to group. These names consisted of a stratified random sample composed of 50 percent of the municipal household heads and 50 percent of the absentee elite. The rankers were told to place these names into as many categories of economic status as necessary. If a name happened to be unfamiliar, or if the rankers did not know enough about the person to accurately classify him or her, they were instructed to set the name aside.

Cucurpeños clearly recognized marked differences of economic status among themselves. Folk models of economic inequality ranged from the ubiquitous "upper–middle–lower class" system (Ranker 5) to groupings of eleven different categories (Ranker 6). Three rankers classified the sample into six categories, and the mean number of groupings was, in fact, 6.64.

By and large, the rankings closely corresponded to more objective measures of economic status such as wealth in livestock (Appendix A). More importantly, they elicited a wide range of information about how the Cucurpeños classified themselves. After the rankers had divided the sample into categories, they were asked to assess the distance between different groups—to determine whether the distances were great or small. Individual hierarchies may have varied in complexity, but all of the rankers recognized three major levels of economic status in the municipio. Furthermore, they often agreed upon what distinguished one level from another. What emerges from their rankings and their words, then, is a glimpse at the symbols of economic status that Cucurpeños themselves employ—symbols often translated into political action in the ongoing struggle for scarce resources.

LOS RICOS

Perhaps the most striking distinction the rankers made was in the position of the top strata. All of the rankers agreed that the uppermost categories enjoy livelihoods much higher than the ones below. These top categories consist entirely of the absentee elite. Cucurpeños clearly recognize that a number of private ranchers are far wealthier than the rest of the people making a living in the municipio.

In the process of classifying the sample, rankers mentioned a number of characteristics distinguishing this "upper class." Members were described as "millionaires" by several men. Ranker 8 stated that these wealthy individuals "have a ranch with many cattle, horses, fields, pump-powered wells, grazing lands. They have a house in Magdalena, an elegant place to live." Ranker 2 pointed out that the upper strata not only possessed land and livestock but other business interests as well. "They have more means of working," he noted, "of embarking upon new ventures. They have feed lots, markets. They dedicate themselves to commerce."

Other rankers observed that the absentee ranchers enjoy access to credit and have substantial savings in the bank. Their monetary reserves and their positions within financial networks, therefore, allow them to invest in new enterprises and expand established ones. They also live off the labor of others. As Ranker 7 said, "They don't work. They only work with their brains." Ranker 9 reiterated this point when he noted, "They live off their wealth. And keep on working to acquire more." Ranker 2 concluded, "Most of them are rich because of their fathers, because of their ancestry, their inheritance. They've been rich for many, many years."

These observations paint a provocative portrait of Cucurpe's absentee elite. First of all, the *ricos* are capitalists rather than peasants, producing entirely for the market rather than for domestic consumption. They view land and livestock as commodities to be bought and sold, and since most of them live elsewhere, they do not have the deep attachment to the region that characterizes many municipal residents. Furthermore, as capitalists, they employ labor to produce their goods but do little or no manual labor themselves. Finally, their wealth often comes to them through inheritance rather than through their own efforts. In the eyes of the rankers, at least, not all of them are self-made men.

Most of these observations clearly function as potential symbols of class conflict, rallying cries in the struggle for scarce resources in Cucurpe. In the northeastern portion of the municipio, for example, ejidatarios employ such symbols in their ongoing battle with neighboring private ranchers. At the same time, however, these same descriptions also reveal a grudging admiration for the men at the apex of the local economic pyramid. The rankers respected the ability of the absentee elite to work with their minds rather than their hands and to manipulate banks and markets to their own advantage. As a poor ejidatario said, *"Los capitalistas son muy vivos," "vivo"* being one of those multivocal words with numerous connotations, signifying that a person is clever while implying a certain amount of ruthlessness as well. Similar semantic tension characterizes other such descriptions of the Cucurpe elite.

This semantic tension is magnified by the fact that many members of the elite remain somewhat shadowy figures to most Cucurpeños. Since they live elsewhere, the private ranchers rarely come into close contact with local inhabitants. Those with ranches in the northern or eastern sections of the municipio often bypass the pueblo of Cucurpe altogether when they visit their holdings. Those who do have to pass through the village hardly ever spend much time there. Some of the comuneros may have worked for these ranchers on roundups at one time or another, but few know them intimately. Consequently, the world of the comuneros and the world of the absentee elite infrequently intersect.

More to the point, the most powerful private ranchers often avoid or deflect direct conflict with the peasant corporate communities. If their property is threatened by expropriation, they either counter that threat in Hermosillo or Mexico City, or they cut the best deal they can and move on. Unlike poorer private cattlemen, they do not curse the bolshevikis with a vitriolic intensity born of desperation. Their resources are simply too great or too varied for them to worry much about Cucurpe affairs.

LA GENTE ORDENADA

The next distinguishable level of stratification might be termed Cucurpe's "middle-class." This level consists of a series of categories in which most of the individuals are rancher-farmers who live in the municipio itself. Interestingly enough, all but one of the rankers placed themselves within these middle-range strata. "We are workers who possess certain things in order to live," Ranker 2 said. "We have a little bit of land and a little bit of livestock." People in these categories may not own an elegant home in Hermosillo or a condominium in Tucson, but they are not landless laborers either. They produce food for their households and surplus for the market, and occasionally a moral note creeps into their descriptions of themselves. As Ranker 11 noted, "We more or less live a moderate life. We don't suffer much from necessity because we are orderly people (*gente ordenada*)."

The differences in wealth among these individuals pale in comparison to the economic distance separating them from the absentee elite. Nonetheless, recognizable variations do exist. Individuals within the higher categories live better than those below because they have enough land and livestock to support themselves. Those in the lower categories, by contrast, have to supplement their calf sales and harvests with occasional wage work. Ranker 7 elaborated upon these differences when he said that those in the upper group "live well, comfortably. They have a quiet, easy way of life." Men like him, on the other hand, "live from blow to blow, with the ax and plow. We also work for wages. But we have livestock and our own land."

As the vignette at the beginning of this chapter suggests, Cucurpe's "upper middle class" often stands in the vortex of local agrarian conflict. Encompassing both private ranchers and wealthy comuneros, these individuals possess more land and cattle than their neighbors. What they do not have, however, are the political connections or the diversified business interests of the absentee elite. Their livelihoods depend entirely upon Cucurpe resources, so local struggles for those resources threaten their very survival in the municipio. Many Cucurpeños, therefore, become mortal enemies of the more radical members of the corporate communities, the bolshevikis.

LOS POBRES

A large number of those enemies fall into the third general level of economic status recognized by Cucurpeños. People in these categories are not self-supporting rancher-farmers, peasant or private. Rather, they are individuals who have to scramble to survive in Cucurpe's agrarian economy, usually as intermittent wage laborers. According to Ranker 2, "They are the persons who live on their salaries. A few have four, five, six cows, no more. The wages they make are very low. Here there's no steady work."

Others painted the same bleak picture. Ranker 4 said, "They don't have anything, the poor people. They make mescal, work a little." Ranker 8 noted, "They live on the minimum wage. At times they work, other times they don't. They live a pretty hard, poor life." Describing one individual within this level, Ranker 11 was even more blunt. "He doesn't have anything more than his house," the man commented. "He's not worth peanuts."

A few of these men make relatively good wages by working as cowboys on private ranches. There they live rent-free with their families and receive steady incomes. Most landless laborers, on the other hand, do not enjoy the luxury of *trabajo corrido* (full-time work). Miners, for example, drift in and out of the municipio, laboring for fifteen- or twenty-day shifts in the mountains of Cucurpe and then seeking employment somewhere else. Cucurpe's decaying mining industry simply cannot support the large and stable work force that it once did.

The rest of the people in these bottom strata belong to the corporate communities, where they eke out a meager existence through a mixture of wage work and subsistence farming. Such individuals are able to meet some of their own needs, but they don't possess enough land or animals to make a living as rancher-farmers alone. They have to scrounge for wage work or produce some other good such as rawhide lariats, cantera *ollas*, or mescal. If they are young and nimble, they break horses. If they are old and stiff, they gather loads of firewood on the back of a burro. Their poverty forces them to be jacks-of-all-trades. In an economy like Cucurpe's, they simply cannot afford to specialize in a single trade.

One of the households belonging to Ejido 6 de Enero exemplifies the hand-to-mouth existence of these people. The family—all ten of them—share two rusty beds or sleep on the floor of their ocotillo *jacal* on the edge of a clearing called Agua en Medio. Although there is no irrigated land in the ejido, the family has planted about 4 ha of temporal in corn, beans, and squash. They also own three cows, two goats, one burro, and four chickens. The father and one of his sons were working for 200 pesos a day (U.S. $8) in 1981, cutting down mesquites and making charcoal (*carbón*) for a man from the Yaqui Valley who had a concession to do so from the ejido. The younger sons make adobe bricks. Like most of their fellow ejidatarios, they are trying to make a living in the countryside with little or no assistance from the government and with few resources of their own.

Not surprisingly, these people often find themselves battling households with more land and livestock. Unlike the prosperous rancher-farmers of San Javier, for example, they want change. They need either land or jobs or both, and if those necessary resources are not forthcoming, many of them have to leave Cucurpe in search of livelihoods somewhere else. They constitute the most unstable element of Cucurpe's population, moving in and out of the municipio according to the prevailing economic currents of the time.

Comunidad and ejido leaders attempt to create power bases for themselves among these individuals by manipulating government programs of rural development or by attempting to expropriate the land of nonmembers. Such political maneuvering plays an important role in all three corporate communities, pitting one faction against the other and engendering constant tension within the organizations themselves. The strategy is a risky one, however, depending almost entirely on outside governmental support. At times it pays off handsomely. The last years of the Echeverría administration witnessed a surge in agrarian populism at the federal level, leading to the creation of the ejido and the reconfirmation of the two comunidades. The apparent oil boom of the early López Portillo years stimulated federal investment in the rural sector as the bureaucrats sought to diversify and revitalize rural economies. But federal political support varies from president to president, and federal economic aid can suddenly evaporate as national economic development founders on the shoals of recession and corruption. The alliance between the power brokers and the poor is, therefore, a fragile one, and is always at the mercy of forces beyond local control.

THE IDEOLOGY OF RESOURCE CONTROL

Politics in Cucurpe are extremely volatile, riven by conflicts arising from an inequitable division of scarce and necessary natural resources. Nevertheless, the conflicts are usually expressed within legal and legitimate channels. Even though both comuneros and private ranchers mutter about taking violent action against each other, violence rarely occurs.

One of the factors that undoubtedly decreases tension in the municipio is the residential patterns of the absentee elite. Great differences of wealth exist, but many of those differences are displaced, both symbolically and concretely, from municipal daily life. The elite build their luxurious homes and drive their new cars in Magdalena or Hermosillo, not Cucurpe. Their sons and daughters do not attend the same schools or go to the same dances as those of poor Cucurpeños. Their wives do not meet the wives of comuneros on the same streets. In short, the elite export not only the surpluses they take from the land but also their most conspicuous displays of conspicuous consumption.

Partible inheritance also acts as a leveling mechanism in the municipio. Ranching families who choose to remain in Cucurpe for one reason or another tend to see their economic status slip from one generation to another. Sons of wealthy fathers often inherit modest patrimonies. Because of such intergenerational fluctuations, a social

gentry has never entrenched itself in the municipio, and since Cucurpeños do not confront great disparities in wealth on a daily basis,
those disparities rarely ruffle the flow of ordinary human interaction.

Among municipal residents themselves, the range of economic
status is not broad enough to create lasting social barriers. Most households, regardless of wealth, make their living off the land. They all
have to plow their fields and chase their cattle, geld their horses and
clean out their corrals. Cucurpe's economy is pared too close to the
bone to allow a "gentleman's complex" despising manual labor to
evolve (Freyre 1964). And because of the nature of their economy,
Cucurpeños share a cultural orientation that values competence rather
than etiquette, education, or family background. People respect men
who are good farmers, good horsemen, good neighbors, and good
providers for their families. They respect women who run their households well and take care of their husbands and children. Cucurpeño
humor—rough, bawdy, and rooted in the land—makes short shrift of
more genteel pretensions.

In this respect, Cucurpe bears more similarity to the frontier community of Ouro Verde in southern Brazil (Margolis 1973) than to the
long-established towns of Spain or the Mediterranean. In Ouro Verde,
economic position, determined primarily by one's relationship to the
land, dominated the rural class structure. Most prosperous landowners originally got their start as small farmers or sharecroppers and
continued to work alongside their employees. According to Margolis
(1973:204):

> Education and "manners" rarely were identified as important criteria of
> upper-class membership, reflecting the fact that many wealthy land-
> owners and shopkeepers have had only one or two years of schooling and
> in this respect differ little from their lower-class neighbors.

Cucurpe, too, has been something of a frontier. Until the late
nineteenth century, Apache attacks prevented the establishment of
large, landed estates in many parts of northern Sonora. Then, soon
after frontier conditions began to disappear, the Mexican Revolution
broke out, bringing in its wake a legacy of land redistribution and
agrarian reform. Such developments allowed a greater degree of social
mobility than in other, more settled regions of the world.

Another long-term social process—*mestizaje*, or racial mixture—
contributed to this mobility. Even though Cucurpe was originally a
mission for Eudeve Indians, Spaniards, mestizos, mulattoes, and
other Indians such as Pimas and Seris settled in the area during the
colonial period. As chapter 1 notes, by the end of the eighteenth

century, only 49.1 percent of Cucurpe's population were Indians while 43.4 percent were mestizos or mulattoes and 7.5 percent were Spaniards (Dobyns 1976). Today there are no identifiably Indian segments of the population, and hence, no stratification system based upon ethnicity. Differences in race have largely disappeared, while differences of class have not had time to rigidify into exaggerated customs of deference, submission, or avoidance.

This relatively open social structure may partially explain why concepts like "respect," "honor," or an extreme emphasis upon *machismo* do not dominate the social arena as they do in some areas of Italy, Spain, and central Mexico (Silverman 1966; Romanucci-Ross 1973; Davis 1977; Galt 1980). Gilmore (1982:191) suggests that conflicts over "immaterial honor" represent cultural displacements "for powerful aggressive energies which might otherwise explode into open hostility." In a place like Cucurpe, by contrast, social position is fairly fluid, and direct means of political protest are available. Aggression, therefore, does not have to be displaced quite so elaborately.[2]

The importance of direct political action cannot be overemphasized. None of the factions engaged in the politics of resource control in Cucurpe are satisfied with the way things are. Private ranchers complain that the government is trying to implant communism in the countryside, while comuneros and ejidatarios are quick to point out how easily the laws of agrarian reform are circumvented or ignored. Nonetheless, the peculiar pluralism of Mexico's political structure keeps everyone in the game. If the mechanisms of agrarian reform, creaky as they are, did not exist, then the peasants might once again march on Mexico City. If, on the other hand, all private holdings were threatened with expropriation, a rightist revolution might take place. So far neither of these extremes has occurred, even though ranchers and campesinos occasionally commit sporadic acts of violence against one another.

A final factor must also be mentioned here, one that will be discussed in greater detail in the next three chapters. Even though their enemies label them bolshevikis, the most radical of comuneros hardly qualify as Marxist revolutionaries. Despite the long-standing existence of corporate communities, truly collectivist ideologies simply do not exist in the municipio. People with no land aspire to be landed peasants. Comuneros with land would love to become private ranchers if they could afford their own spreads. Members of the corporate communities do not challenge the right of the private ranchers to exist. Rather the comuneros demand that their corporate boundaries be respected. Consequently, the terms "capitalista" and "bolsheviki" are

146 CAPITALISTAS Y BOLSHEVIKIS

in essence misnomers. Cucurpe is not a battleground between collectivism and free enterprise. On the contrary, most Cucurpeños want to be as independent as possible—to run their own cattle, to farm their own fields. The phrase *"Quiero vivir muy agusto con mi milpa y mis animales"* (I want to live contentedly with my milpa and my animals) expresses the deepest sentiments of agrarian life. Those without land or animals may try to manipulate the forces of agrarian reform to acquire such resources. Once they have them, however, they bitterly resent any attempt to take them away.

8. Los Comuneros

THE HISTORY AND STRUCTURE
OF THE COMUNIDAD OF CUCURPE

The government representatives have driven in from Magdalena again for another interminable meeting of the comunidad. They and the comuneros gather in the hall of the local stockmen's association to talk about the stonecutting plant the government is building on the mesa above Cucurpe near the ruins of the Franciscan mission. The brother of the comunidad's president is elected sergeant-at-arms even though a few minutes earlier, he was tossing pebbles at the speakers sitting at the head table. He keeps shouting for order, but as the meeting drags on, the horseplay grows louder as the comuneros get more rambunctious. The meetings bore them; besides, they don't trust the government anyway.

After the junta is over, Juan, the president, invites the government officials back to his house for a carne asada. Strips of fresh beef are roasted over an open fire and then wrapped in tortillas and drenched in homemade salsa. There are also green onions and refried beans, cold beer, and a gallon of lechuguilla which the men pass around. Juan and the bureaucrats laugh about Juan's nemesis, the former leader of the comunidad, who as always made trouble for everybody involved, and prolonged the meeting by at least an hour. His obstinacy is a standing joke among the officials. Juan, on the other hand, is as cosmopolitan as they come—suave, friendly, diplomatic, a consummate politician who knows that most important business gets done outside official channels.

As people relax and tongues get looser, the bureaucrats talk about the inertia of the government and the inescapable web of corruption that makes it so hard to get anything done. They discuss the failure of the three wells the government drilled in the side canyons of the San Miguel drainage, noting that private wells forty feet deep yield more water than the 600-foot-deep wells just completed. The two younger men say that when they first went to work, they were bursting with enthusiasm and idealism, committed both to rural development and to agrarian reform. But they quickly learned how unresponsive the

Comuneros cutting slabs of volcanic tuff at the ill-fated Canteras de Cucurpe.

government was, half-seriously concluding that Mexico needs another revolution. The older official sardonically comments that I could supply them with guns.

He then walks over to his truck and slips a tape into his cassette player. I expect to hear norteño music; instead, Glen Miller's band glides through the "Hokey Pokey" and "As Time Goes By." As we drink more beer and eat more meat, the songs of the big band era mingle with the sights and sounds of la vida Sonorense: *crowing roosters, grunting pigs, and comuneros riding up on horseback to renew their ties with Juan and to observe the men who control access to the money and power their comunidad needs in order to survive.*

Meanwhile, Juan, in his gray felt cowboy hat and his boots with the silver toe tips, slips easily through the crowd, joking with the dignitaries and swigging lechuguilla with his friends and neighbors. He's the bridge, the broker, the man who brings the bureaucrats and the comuneros together. He understands the expectations and limitations of both groups, and he constantly explains one group to the other, lining up support among the Cucurpeños in order to manipulate the powers-that-be in Magdalena and Hermosillo. Even his followers laugh and say he's sin vergüenza—*without shame—but no one else in the comunidad knows how to move through the Mexican bureaucratic jungle as deftly.*

The last two chapters showed significant levels of economic inequality in the municipio of Cucurpe. They also demonstrated that differences in wealth and land tenure directly affect the politics of resource control. As we saw, private ranchers and three peasant corporate communities are locked in a continuing battle for Cucurpe's land and water. What remains to be done is to assemble the bits and pieces of information into a comprehensible mosaic that depicts as clearly as possible the politics of resource control in one municipio in northern Mexico.

The best way to do so is to focus on the Comunidad of Cucurpe—the largest and most powerful corporate community in the municipio. The Cucurpe comunidad has more members than the other two peasant organizations combined. Moreover, it represents about 45 percent of the total municipal population itself, making it the most important institution of resource control in the region. Even though the tribulations of Ejido 6 de Enero appeal more dramatically to the imagination, the legal battles and internal squabbles of the Comunidad of Cucurpe affect many more people. In its cumbersome and convoluted fashion, the comunidad is spearheading the drive to preserve Cucurpe's peasantry by fighting to protect corporate grazing land and struggling, often with itself, to define the status of arable land within its boundaries. It also is attempting to expand and diversify the local economy by undertaking new enterprises such as Canteras de Cucurpe, the quarrying operation and stonecutting plant. If the comunidad flourishes, Cucurpe may reverse a historic trend toward demographic decline and economic stagnation. If it fails, however, the dreary juggernaut of rural depopulation and economic marginalization will undoubtedly roll on.

HISTORY

No one really knows when the comunidad first came into being. Comuneros talk about an ancient colonial title to their land, but if that document ever existed, it has long since been lost. Nonetheless, generations of fathers have passed down knowledge of comunidad boundaries to their sons. At some time in the past, comuneros marked those boundaries with piles of stones (*mojones*), giving them names like Cabeza de León, Piedra Blanca, Tío Cheto, Purgatorio, Manzano, and Puerto Viejo. Even though the markers themselves were occasionally torn down by private ranchers, a small group of comuneros remembered where they had been located. These individuals considered that all the land enclosed within these boundaries belonged to the traditional corporate community, and for years they fought to win reconfirmation of title to that land from the federal government. Their struggle in the face of conflicting documentation, bureaucratic inertia, internal dissent, and the occasional threat of violence illuminates many of the problems of agrarian reform not only in Cucurpe but throughout the Mexican countryside as well.

At present, the earliest document concerning Cucurpe in the possession of the Department of Agrarian Reform was written on October 4, 1878. This document discusses the need to resurvey the "ejidos de Cucurpe" because previous records of those lands "had been destroyed in one of the different pillages of the municipio's archives suffered during past revolutions."[1]

Succeeding documents describe the resurvey, which was conducted by an English mining engineer named Col. Juan Denton Hall that same year. Appointed "surveyor of the ejidos of the villa of Cucurpe" by the governor of Sonora, Denton Hall began work on October 21. For the next month, he and his assistants measured distances from "the door of the old church" (probably the Franciscan mission located on the mesa above the river) using a "cord of fifty Castilian *varas*" (a *vara* equals 32.9 inches).[2]

The surveying party first struck out in a northwesterly direction towards El Pintor. One hundred and one cord-lengths later, they encountered Rafael Fernández, the owner of the hacienda at El Pintor, who showed Denton Hall a bill of sale (*escritura de venta*) for the land executed by none other than Francisco Montés, the infamous Piman interloper who had given his nickname (El Pintor) to the place itself (*see* chapter 1). Fernández did not know where the boundary markers of his property lay, so Denton Hall had to appeal for help to Ursulo Ramos, president of the municipio of Cucurpe. Ramos told the surveyor that all the land north of a large white rock outcrop belonged to the former pueblo of Dolores. The inhabitants of El Pintor, including Fernández, received legal grants to this terrain after the old mission lands of Dolores had been redistributed in 1852. The people of El Pintor, however, had been in actual possession of this ground, including "water rights to arable land with the use of pasture, woodland, firewood, etc." (*hijuelas de tierra de pan llevar, con el uso de los pastos y maderas, leñas, etc.*) from "time immemorial." The president resolved to place a boundary marker dividing the ejidos of Cucurpe from the Dolores lands at the very same rock outcrop in order to avoid future disputes.

Denton Hall and his party then proceeded east to the rancho of Saracachi, which later became part of the hacienda of Agua Fría, and south to Rancho El Bajío, measuring the "ejido" boundaries as they went. After that, they headed west to the settlement of El Tren de Guadalupe, which marked the boundary between Cucurpe and San Javier. They encountered no further boundary disputes, completing their survey in late November. Denton Hall's report was sent to the state treasury in Ures, which was the capital of Sonora at that time.

The survey is important because it served as the instrument upon which the federal land grants of 1882 were based. In that year, Manuel González, the president of Mexico, awarded parcels of 145 ha to 92 *"vecinos de la Villa de Cucurpe,"* presumably as a reward for service against enemies of the republic. A crude map, entitled *"Plano de los Egidos [sic] de Cucurpe,"* delineated those individual lots as well as the boundaries of the ejido lands (*terrenos de los egidos*) themselves. It shows the *"egidos de Cucurpe"* bordered by El Torreón and El Pintor on the northwest, by unoccupied land (*baldíos*) on the northeast, by Rancho Saracachi and Rancho Bajío on the east, by San Javier on the south, and by more unoccupied land on the west. According to the *Plano*, the entire area encompassed 16,234 ha, of which 25 ha fell within the *fundo legal*, or land set aside for the villa of Cucurpe itself. Private owners remained in control of 2,799 ha. The remaining 13,430 ha were divided among the 92 grantees.[3]

This *Plano* is the only documentary basis upon which the modern Comunidad of Cucurpe is founded. Comuneros and officials from the Department of Agrarian Reform searched archives in Sonora, Guadalajara, and Mexico City for earlier titles to the land, but were unable to discover anything. From the very beginning, then, the claims of the comuneros rested upon a fragmentary and ambiguous documentary foundation.

Furthermore, the exact nature of these "egidos de Cucurpe" is not known, partly because the term "ejido" itself has changed meaning several different times. For example, Vassberg (1974:391) states that in sixteenth-century Castile:

> The exido was a multipurpose piece of land that could be used as pasture. The exido (derived from the Latin *exitus*, meaning exit) was an area of land situated just outside the town, or at its exit. It was not planted or cultivated because it was reserved for use as a threshing floor, as a garbage dump, for loafing, and as a keeping place for stray animals.

Castilian communities of that time controlled other types of corporate land as well, including *dehesa* (enclosed land), *monte* (land covered with trees and brush), and *coto* (enclosed, cultivated fields) (Vassberg 1974, 1984). During the first century of Spanish colonization of the Americas, then, the term ejido possessed a limited and quite specific meaning. It did not encompass all or even the most important types of communal terrain.

Somehow it lost that specificity in the New World. The jurist Escriche (quoted in Orozco 1975:49) defined the ejido as "the open country or land on the outskirts of a village, which is neither planted nor tilled and is common to all the inhabitants." As terms like dehesa fell out of usage, however, ejido came to signify all common lands which were neither cultivated or apportioned among individuals (Figueroa 1970). The phrase "egidos de Cucurpe" may very well have applied to just such lands surrounding the settlement of Cucurpe itself.

Unfortunately, ejido was never defined in any strict legal sense. The *Recopilación de leyes de los Reynos de las Indias*, the massive compendium of colonial legislation first published in 1682, stipulated that every Indian community was to receive a minimum concession of one *sitio de ganado mayor* (5,000 square *varas*, or 1,746.8 ha) for the communal use of its inhabitants. *Exido* was the term used to describe such a grant. As Orozco (1975) points out, however, neither the *Recopilación* nor any other source describes the nature of these ejidos or the manner in which their boundaries were established. It is not clear, for example, whether the "egidos de Cucurpe" included only pasture and wasteland, or arable land and irrigation water as well.

Whatever the situation in the nineteenth century, two related inferences can be drawn. In the first place, the inhabitants of Cucurpe undoubtedly have enjoyed corporate control over surrounding uplands since the colonial period. Secondly, such control apparently was not vested in a formally chartered body of comuneros. In contrast to a highly regulated corporate community like the Swiss village of Törbel, which was acting as a legal entity as early as the thirteenth century (Netting 1981), the Cucurpe "egidos" appear rather amorphous, governed by unwritten custom rather than written law. The corporate community a century ago probably bore little resemblance to the federally chartered comunidad today.

That transformation was a long and arduous one, fraught with many setbacks and delays. As early as 1918, residents of Cucurpe were appealing to outside authorities to prevent neighboring ranchers from invading corporate lands.[4] That year a number of Cucurpeños petitioned the state governor to remedy the situation but were unable to present any documentary evidence supporting their claim. Consequently, the governor did nothing about their request.

During that period, local ranchers were beginning to encroach upon corporate lands from the hacienda of Agua Fría to the east and from Predio Torreón to the north. One older comunero told me that the *"capitalistas"* were able to do so because they controlled the municipal government. By 1935, he added, "capital was fencing off" (*el capital estaba cercando*) many portions of the comunidad. The man's parents and others tried to fight the private ranchers, but they did not have the money or the political experience to offer much resistance.

The first documented evidence of effective action taken by Cucurpe residents in defense of their corporate lands did not appear for another two decades. In March 1955, a majority of the local inhabitants elected a representative and his substitute to "intervene" in a boundary conflict "which the communal lands (*terrenos comunales*) sustain with the owners of the properties known, to the north, as the lands of Torreón, to the south, as the lands of San Javier, to the east, as the lands of Saracachi and El Bajío, and to the west, as the lands of El Otate and Torreón."[5]

In response to this petition, which called for the reconfirmation of "the communal property of the campesinos residing in the previously mentioned ancient Ejido of the Pueblo," a formal request for "recognition and entitlement" (*reconocimiento y titulación*) was instituted on July 4, 1955. The chief of the federal Agrarian Department, as it was then called, appointed an engineer to survey and mark the boundaries of these corporate lands. In 1959, however, Cucurpe's municipal president wrote that this engineer "only effected some estimations, repeatedly abandoning all activities without leaving a trace of his work."[6]

That same year, the residents of Cucurpe marshalled their forces once again. Alarmed because the ranchers of Torreón were threatening to fence off corporate lands, the Cucurpeños themselves offered to pay an engineer to survey their boundaries. The municipal president, in fact, told the head of the Agrarian Department that a surveyor had been contracted to perform the task "in conformity with the official blueprint (*plano*) carried out in 1908 by the engineer William Roppher."[7] This 1908 map may very well have been based on Denton Hall's survey of 1878, because it indicated that the *"Antiguo Ejido de Cucurpe"* consisted of 16,254 ha, nearly the same figure as reported in the *Plano* of 1882.

Apparently nothing substantial came of this petition either. Nevertheless, the next decade witnessed an increase in both organization and militancy on the part of the Cucurpeños. In 1960, more than two hundred of them formed the Agrarian Committee of the Ancient Ejidos of Cucurpe, Sonora (*Comité Agrario de los Antiguos Ejidos de Cucurpe, Sonora*). They did so because some of their neighbors were trying to acquire title to corporate territory on the ground that these lands belonged to the nation (*terrenos nacionales*) and therefore could be parcelled out.

The first order of business was to search archives in Mexico City, Guadalajara, and Sonora to locate the "primordial title" (*título primordial*) to Cucurpe's corporate lands. No primordial title surfaced, but the committee under new and dynamic leadership pressed on. In 1963, the municipal president even wrote to the president of Mexico, stating:

> Knowledge of these boundaries was obtained from accounts transmitted from the fathers to the sons of people who populated the area in the past. Today one can locate vestiges of the ancient boundary markers that used to exist and that the actions of time as well as of interested parties have destroyed. In the same fashion it is possible to locate natural landmarks along these boundaries. Through such means, it is easy to identify the ancient perimeter forming the land in question.[8]

During this period of increasing tension, the surrounding ranchers were also amassing documentation and hiring legal counsel to defend their own claims. Their precautions paid off handsomely for some of them on November 25, 1964, when President Adolfo López Mateos awarded forty co-owners (*condueños*) of Predio Torreón joint title (*título de propiedad mancomunada*) to 19,247 ha of grazing land. According to the presidential resolution, these forty condueños and their ancestors had enjoyed possession of this terrain "in a peaceful, public and uninterrupted manner" since 1793, when Viceroy Conde de Revillagigedo had conferred a grant of *merced* upon their "progenitor," Francisco Xavier Gil Robles. The resolution then listed the number of hectares to which each co-owner was entitled even though the area remained open range.[9]

The corporate community of Cucurpe reacted by forming a new Committee for the Defense of the Ancient Lands of the Comunidad of the Pueblo of Cucurpe, Sonora (*Comité Pro-Defensa de los Antiguos Terrenos de la Comunidad del Pueblo de Cucurpe, Sonora*), on March 7, 1965.[10] The same day, the committee once again solicited the Department of Agrarian Affairs and Colonization, a predecessor of Agrarian Reform, to confirm the comunidad's title to lands awarded when the pueblo was founded in 1647. According to this document, those lands were delineated by four boundary markers—Babirochón to the northeast, Tierra Blanca to the southeast, Pueblo Viejo de Cucurpe to the northwest, and Otate or Purgatorio to the southwest.[11]

The two documents are interesting because they refer to Cucurpe as a comunidad, not an ejido, for the first time. Furthermore, they clearly distinguish between the Comunidad of Cucurpe and the actual

pueblo itself, indicating that the corporate community was not necessarily coterminous with the village. The new terminology probably
reflected the growing political sophistication among Cucurpeños. In a
paragraph of the letter addressed to the head of Agrarian Affairs, for
example, the comunidad authorized the National Confederation of
Campesinos (*Confederación Nacional de Campesinos*; CNC), the largest
and most influential peasant organization in Mexico, to transfer the
comunidad's title from one branch of Agrarian Affairs to another. This
reference to CNC suggests that the comunidad had become affiliated
with the organization by 1965 and was receiving guidance and support
from it.

The official process of "recognition and entitlement" creaked into
action during the following years. In 1967, Bienes Comunales took a
census of all male comuneros and unmarried or widowed female
comuneros sixteen years of age or older, arriving at a total of 336
members of the organization. The census included their age, sex,
number of livestock, amount of land owned, whether they were born
in the municipio, and, if they were not, how long they had resided
there. Sometime during this period, Bienes Comunales also dispatched an engineer to survey and demarcate comunidad lands. According to the president of the committee at the time, he and the
engineer and eleven other workers spent nearly two weeks in June
"battling the hills, surveying, with axes, with machetes." As soon as
the engineer finished measuring the boundaries of the Comunidad of
Cucurpe, he carried out the same task for San Javier.

The president of the committee was pleased with the engineer's
efforts, describing him as "very well prepared and competent." Unfortunately for the comunidad, however, the engineer had one major
weakness—a strong taste for alcohol and an inability to stop drinking
once he started. When he left Cucurpe, measurements and recommendations in hand, he stopped at a hotel in Magdalena where "all
the little rich men" (*todos los riquitos*) were waiting for him. According
to the president of the committee, the wealthy ranchers got him drunk
and then drove him to Nogales, where they bought him clothes and
gave him money. By the time he sobered up, he had lost all of the
documentation concerning the comunidad, so he returned to his
home in San Luis Potosí rather than reporting to Agrarian Affairs in
Mexico City. Once again the neighboring ranchers—"the whole gang
who had invaded our land"—managed to thwart the attempts of the
comunidad to legitimize itself in the eyes of the government.

This setback only angered the president of the committee and
roused him to greater efforts. A little bulldog of a man, described by

another comunero as "very frank, very obstinate," the president made at least five trips to Mexico City to plead the comunidad's case with agrarian officials. On his first trip in January 1970, he and several representatives from the Comunidad of San Javier discovered, much to their dismay, that none of their documentation had reached Agrarian Affairs. They were forced to return to Cucurpe then, but they soon organized another delegation of fourteen men that included representatives from Cucurpe, San Javier, and the group that would form Ejido 6 de Enero. This delegation spent a month in Mexico City, sitting at one point in the offices of Agrarian Affairs from eight in the morning until two the next morning for five straight days waiting for an audience with the head of the department. The president told me they were afraid to leave their seats because they would have lost their place in line. Finally, on the afternoon of the fifth day, the official received them for fifteen minutes. Following this brief discussion, "things began to change a little."

The next year, in 1971, Agrarian Affairs sent another engineer to survey comunidad boundaries. Utilizing aerial photos, he was able to complete his task and send the results to Mexico City without falling prey to the enemies of the comunidad. First, he measured the total amount of land falling within the comunidad's traditional boundary markers. Then he gathered information on parcels held by private ranchers within those boundaries. His conclusions were startling: the entire area encompassed 32,638 ha, of which 11,438 ha (35 percent) were in private hands. More to the point, boundary disputes existed along the northern, western, and eastern margins of the comunidad. In the engineer's own rather plaintive words, "I am obliged to declare that a conformity of boundaries only exists between the Comunidad of Cucurpe and that of San Javier."[12]

With this information in hand, the president of the committee launched a determined attack on the claims of the private ranchers. After three meetings before the Technical Board of Agrarian Conciliators (*Cuerpo Técnico de Conciliadores Agrarios*), however, the disputants still were unable to resolve their differences. The president of the committee, now known as the Representative of the Communal Lands of Cucurpe (*Representante Propietario de Bienes Comunales de Cucurpe*), wrote a long letter to the head of Agrarian Affairs denouncing the invasion of comunidad lands. He devoted particular attention to the co-owners of Predio Torreón, who in his opinion occupied 6,120 ha of corporate terrain. The condueños of Torreón argued that this land was part of the 19,247 ha granted them by the presidential decree of 1964. According to the comunidad's representative, however, that title was "apocryphal and totally void of effect." Citing Article 27 of the Mexican constitution, the representative pointed out that all alienations of ejidal or communal lands carried out by "political officials, state governors, or any other official authorities" from 1876 until the present were null and void. Consequently, the presidential decree of 1964 was unconstitutional because it failed to take into account the comunidad's petition for "recognition and entitlement" filed on July 4, 1955, a petition which laid claim to nearly 32 percent of Predio Torreón's 1964 grant.[13]

By this time, the official machinery of agrarian reform was rolling. Following completion of the survey, the same engineer carried out a census of comunidad members in October 1971. According to his figures, the comunidad consisted of 116 male heads of households, 103 single males aged sixteen or older, and 21 widows. These 240 comuneros supported 662 additional family members, giving the comunidad a total population of 902.[14]

On February 2, 1972, the National Indian Institute (*Instituto Nacional Indigenista;* INI) wrote the Department of Agrarian Affairs in support of the comunidad's solicitation. The general director of INI argued that since neighboring ranchers could not meet the criteria of Article 27 of the federal constitution, the comunidad was entitled to the 32,852 ha it claimed. This higher figure resulted from a revision of the 1971 survey which added 214 ha to comunidad terrain. Interestingly enough, the letter also cited the *"plano de 1878"* as the documentary basis for the comunidad's suit, even though that document noted only 16,234 ha within the boundaries of the *"egidos de Cucurpe."*[15]

The private ranchers soon launched a devastating counterattack against the comunidad. On January 19, 1973, attorney Mario Cano Cano sent a letter to the Department of Agrarian Affairs detailing a long series of objections to the comuneros' claims. Representing nearly all the individuals involved in boundary disputes with the comunidad, Cano declared that his clients were "owners in full possession" of their lands "in a peaceful, continuous, and public manner since time immemorial." He also stated that none of them exceeded the legal limits of tenure for small private landowners and that they had always exploited the land themselves. Many of the comuneros, on the other hand, were not actively ranching in the area but instead were living in the United States.[16]

Cano then proceeded to challenge the very existence of the comunidad itself. He argued that the organization had never presented any documentation proving it was an "authentic Indian community."

On the contrary, the 1878 Denton Hall survey referred to an "ejido," not a "*comunidad indígena*," and therefore could not be "considered as a communal title." Furthermore, that document may not have been legally binding in the first place, rendering the comunidad's claim unjustified and invalid.

Cano also pointed out that the 1878 *plano* barely encompassed 15,000 ha, less than half the acreage the comunidad was asking for. And of that acreage, only 21,000 ha were not under litigation at the time. Offering a compromise, the attorney stated that he and his clients would not oppose granting the "settlement" (*poblado*) of Cucurpe title to those lands as long as the rights of the surrounding ranchers were respected. In other words, the people he represented were willing to recognize the existence of a corporate community in the area if agrarian officials stopped trying to expropriate the private parcels in question.

Cano concluded his letter on an aggressive and antagonistic note, however, stating that the Department of Agrarian Affairs

> should resolve to negate and declare contrary to law the Procedure of Recognition and Entitlement of Communal Land solicited by the inhabitants of the supposed Comunidad of Cucurpe, of the municipio of the same name, of the state of Sonora. Such action should be taken in virtue of the fact that no title of any sort has ever been provided which proves that the supposedly communal lands of Cucurpe belonged to an Indian Community. Furthermore, one is not dealing with an Indian group which has always and without a property title retained possession of its lands in accordance with the stipulated conditions of Articles 199 and 359 of the Federal Law of Agrarian Reform. Rather, one is dealing with the nucleus of an ejido whose lands were located in accordance with the measurement and survey of Surveyor Juan Denton Hall on the 20th of October, 1878.

In the midst of these murky waters of claim and counterclaim, the Hermosillo branch of Bienes Comunales slowly began to process the information and make its recommendations. According to the comunidad's representative, two agrarian officials—one in Hermosillo, another in Mexico City—were related to families fighting the comunidad and sought, therefore, to delay or sabotage the comunidad's solicitation. Nevertheless, the process of "recognition and entitlement" had been set in motion and could not be stopped.

According to the Federal Law of Agrarian Reform,[17] the comunidad in question presents its solicitation, an action undertaken by the Cucurpeños in 1955. Then the solicitation is published in the "Official Record" (*Diario Oficial*) of the Mexican republic. After these initial steps have been taken, the group petitioning for land elects a

representative and his substitute to organize and present the necessary documentation to support their claim. As the reader will recall,
the comuneros carried out this requirement in 1965.

At this point, the agrarian authorities begin to take a more active
role by completing a census of the comunidad. After the first attempt
in Cucurpe ended in drunken failure in 1967, the comunidad was
again surveyed and a census taken in 1971. If procedure is followed,
the results of these activities are then published. From the date of their
printing, other parties with claims to the same lands have thirty days
to present their cases to the agrarian officials. Because nearly all the
approximately 1900 comunidades in Mexico are Indian (Reyes Osorio
et al. 1974), the National Indian Institute examines the documentation
and issues an opinion. All of these steps had been carried out in
Cucurpe by the beginning of 1973.

Next, Bienes Comunales weighs the evidence and presents its
own official opinion (*dictamen*). The report on Cucurpe was a masterful
example of political compromise. It declared that the "nucleus of
population known as Cucurpe" enjoyed the "legal capacity" for the
"entitlement and confirmation of its communal lands." On the other
hand, Bienes Comunales also recognized the validity of all private
claims to disputed territory. According to the report, the forty co-
owners of Predio Torreón possessed "legitimate title" to 6,120 ha of
terrain within the traditional boundaries of the comunidad. The titles
of eight other parties were also respected, removing an additional
5,318 ha from comunidad jurisdiction. In short, Bienes Comunales
acquiesced to the arguments advanced by Cano, the lawyer of the
private ranchers, by stating that the Comunidad of Cucurpe was only
entitled to 21,050 ha, or 64 percent of the territory it claimed. Of the
entire 32,638 ha in question, 11,438 ha belonged to private individuals,
while 150 ha constituted the "urban zone" of the pueblo of Cucurpe
itself.[18]

The recommendations of Bienes Comunales were accepted by the
Cuerpo Consultivo Agrario (Consulting Agrarian Body), the highest tribunal within the Department of Agrarian Reform dealing with such
matters. This body proclaimed that "recognition and entitlement"
would be granted to 21,050 ha of land which the "nucleus of population" of Cucurpe "had possessed in a continuous, public, and peaceful
manner since time immemorial." It went on to state that "no properties or possessions of private individuals existed" within that land, a
point that later became a bitter bone of contention among the comuneros themselves. Following the legal formulas of agrarian reform,
the report concluded:

Be it declared that the communal lands so recognized and entitled are inalienable, imprescriptible, and not able to be embargoed. They will be subject to the provisions and regulations of the Federal Law of Agrarian Reform only in order to guarantee their possession and enjoyment to those who belong to the comunidad.[19]

On September 22, 1975, the last stage of the tortuous process took place when President Luis Echeverría issued the presidential resolution of "recognition and entitlement" itself. Published in the *Diario Oficial*, this resolution granted the comunidad legal status in the eyes of the federal government. It also listed the names of the 240 comuneros recognized by the census of 1971, described the comunidad's boundaries, and stated that no conflicts over those boundaries existed with the organization's neighbors.[20] After at least sixty years of bureaucratic wrangling, the bolshevikis had finally won a victory. It was a partial victory to be sure, but a victory nonetheless.

As a result, the Comunidad of Cucurpe finally enjoyed the imprimatur of the highest executive authority in Mexico. Despite the fact that its claim to corporate terrain rested upon little more than custom and an 1878 survey that agrarian officials themselves admitted may not have been legally binding, Cucurpe was recognized as a full-fledged "Indian community." Unknown to many comuneros, it also became bound by the multitude of rules and regulations generated by Mexico's post-revolutionary process of agrarian reform.

ORGANIZATION AND MEMBERSHIP

Not surprisingly, most of those rules and regulations dealt specifically with ejidos rather than comunidades. An old term for a new entity, the ejido dominates the Mexican countryside; in 1970, for example, there were more than 21,000 ejidos nationwide compared to only 1,231 comunidades. More to the point, ejidos controlled about 60,577,490 ha while comunidades enjoyed jurisdiction over 9,195,142 ha. Between 1930 and 1970, the total amount of ejidal acreage increased by 52,631,579 ha; comunidades, in contrast, gained only 3,238,866 ha (Yates 1981).

The Federal Law of Agrarian Reform even allows comunidades to transform themselves into ejidos if they so desire. According to an official of Bienes Comunales in Hermosillo, roughly 25 percent of the comunidades in the northwestern district (Sonora and Baja California) eventually choose to do so, largely because people equate being a comunero with being Indian and poor. The status of ejidatario, on the other hand, possesses a more modern and progressive connotation. As Figueroa (1970:159) rather tartly points out:

> The Agrarian Code has merited with surpassing reason the title of Ejidal Code, because it treats almost exclusively themes relating to the ejidos. . . . The prejudice of the law in favor of the ejido could not be more infamous, because it ignores the historic preeminence of the comunidades and substitutes the ejido as the original organization.

The ejido, it must be noted, is a twentieth-century development in Mexico. A modern ejido does not necessarily enjoy jurisdiction over resources which were corporately controlled prior to the Mexican Revolution. Instead, the ejido is a creation of that revolution, designed to give campesinos access to land and water they may never have possessed in the past. Prospective ejidatarios do not have to prove title to the lands they claim. All they have to do is organize a group of twenty or more Mexican citizens sixteen years or older who do not already control property exceeding the legal limits. This group then forms a "new center of population" (*nuevo centro de población*) which has the right to lay claim to any lands within a seven-kilometer radius that are not legally held as "small private properties" (*pequeñas propiedades*).

Comunidades, in contrast, must demonstrate long-standing corporate control of land and water. Because of this stipulation, most groups solicit lands as "new centers of population" rather than subjecting themselves to the byzantine process of "recognition and entitlement" described above. Aside from this difference of origin, however, the dissimilarities between ejidos and comunidades are hard to define. According to the Federal Law of Agrarian Reform's Article 52, the resources of both types of institutions cannot be "alienated, ceded, transferred, rented, mortgaged or encumbered." In other words, both are peasant corporations whose members hold land and water in common but who cannot legally sell that land or water to any party outside the corporate community itself.

Furthermore, the organization of comunidades and ejidos is exactly the same. Both must elect a president, secretary, treasurer, and substitute as well as a council of vigilance (*consejo de vigilancia*). Both must hold a general assembly (*junta ordinaria*) open to all members on the last Sunday of each month. Members have an obligation to attend these meetings, and may be fined if they do not. All major decisions affecting the ejido or comunidad must be decided by majority vote, either in the monthly general assemblies or in specially scheduled sessions (*juntas extraordinarias*). The intent of agrarian reform law clearly is to organize both comunidades and ejidos as democratic institutions in which "the general assembly is the principal internal authority, integrating all ejidatarios or comuneros in full possession of their rights."[21]

Nevertheless, one potentially major difference between the two institutions concerns the status of lands held in usufruct by individual members. Article 52 of the Federal Law of Agrarian Reform (1981) states, "In accordance with the law cultivated lands can be the object of individual adjudication among members of the ejido; at no time will these lands stop being the property of the nucleus of the ejido's population." The article does not specifically declare that individual allotment can also be carried out in comunidades. Article 267, the only article referring to comunidades alone, notes:

> The nuclei of population that by act or by right (*de hecho o por derecho*) observe the communal estate will have the capacity to enjoy in common the lands, forests, and waters that belong to them or that have been or will be restored to them.

Neither of these statements definitely prohibit the allocation of comunidad lands to individual members, but at the same time, they do not unequivocally declare that such a practice is permitted. In this case the law regarding comunidades is remarkably ambiguous. According to Reyes Osorio et al. (1974:539), however, the cultivated lands of comunidades:

> in practice, in the majority of cases, function as private property; the parcels possessed individually by comuneros are treated and respected as such by all the members of the comunidad. These "properties" are frequently the objects of sale, partnership, or lease.

The authors go on to say:

> The Agrarian Code cited above and those which followed it do not devote much space to communal property. Aspects of their functioning as well as the identification of their members, the distribution of property, etc. also are not treated (Reyes Osorio et al. 1974:539).

Several pages later, the authors conclude:

> The preceding brief analysis demonstrates that the legislation relating to the communal properties of the pueblos is not clear, and that various of its dispositions have permitted the appearance of confusing and even conflicting situations (Reyes Osorio et al. 1974:540).

As the following chapter demonstrates, the ambiguities of the law do indeed cause conflict and confusion, especially in regard to the status of arable land. Members do not agree with one another about where the jurisdiction of the Comunidad of Cucurpe begins and where it ends, and these disagreements cause deep and potentially violent factionalism within the organization. They also exacerbate relations with the state and federal governments.

A certain amount of uncertainty also surrounds the necessary qualifications to become a comunero. According to Article 267 of the Federal Agrarian Reform Law, members have to be campesinos who meet the requirements of Article 200. In other words, they have to be Mexicans by birth, sixteen years or older, who do not already possess more than the legal limit of land allowed ejidatarios. Moreover, they also must have resided within comunidad boundaries for at least five years before the census of membership is taken.

As noted earlier in the chapter, the original census of the Comunidad of Cucurpe was conducted in 1971, enumerating 240 members. By the time of the presidential resolution in December 1975, however, that roster no longer reflected the reality of the comunidad's population. The Department of Agrarian Reform carried out, therefore, a new census on February 23, 1979. Interestingly enough, only 110 comuneros listed in the original document were still making their living from comunidad land, a figure which casts considerable doubt on the accuracy of the 1971 document. Despite high rates of emigration, it is hard to believe that 54 percent of the original membership died or moved away within the space of eight years. More likely, the official in charge of the earlier census simply granted membership more freely than the authorities who followed.

Different political priorities may also have shaped the criteria by which members were chosen. In 1971, the Cucurpeños were struggling with an indifferent bureaucracy and with hostile neighbors to win title to their land. Greater numbers, even on paper, undoubtedly gave them more pull with officials in Hermosillo and Mexico City, so relatives living in Magdalena, Nogales, or the United States may have padded the 1971 rolls. By 1979, the situation had changed. The comunidad was firmly established as a legal entity in the eyes of the law. Comuneros who were actually farming and ranching the land may have wanted to limit rights to corporate resources by purging nonresidents.

Such action would have been relatively easy to take because of the procedures to be followed by the comunidad. At each monthly meeting, the secretary of the comunidad calls roll. If a comunero is not present, he is fined 100 pesos in addition to his 25-peso monthly dues. Comuneros with more than ten absences are suspended from the organization, and unless they pay the substantial fines they have accumulated, they can be expunged from the rolls the next time a census is conducted. In 1981, for example, thirty-five comuneros were listed as being suspended. Since many of them owed several thousand pesos in back dues and fines, it is quite possible they ultimately will be expelled.

The 1979 census also may have been used to evict comuneros who publically opposed comunidad policies. At least three men listed as comuneros by the presidential resolution were denied membership then, even though they continued to live and work land within comunidad boundaries. One such individual—a member of the *consejo de vigilancia* before he was purged—clashed with other comunidad leaders as well as with the official from Agrarian Reform charged with reorganizing the institution because he refused to accept the corporate control of arable land. In his own words:

> I was disgusted with the executive engineer. I wasn't in accord with the way the engineer operated. The agricultural lands were not communal. They were the property of everyone who already possessed them.

In his opinion, the comunidad was limited to grazing lands, and these lands were to be exploited only by "authentic comuneros." According to him, "There are many authentic comuneros who are not mentioned in the presidential resolution." On the other hand, many actual comuneros should never have been granted membership in the first place. To illustrate his point, he cited the president of the comunidad himself:

> First of all, he has a brand-new car. Secondly, he has a tractor with all the machinery. He has his land; he has a well with a pump. He has his house of residence in Magdalena without paying five centavos. How can he be an authentic comunero?

Political housecleaning was not the only purpose of the 1979 census, however. At that time, the general assembly of the comunidad also petitioned Agrarian Reform to admit seventy-eight new members to the organization, most of whom were either sons of comuneros or their widows. In contrast to the transmission of ejido membership, the heirs of comuneros do not automatically become members themselves. Instead, they have to be approved by a majority of the general assembly, and even then, they cannot formally enter the comunidad until a new census is taken.

An example of this restriction occurred in 1981. In May of that year, a man who had returned to Cucurpe after working for the railroad for more than twenty years petitioned for membership, a status all of his brothers enjoyed. The president told him that although the comunidad sympathized with his plight, he could not join the corporate community until vacancies arose and Agrarian Reform conducted another census. At that point, another comunero rose and argued that sons of comuneros should be admitted first. The petitioner protested that he was a native son of Cucurpe (*hijo del pueblo*) and therefore deserved membership, but his argument was to no avail. As his petition was shelved, he quickly learned that simply being born in the region was not enough. Four-fifths of all comuneros were natives of the municipio. Nevertheless, place of birth was not the only, or even the most important, criterion for membership. The corporate community no longer was open to any Cucurpeño. On the contrary, admittance depended upon complex political considerations operating under the guise of the agrarian reform laws.

LEADERSHIP

On paper, the comunidad is a democracy in which every member has the right to voice his opinion and to vote on matters of importance. In practice, a handful of comuneros—perhaps ten or twelve of them— actively shape comunidad policy. During the monthly meetings, these are the men who dominate the interminable discussions. The rest of the comuneros, in contrast, usually keep silent, too shy, bored, or afraid to express their own thoughts. Even though deep and bitter divisions characterize the organization, these divisions rarely ruffle the surface of public discourse. Instead, dissidents savage the comunidad and its leaders in private while keeping their own council during the general assemblies. As several disaffected comuneros told me, it is better to say nothing than to be labeled as an enemy of the comunidad. One man's advice was, "Pay your quotas and don't get involved."

Such apathy stems in part from the formal trappings of the organization itself. Most comuneros distrust or do not understand the regulations of agrarian reform. They are farmers, not lawyers, and the rules and rhetoric confuse or bore them. When a truly important issue surfaces, they may make their stand. The rest of the time, however, they let others do the talking while they poke fun at the proceedings with their friends. At every assembly, the comuneros elect a sergeant-at-arms (*presidente de batis*) and at every assembly this hapless official shouts at his companions to quiet down, to pay attention to the debate, to stop drifting away before the meeting is over and the dues are paid.

Even in the days when it was fighting for its life, the comunidad never enjoyed a particularly active membership. According to the man who led the organization then, most of his support came from a nucleus of eight to ten men. In his own words:

> These men never abandoned me. They never got discouraged. Many times I had to go to Nogales, Hermosillo, Mexico City alone because the people did not want to go. On many occasions I had to pay for these trips with money out of my own pocket. When I asked these men to lend me money for these trips, they would lend me 1,000 pesos or more. When our commission had to go to Mexico, I asked these friends for the money.

All of these staunch supporters of the comunidad were lifelong residents of Cucurpe who controlled both land and livestock. By local standards, they were men of substance, prosperous rancher-farmers rather than landless laborers like the campesinos who organized Ejido 6 de Enero. Nevertheless, their livelihoods depended upon corporate resources. They viewed with alarm, therefore, the encroachment of private ranchers upon communal lands.

The former representative of the comunidad came from a different background. When he was a young man, his family moved to Hermosillo where he learned carpentry and the construction business; he did not return to Cucurpe until the late 1950s. By 1961, however, he had been elected president of the municipio, an office he held for the standard term of three years. During that term, he began to take an active interest in the comunidad's struggles, assisting the cause in whatever way he could with the powers of his position. After his term was over, he became the elected leader of the Cucurpeños fighting to win "recognition and entitlement" to their corporate lands. At the same time, he continued to make his living as a mason and carpenter rather than as a farmer like most of his neighbors.

As a result, the comunidad achieved its first successes under the leadership of a man who spent nearly half his adult life away from Cucurpe. The former representative only completed the third grade, but his residence in the state capital of Sonora undoubtedly exposed him to new ideas and new methods of organization. It also familiarized him with the workings of the state and federal bureaucracy. Unlike many Cucurpeños who remained in the municipio, he did not feel a countryman's insecurity in the presence of government officials. As another comunero commented, "He's never afraid to stick his nose in anywhere."

Nevertheless, his obstinacy and his single-minded devotion to the comunidad won him many enemies in and out of Cucurpe. One local resident expressed the sentiments of many Cucurpeños when he told me there was no conflict over land until this man returned and "began to divide the people." Another individual—one of those comuneros who disagrees violently, but in private, with the course that the comunidad is following—used even stronger language to describe the former representative. "He was a bad leader," the man said. "He is very jealous. He wants everything, everything, even the women. He was a red. A red, a communist."

Because of his reputation as a firebrand, the former representative was not chosen as first president of the organization following the presidential resolution of 1975. Instead, that office went to another man who was much more polished and diplomatic. Like his predecessor, however, the comunidad's first president also left Cucurpe as a young boy and spent most of his life elsewhere in Sonora. Born into a poor family, this man realized at an early age that there were no opportunities for him in the municipio, so he emigrated to Hermosillo in the early 1940s to work as a laborer. Even though he failed to complete primary school, he was smart, aggressive, and ambitious. Quickly tiring of the backbreaking work of a laborer, he told his boss he was an ironworker and asked for a skilled job with better pay. The boss soon found out he was bluffing. Nonetheless, he liked the young man's personality and drive, and he agreed to teach him ironworking and carpentry.

With the support of his employer, the young man quickly advanced in the construction industry. He was sent to Guaymas as the foreman on a big job, and from there he moved to Ciudad Obregón, the bustling center of a postwar agricultural boom in the fertile Yaqui Valley. In Obregón he met and married his wife and formed a construction company with another man. Contracting jobs all over the state, the man made influential contacts among private individuals and public officials alike, learning how to administer a company and oversee large numbers of employees. More importantly, he moved at ease in important circles, entertaining government officials and manipulating bureaucracies to get things done. These skills proved invaluable when he took over leadership of the comunidad.

He might never have left Obregón if his construction business had not folded in the late 1960s. Broke, his future as a contractor shattered, he returned to Cucurpe to make a living as a traveling peddler (*fallu-quero*) in the region. After saving a little money, however, he built a ranch on corporate land and began to raise goats. Then he purchased some farmland in a side canyon of the San Miguel and started to farm. After living away from Cucurpe for so long, his destiny suddenly intertwined with that of the comunidad.

In the 1970s, his fortunes improved. Calling upon his old friends in the government, he landed a series of contracts with the state Department of Public Works, building schools and restoring historic monuments like the Franciscan mission of Tubutama. By 1981, he was renovating a Porfirian-era home in the pueblo of Arispe and rehabilitating the famous mission of Caborca, where Sonorans defeated and killed North American filibusterers led by Henry Crabb in 1857. But even though the man maintained a residence in Magdalena, he remained deeply involved in municipal affairs. He served a three-year term as president of the comunidad and then was easily reelected. He also headed the municipal chapter of PRI, and chaired the local Committee of Progress and Welfare (*Comité de Progresar y Bienestar*). Because of his diplomacy and sophistication, he quickly became the principal node in a political network extending throughout the municipio and beyond.

Like his predecessor, he antagonized many people along the way. People complained about his frequent absences from Cucurpe, his obvious wealth, and his contracts with the government. One woman—the daughter of a White Russian who had fled his homeland after the Russian Revolution—fulminated about the president and his supporters who were trying to expropriate her land. A sharp-tongued individual with a caustic wit, she noted that both the president and his predecessor had left Cucurpe "for more than thirty years" before returning "to cause trouble." Commenting on their current prosperity, she also pointed out that in the past, these two leaders of the comunidad "had no land. They were bootleggers, scoundrels, cattle thieves, wretches. Before they rode on burros and now they ride in cars."

Nevertheless, the president enjoyed the enthusiastic support of the comunidad's most powerful faction, an alliance of established rancher-farmers and landless laborers, many of whom were employed by the man on his numerous restoration projects. One old comunero confided that no one could really take the president's place. "He has many friendships among all types of people, little ones and big ones," the old man said. "Besides, he's very meddlesome. He has no shame. He's fought much for the comunidad." The old man clearly realized that the comuneros needed such a man to lead them, one with the contacts and experience to pull strings and manipulate the government bureaucracy, to beat the wealthy enemies of the comunidad at their own game.

Interestingly enough, then, the comunidad seemed to acquire the leaders it needed at different stages in its recent history. During the

1960s, when the corporate community was fighting to defend its traditional rights, the dogged determination of the first man forced the bureaucratic wheels to start rolling. Once the comunidad was recognized as a legal entity, however, the institution required more flexible and sophisticated leadership. The second individual provided those qualities, working closely with government officials to broaden the comunidad's scope as well as to safeguard its corporate land. Both of these leaders were native Cucurpeños, but both developed their administrative skills far from Cucurpe's isolated rural society. Honed in Sonora's cities, these skills helped comuneros bridge the gap between the agrarian world of the municipio and the world of credit, capital, and the government outside.

An earlier *día de San Isidro* at El Ranchito south of Cucurpe, May 15, 1981.

9. *Los Comuneros*

THE FUNCTIONS OF THE
COMUNIDAD OF CUCURPE

The day is May 15, 1985, and the bolshevikis have gathered at Milpa Grande to honor San Isidro Labrador. San Isidro is the patron saint of farmers, so every year small groups of Cucurpeños carry his image through their fields after a velorio on the previous night. But these particular people have even more reason to be thankful than their neighbors: four years ago, many of them had no land at all. They were comuneros, and Milpa Grande fell within comunidad boundaries, but it still remained in the possession of a wealthy man from Magdalena who was fighting the comunidad tooth and nail. For years the lawsuits dragged on, and for years these poor comuneros waited for the government to hand over irrigated fields like Milpa Grande to them. Nothing happened, so finally, in the spring of 1982, they took matters into their own hands and seized the land themselves.

Now, at least eight families are planting crops on the property, which lies along the Río Dolores a few kilometers north of Cucurpe. Some grow wheat or barley, others corn and beans, but today they are enjoying the fruits of their labors, honoring the santo and basking in the warm spring air. After the procession, they place their images of San Isidro on the ground and surround it with flowers, and then they eat and drink and listen to the corridos of El Gavilán in the shade of a huge cottonwood tree.

A tall, thin man with dark, piercing eyes and tatoos on his arms, El Gavilán (The Hawk) wasn't born in Cucurpe, but he married a local woman and became a bolsheviki anyway. He is also the best songwriter in the region. He plays his "Corrido de los Bolshevikis" to everyone's amusement, and then he sings his most famous song, "La Yegua Mariscaleña," a ballad that describes the victory of a comunero's stallion over a private rancher's mare. It is an inspired wedding of one genre with another, a song that transforms a local horse race into a triumphant affirmation of the comunidad itself.

After he finishes, one man passes out, while a little girl curls up between the roots of the cottonwood and falls asleep. Faustino, a great jovial bear of a man, informs me that the bolshevikis are taking up a collection to buy me a new hat. Everyone talks about the horse races that are scheduled to take place at El Júparo along the floodplain of the Río Saracachi later that afternoon.

Before leaving for those races, my wife and I ask about one of the images of the saint, a wooden carving of San Isidro plowing behind two oxen. An old woman replies that the bulto *belonged to her father, who passed it down to her. The woman, who also runs the Holy Week festivities in town, bears one of the few identifiably Opata surnames in the region. So does El Gavilán's wife. This little band of bolshevikis, therefore, includes people who can trace their ancestry back to the time when Cucurpe was an Indian mission rather than a mestizo community. Like their forefathers, all they want is enough land to live on, which is why they challenged the government and the landowners in the first place. They are relaxed and cheerful now, confident for the time being that the government won't take the land away from them. They also hope that San Isidro will bless their fields and protect them from flood and drought. It is easy to be optimistic on a day like this when the winter wheat ripens and the young corn and bean plants spread in the sun. Down deep, however, they know how fickle and treacherous both the weather and the government can be.*

As the previous chapter suggests, the Comunidad of Cucurpe does not conform in many respects to the traditional model of the peasant corporate community. It possesses no civil-religious hierarchy like the corporate communities of Mesoamerica or Andean South America. It enjoys no stable pattern of resource distribution and control similar to that of the village of Törbel in the Swiss alps (Netting 1981). Even though it claims a colonial heritage, the comunidad today is a contradictory mixture of the old and the new, busily and often messily defining itself in response to a multitude of modern problems. With one foot enmeshed in the web of Mexican agrarian reform laws and the other in three centuries of unwritten frontier custom, the organization is composed of members with radically different notions of its fundamental purposes and goals. These ideas, in turn, frequently collide with the blueprints of state and federal officials overseeing various aspects of comunidad administration. Such differences spawn both conflict and confusion, factionalizing the organization and engendering cynicism and distrust between comuneros and government bureaucrats.

At the same time, these conflicts also imbue the comunidad with a dynamism that vibrates through every aspect of Cucurpe resource control. What the comunidad does is important, and everyone, even its enemies, realizes that. The debate over its proper scope and functions, carried out in meetings, on street corners, and in the offices of the *dependencias* (regional offices of government agencies) rages with a fervor fueled by the knowledge that the future of the comunidad may well determine the future of the municipio itself.

THE CONTROL OF COMUNIDAD GRAZING LANDS

The greatest amount of consensus within the organization concerns the corporate grazing lands. Nearly all comuneros believe this land should remain open range, accessible to all members. Defense of the communal rangeland, in fact, was the driving force in the comunidad's long struggle to win "recognition and entitlement" from the federal government. Wealthy comuneros who vilify their neighbors for attempting to expropriate farmland agree that the corporate grazing lands need to be protected from the grasp of private ranchers. In their opinion, such protection is the only legitimate function of the corporate community. As one comunero stated, "I am in the comunidad for my cattle. I fought for the grazing lands so that no one would bother me."

Despite this apparent unity of purpose, however, the comunidad is divided over whether or not to seize the nearly 12,000 ha of corporate land remaining in private hands. A number of comuneros still do not accept the boundaries of the comunidad established by the presidential resolution of 1975, claiming that collusion between rich ranchers and government officials cheated them of more than one-third of their traditional corporate community. At a comunidad meeting in February 1982, for example, the former representative of the comunidad exhorted his fellow members to "put on their pants" and tear the fences down. He said they could no longer rely on the government to fight their battles for them and argued that the comuneros should follow the example of the ejidatarios from Ejido 6 de Enero, who were aggressively defending themselves against their enemies. At that point, to everyone's amusement, someone shouted, "Bring on those from 6 de Enero then!"

Surprisingly, the president of the comunidad agreed with his predecessor. Nonetheless, he pointed out that many comuneros, not just "ten or twenty sacrificial lambs," had to participate if the action were to be effective. Earlier, the president confided to me that friends of his at Bienes Comunales had told him they would support such an act once it had been accomplished. The president claimed that 120 "united comuneros" were ready to carry out the task.

Not so unexpectedly, the fencecutting never took place. Despite their fiery rhetoric, the bolshevikis were not prepared to challenge head on the ranchers or the government. One reason was the opposition of many other comuneros to such a risky and illegal venture. Even if they agreed with the bolshevikis in principle, their prudence far outweighed their ideological fervor. After the former representative's call to arms, another sharp-tongued Cucurpeño commented privately that the man "spoke nonsense. He is very foolish." Without legal authority to do so, comuneros could be fined, jailed, or even shot if they tried to remove the fences. The president of the comunidad himself consistently called for caution in the general assemblies. Therefore, his figure of "120 united comuneros" clearly was an exaggeration.

The president also admitted in private that a better way to enlarge the comunidad was to petition the government to grant more land to the sons of comuneros. During the early 1980s, however, the comunidad took no formal action to expand beyond its 1976 boundaries. The organization no longer felt that its very survival was at stake. After all, the comunidad enjoyed secure title to 21,050 ha, and a number of lawsuits by private ranchers to reclaim this land had already been defeated in Mexican courts. Consequently, most members seemed satisfied with the present situation, or at least resigned to it.

The comunidad did make an effort to evict the livestock of non-members, or at least nonmembers who opposed and antagonized the organization. In November 1979, for example, at least eleven individuals received notifications of eviction (*notificación de desalojo*) ordering the people in question to remove their animals from corporate lands by January 15, 1980. If they failed to comply, municipal officials were empowered to round up their livestock and intern them. Six of these individuals lived outside the municipio but five were lifelong residents of Cucurpe who had either refused to join the comunidad or who belonged to Comunidad San Javier. The comunidad was attempting, therefore, to deny them access to resources they had exploited all their lives.

Like so many of the comunidad's other endeavors, the eviction notices were never carried out. Nevertheless, the letters further embittered local relationships in Cucurpe. As one of the men who received a notice said:

> How can they say I have no rights? I have never left here. But the head of the comunidad comes here only to visit. He lived for more than forty years in Obregón. The comunidad does nothing but cause harm and screw things up.

The failure to enforce the eviction notices indicates that the comunidad has little power to interfere in the day-to-day business of raising livestock on corporate land. At least fourteen nonmember households continued to pasture their livestock on comunidad agostadero, while the regulation limiting comuneros to fifty head of livestock apiece was ignored. Local inhabitants are accustomed to grazing their cattle on corporate range. For the present, custom, not law, prevails.

The comunidad also does little or nothing to improve that range. Although a number of cattle tanks have been excavated, they were constructed by stockmen who run their animals in the areas they serve. The only venture designed to stimulate the livestock industry in which the comunidad was involved was a government-financed plan to build corrals and install a scale for weighing cattle on the outskirts of Cucurpe. And even this plan was the project of the local cattlemen's association (*Asociación Ganadera Local de Cucurpe*); all the comunidad did was agree to allow the facilities to be built on comunidad land.

As chapter 4 revealed, cattle are the lifeblood of the Cucurpe economy. Why, then, does the comunidad not exercise more control over its most important resource, the corporate grazing lands? One of the reasons is historical: despite its colonial roots, the modern corporate community only has enjoyed legal recognition and formal authority since 1976. Consequently, it has not had time to consolidate its power or extend its control over a resource notoriously resistant to effective corporate management (Bennett 1969).

A second reason for comunidad inaction may be the high rate of emigration from Cucurpe itself. The municipio is not a closed system, and the number of people making their living as stock raisers is declining rather than increasing. Since the human population has not reached any sort of demographic equilibrium, the need to maintain a careful balance between livestock and their environment has not been perceived. As chapter 4 notes, the Cucurpeños refuse to acknowledge their role in the degradation of the range. Therefore, it is doubtful that they will begin to reduce livestock numbers unless pressured to do so by the government.

Thirdly, and most importantly, a serious livestock reduction program would devastate the local economy unless alternate sources of income were provided. Livestock sales account for a median 92 percent of yearly income other than wage work for households belonging to the comunidad. Since wage work at present is so sporadic, cattle remain the foundation of Cucurpe life. Moreover, Cucurpe's position at the bottom of the international livestock industry severely restricts the ability of local stockmen to limit their number of animals. Cucurpeños, after all, must maintain breeding stock as well as calves on their range. They cannot afford to specialize in any phase of cattle production other than the most basic one, that of running cow-calf operations.

Finally, once again, there is the heritage of the frontier. Until the advent of barbed wire, cattle roamed over the entire region, making systematic range management impossible. Even after fencing became feasible, vast tracts of open range remained, shaping a mentality that simply did not see the need to husband grazing land as carefully as floodplain fields. The frontier has disappeared but the mentality survives. So far, the comunidad has not attempted to substitute an ethic of conservation for the ethic of individual freedom that prevails.

THE CONTROL OF COMUNIDAD ARABLE LAND

If livestock reduction is ever instituted, tremendous contention will undoubtedly result. At present, however, most of the serious conflict in the comunidad can be traced to one issue: the control of arable land. When officials of Agrarian Reform were surveying the comunidad in the early 1970s, Cucurpe landowners were given a chance to present their titles to fields or pasture. After examining such documents, the authorities determined that none were authentic "small private properties" (*pequeñas propiedades*). Several years later, when the presidential resolution transformed the traditional *comunidad de hecho* (de facto comunidad) into a *comunidad de derecho* (legal comunidad), all milpas and temporales within its boundaries were recognized as corporate land. Comuneros retained control of the fields they farmed, but they no longer could sell, rent, or mortgage those fields. Moreover, individuals excluded from the comunidad were threatened with expropriation. To keep from losing their land, they instituted a series of *amparos* (injunctions) giving them time to plead their cases before judicial authorities.

No other conflict reveals the historical contradictions of the comunidad more clearly. Prior to the presidential resolution, agricultural land was considered private property. Fields were bought, sold, or rented at will, and milpas formed the very heart of a man's patrimony to his children. With a stroke of a pen, however, Cucurpeños suddenly found that these fields no longer belonged to them but were vested in the corporate community itself. Their bitterness concerning this sudden change in the status of arable land poisoned the political climate of Cucurpe in profound and potentially violent ways.

A prominent merchant and member of the comunidad eloquently expressed the outrage many residents felt at this turn of events. He talked at length about how hard a man had to work to make his land produce so that it would sustain him in his old age and be worth passing on to his children. In the past, he said, "rights to arable land (*terrenos de pan llevar*) were always respected." During the long struggle to reconfirm the comunidad's title, arable land was never mentioned as part of the corporate community. Instead, most comuneros were only fighting to defend its boundaries against "neighbors invading the grazing lands of the comunidad."

Now, however, comuneros could not sell their land to pay their medical expenses or use their milpas as collateral to borrow money from a bank. The government with its arcane rules and regulations had taken away the patrimonies of the Cucurpeños and substituted a foreign body of agrarian laws in their place. The injustice of the situation deeply rankled this ordinarily phlegmatic man. According to him, the government had no right to impose its authority over the comunidad. In his words:

> Here the government granted nothing. Even though we were disorganized, we were an old comunidad. The government merely reconfirmed what we already had. This is a very, very old comunidad. All my life this right [private ownership of milpas] has been respected. To consider these milpas as communal lands was a most absurd determination.

This man and others said that most comuneros did not understand all the implications of becoming a *comunidad de derecho* when the presidential resolution was promulgated. Unfamiliar with the intricacies of agrarian reform, Cucurpeños assumed that things would continue as they always had, so they did not bring forth their land titles, bills of sale, tax receipts, and other documentation. Furthermore, the man in charge of defending private property within the comunidad failed to carry out his responsibilities. "He should have defended the cause at that time," the man argued. "He made a list of all the private property owners living on comunidad land but he never went to the offices of National Lands (*Terrenos Nacionales*) or to Mexico City." Such "errors" were committed "because of the ignorance of the people." Comunidad leaders, on the other hand, comprehended the situation and exploited the inexperience of their followers. The comunero warned that, "Peace will be restored here when these private property owners are respected." Needless to say, this man controlled a considerable amount of irrigated land in one of the most fertile areas of the comunidad.

There was plenty of support for his position within the organization. In a random sample of 75 percent of comunidad household heads (seventy-four of ninety-nine individuals), 44.6 percent (thirty-three persons) thought the milpas should be considered private property. Only twenty, on the other hand, felt that arable land should be vested in the comunidad, while twenty-one expressed no opinion. A large number of comuneros, therefore, strongly disagree with one of the most important functions of their organization: the distribution and control of farmland. Ironically, both the president of the comunidad and its treasurer were among these dissenters.

The belief that arable land belongs to the households who work it cuts across economic strata within the corporate community. Nevertheless, differences in wealth do appear to influence attitudes toward its status. Breaking the sample into quartiles based upon their indexes of total wealth, a chi-square test of the relationship between household wealth and attitude toward the status of arable land was performed. This relationship was significant at the .05 level. Forty-seven percent of the comuneros in the bottom three quartiles thought that milpas should be considered a corporate resource. In contrast, only 12 percent of the top quartile felt the same way. Landed comuneros do not want to lose control of their fields to government officials or fellow members. In the words of the comunidad's president in 1981, "For my sake, I wish the milpas were private property. Then you could work without any disturbance, with complete liberty." This statement came from a man reviled by his enemies as *"el bolsheviki mayor."* Nowhere is the ideological disjunction between national laws and local opinions broader or more volatile.

Much of this sentiment spills over into the debate about whether or not the comunidad should expropriate the land of nonmembers within its boundaries. As late as 1981, four individuals antagonistic to the comunidad remained in control of more than 100 ha of prime floodplain. When the comunidad was recognized, these landowners were told that they had to give up their fields. Therefore, they instituted a series of injunctions and lawsuits to protect their property.

Their struggle factionalized the comunidad along much the same lines as the controversy concerning arable land. Forty-two percent of all comuneros in the sample cited above opposed expropriation while 41 percent felt that expropriation was justified. The remaining thirteen members of the sample voiced no opinion. Consequently, the comunidad was evenly split over an issue that should have generated much more support.

Again, wealth differences clearly influence attitudes towards expropriation. A chi-square test of the relationship between total wealth and expropriation was significant at the .05 level. Seventy-four percent of the comuneros in the highest quartile of wealth opposed taking away the land of others. In the two middle quartiles, a small majority (53 percent) favored expropriation, while 70 percent of those in the lowest quartile strongly supported the comunidad's efforts to gain control of the land. In other words, relatively minor variations in economic status strongly affect how people feel about important issues of resource control.

Insight into just how deeply these differences cut may be gleaned from the words of the people themselves. One comunero who controls 9 ha of floodplain scathingly indicted his fellow members who favored expropriation. "The bad people here want to kick them [the nonmembers] out," he spat. "They want to take what they don't have. They want to screw things up. All the pueblos have those who create turmoil. They're bolshevikis." Then he extended his diatribe to include the comunidad itself, saying, "The comunidad is not a good system. What a fucking comunidad! It's not worth cock!"

Comuneros who oppose expropriation offer a number of arguments to support their position. Noting that none of the people in question possessed more than the 100 ha of irrigated land permitted small property owners under Mexican agrarian law, one disgruntled individual asked, "Why are they going to take away the land from someone who is working it?" He pointed out that one of his neighbors battling the comunidad owned 40 ha of poor land that only produced because he fertilized it. If that land were seized and divided among ten families, however, "They couldn't make a living off it," he said. Besides, he added contemptuously, "How are they going to work it with nothing more than a burro?"

Other comuneros who object to expropriation argued that three of the four nonmembers were native sons or daughters of Cucurpe. Describing a wealthy hardware store owner in Magdalena who possessed 8 ha of land across from the village of Cucurpe itself, another man said, "He was born here, he grew up here, he's a son of the pueblo. All the years he works the land. All the years he pays taxes on the land. He has children. The comunidad can't remove him."

The bolshevikis, on the other hand, take issue with these contentions. First, they claim that the nonmembers do not really need their land. Speaking of the same man described above, the president of the municipio in 1981 said, "The man is an industrialist. He has millions of pesos. The assembly [of the comunidad] won't let him be an ejidatario."

Another comunero who strongly supports expropriation reiterated this theme, calling the landowners "capitalists" and noting that
only one of them actually lived in Cucurpe. He went on to say that the
one who resided in the municipio only cultivated 2 of her 52 ha herself.
The rest she rented out to other private landowners or to "capitalists"
from Magdalena.

In at least two of the four cases, the bolshevikis' characterization of
the landowners as "capitalists" and "millionaires" is correct. The man
with the hardware store in Magdalena also owns land and cattle
around that commercial center. Very little of his total income derives
from his Cucurpe estate. His brother depends more upon his landholdings in the municipio, but even he has considerable business
interests in Magdalena. Discussing his problems with the comunidad,
he said, "They're all sons of bitches, a gang of lazy bums."

The third person fighting expropriation was born in Cananea, not
Cucurpe, and resides in Magdalena like the other two men. Unlike
them, however, he has never been "a son of the pueblo." He purchased the floodplain in his possession. A number of comuneros also
believe that he and the others obtained their land unethically, paying
practically nothing to former owners desperate for money and then
renting the land back to them until they were too old to work it. In the
words of a comunidad leader, the actions of these men were "criminal." Old renters were turned out "without reimbursement, without
anything." Then the land was rented to someone else. Needless to
say, this comunero vehemently favored expropriation. In his opinion,
the fields should be distributed to comuneros willing to work it themselves. Without the comunidad to regulate such affairs, he felt that
most of the corporate lands would wind up in the hands of "three or
four rich men."

The fourth person fighting expropriation is the daughter, mentioned earlier, of a Russian emigrant who settled in Cucurpe. In contrast to the others, she and her husband live in the municipio along the
Río Dolores, where they operate a small rural grocery store. They also
rent out the 52 ha she owns and run a few cattle. They have no
business interests outside Cucurpe, and according to the woman, the
land belongs to her by birthright. "We were born here," she said.
"We're part of the comunidad." Naturally, the bolshevikis disagreed.
Nevertheless, a number of them were willing to allow her to keep 4 or
5 ha and "rights to pasture" (derecho de campo) if she accepted the
jurisdiction of the comunidad.

In 1981, the situation was at a stalemate. During the previous five
years, a number of lower courts had ruled in favor of the comunidad

but the *quejosos*, or "complainers," as the four landowners were locally known, continued their fight to the Mexican supreme court. Since they had plenty of money and powerful friends, many Cucurpeños believed that they, not the comunidad, would ultimately triumph.

In the spring of 1982, however, the situation came to a head. Comunidad leaders were notified by a longtime ally in the Department of Agrarian Reform that the supreme court had finally handed down a decision supporting their position. Without waiting for governmental approval, forty-two comuneros seized the land of the four plaintiffs and planted spring crops. After years of bureaucratic delay and indecision, the comuneros suddenly took matters into their own hands.

The landowners immediately protested the occupation, so the government dispatched representatives from the state governor's office as well as the federal Department of Agrarian Reform to seek a solution to the problem in a special meeting of the comunidad. As a result, government officials, landowners, and comuneros squared off against one another in the most dramatic public confrontation since the reconfirmation of the comunidad itself.

The meeting opened with a long and flowery appeal for a "just and humane solution to the problem" from the various government agents. The officials talked about restoring "equilibrium and tranquility" to the municipio, and they pleaded for a peaceful resolution in the "common interest." Finally, they expressed "certain doubts" about the comunidad's "seizure of land," stating that the authorities might not be able to support such an action.

The comuneros listened to the rhetoric, and then the president's substitute bluntly told the bureaucrats that they were tired of the delays. They had waited twenty years for the government to support them and they were not going to wait any longer. The land was theirs. From then on, the debate ricocheted among the three groups.

One comunero suggested that the quejosos be allowed access to comunidad resources. Another disagreed, stating that the four individuals in question had been invited to join the corporate community but had refused. The woman fighting expropriation countered that the offer to join had been "shameless" (*vergonzoso*), since the comunidad leaders had offered a mere 25,000 pesos (U.S. $1,000) for her 52 ha of irrigated land.

The government officials kept trying to cool flaring tempers and to reach an accord acceptable to both sides. Like bureaucrats everywhere, they also proposed that a commission be formed to resolve the dispute. The comuneros agreed, electing six of their most radical members to fill the slots.

At that point, the officials tried to get tough. Arguing that the occupation of disputed lands was an "illegal act," they demanded that the comuneros remove themselves until the commission made a decision. The comuneros adamantly refused. The son of the comunidad president, a young man studying veterinary medicine in central Mexico, pointed out that at a previous meeting, the comunidad had agreed to abide by the opinion of a lawyer appointed to review the case. The lawyer had determined that the land in question belonged to the corporate community. Therefore, the issue had already been settled. Everyone at the meeting understood the implication of the young man's argument. In the eyes of many comuneros, waiting for another commission to make yet another decision was merely a way to delay the just reclamation of comunidad land.

The young man's comment triggered a lengthy exchange between the comuneros and the landowners. The woman plaintiff angrily denounced the young man, asking what right he had to say what he did when neither he nor his mother had been born in Cucurpe. A comunero once again offered to let the woman keep one of her fields and have the right to run livestock on corporate land. The former representative of the comunidad, the most hard-nosed of the bolshevikis, said he would agree to such an arrangement only if the woman were not declared a comunera. He added that if she behaved herself and quit causing trouble, she might be admitted to the corporate community at a later date. As for the other quejosos, the two men who had been born in Cucurpe should be allowed to keep their homes and a small portion of their land. The quejoso from Cananea, on the other hand, was not an *hijo del pueblo* and had no right to comunidad resources. That man then rose to his feet and passionately defended himself, proclaiming that he had paid for his land and that he held title to it as a small private property (*pequeña propriedad*). Furthermore, he thundered, "I'm not a foreigner! I'm a Mexican! I also have a right to produce! Don't rob me of my land!"

The debate dragged on and on, with the quejosos asserting their claims, and the bolshevikis denouncing the injustice of the situation. How can four individuals possess so much land, they argued, while many comuneros are landless? In the midst of these angry charges, the government officials repeatedly tried to arrange a peaceful, if temporary, truce, talking about the need to seek a "just and humane" solution on the one hand and threatening the comuneros with jail on the other. Finally, in desperation, one harried bureaucrat proposed to put matters to a vote. He asked those who agreed to obey the law and leave the disputed land to remain seated. Those who wanted to continue to defy the legal authorities, however, should stand up and line themselves against the wall.

In the most dramatic show of unity I observed in two years of comunidad meetings, the great majority of the comuneros, led by the president's substitute and the former representative, headed for the wall. Only a handful kept their seats. Although a number of comuneros undoubtedly were swayed by the determination of their neighbors, the comunidad clearly and unequivocally stood its ground. The defiant members even signed a statement expressing their resolve to remain on the land.

To keep the meeting from ending in a complete standoff, the comuneros did agree to send a representative to meet with the governor of Sonora. There was also some talk about leaving the land if the governor so ordered. By occupying the fields, however, the comuneros had taken a major step toward making those fields their own. Given its fear of conflict and agrarian unrest, it seemed unlikely that the Mexican government would risk possible bloodshed for the sake of a few relatively insignificant private landowners.

Such turned out to be the case. As the vignette at the beginning of the chapter reveals, the comuneros still remained in possession of those lands three years later. Actions proved stronger than words. Despite official threats, no one attempted to drive the comuneros from the fields they had seized.

The confrontation over expropriation reveals some interesting insights into the workings of the Cucurpe comunidad. First of all, it demonstrates that a determined minority can often sway a less committed majority, at least in the public arena. Even though thirty-one comuneros claimed a few months before the invasion to be opposed to expropriation, few of those individuals opposed the bolshevikis by remaining in their seats. The only ones who did, in fact, were a handful of members with strong personal ties to the quejosos themselves. As long as the more radical comuneros were willing to take forceful action, most of the other members followed. The organization's chronic factionalism could be overcome, at least temporarily, when leadership was dynamic and the issue was clear-cut.

The occupation of the disputed fields also suggests that the comunidad was most likely to commit itself to a course of action which promised immediate and tangible results, especially if those results benefited a sizeable number of individual comuneros. The families that confiscated the fields automatically had a stake in the organization, so it was in their best interests to maintain a strong, aggressive corporate community.

Long-term benefits, such as range management, on the other hand, promise no such prompt rewards. Quite the contrary, a program of livestock reduction would involve great financial and psychological hardship. The comunidad is capable of the dramatic gesture, but whether it possesses the leadership to make difficult, long-range decisions remains to be seen.

The actions of the government officials also were illuminating. During the confrontation over expropriation, the basic function of the bureaucrats was to keep the conflict contained and controlled. Even though the comunidad seemed to have a legal right to the land, the officials still tried to seek a solution that included the landowners. Cynics might be tempted to search for evidence of bribery or collusion. Others might argue that the bureaucrats were genuinely trying to keep the peace. The results were the same, however: more delay, more debate, more vacillation. By breaking that pattern and refusing to back down, the comuneros forced the issue. Given the stakes involved, the government tacitly conceded the land to the corporate community.

In Cucurpe at least, agrarian politics must be viewed as an elaborate balancing act in which the government attempts to placate or control all of the parties involved. Peasant organizations such as the comunidades and the ejido are granted land, but the land more often than not is marginal or carved from the estates of small landowners rather than large ones. Whoever has the most pull at the moment wins the battle. The war, on the other hand, is much more complicated—an exhausting struggle of compromise and co-optation, of provocation and delay. Neither the campesinos nor the private landowners are satisfied with the process. Nevertheless, the government, with its fine-tuned sense of how far people can be pushed before they push back, usually manages to prevent the confrontations from escalating into physical violence.

THE COMUNIDAD AS RURAL DEVELOPMENT AGENCY

The control of natural resources such as grazing land or arable land is a traditional function of corporate communities across the world. Therefore, it comes as no surprise to learn that the comunidad devotes so much of its time and energy to such tasks. During the early 1980s, however, the comunidad also concentrated on a more contemporary concern: the need to modernize and diversify the Cucurpe economy. In particular, the comunidad functioned as a local agency through which various branches of the Mexican government funneled money, credit, and technological assistance to Cucurpeños. The struggle for land was an important preoccupation, but so was the need for agricultural expansion, the modernization of water control, and the creation of more local jobs. Although comuneros disagreed violently with one another about the comunidad's jurisdiction over farmland, an overwhelming majority of them concurred that one of the organization's proper functions was, in the words of one poor comunero, "to put people to work."

Diversification of the Local Economy

Chapter 5 briefly detailed the history of the comunidad's *cantera* quarrying operation. Conceived and funded under the López Portillo administration (1976–82) when oil revenues were supposed to fund a massive program of rural development, the cantera plant represented the most ambitious effort in recent years to provide nonagrarian employment for Cucurpe's work force. Like many such development projects, however, it foundered on the shoals of corruption and mismanagement until it was finally abandoned several years later.

During the same period, other schemes to create more jobs were topics of discussion, but little else. There was talk that the Mexican government planned to build an ore-processing plant on comunidad land north of the pueblo of Cucurpe, but the plant never materialized. Comunidad leaders also speculated about the possibility of launching a cantera crafts program under the guidance of several local artisans. Again, nothing happened. Meanwhile, young men and women continued to emigrate from the municipio in search of jobs in Magdalena or the United States.

Despite these failures, comuneros still clung to the hope that the comunidad would somehow be able to secure the funding to diversify their economy and provide jobs for themselves and their children. The treasurer of the comunidad voiced the opinion of many when he said, "The comunidad should open up more sources of work so that the comuneros can make a living, so that they don't have to leave for lack of work."

Water Control

A second important theme expressed by comuneros was the abiding need to bring more water to local farmers. As one wiry eighty-two-year-old man said, "The first thing is to get more water, to produce. Without water you can't produce anything."

A number of solutions to this eternal problem were discussed, most of them revolving around the drilling of pump-powered wells. Comuneros debated a series of proposals to tap floodplain aquifers after wells in the side canyons of the San Miguel drainage failed in the late 1970s. One plan involved drilling wells along the river and then pumping water up and over the mesas to irrigate temporales in the arroyos. Another called for the construction of subsurface concrete plugs or dams (cortinas) to intercept groundwater and force it to the surface. Needless to say, both of these projects were beyond the financial capabilities of the comuneros themselves.

In order to come up with the necessary funding, several meetings were held with government representatives. While no agency seemed willing to capitalize the entire venture, an official from the governor's office finally promised that the state would furnish pumps and tubing if the comunidad drilled the wells at its own expense. By late 1981, drilling rigs were probing for water in several locations. Several years later, crops were successfully being irrigated from a pump-powered well in a drainage of the Río Dolores called Cañada Baisimaco, where several comunidad leaders had their fields.

Agricultural Intensification

These wells were not financed by the organization as a whole. Instead, they were part of a much larger plan to divide comuneros into "collective groups" (grupos colectivos) which would receive credit and assistance from the government. No other government program, even the cantera plant, represented a more far-reaching attempt to transform Cucurpe's economy.

These collective groups were first proposed by representatives from four federal agencies at a special meeting of the comunidad in February 1981. According to the officials, technical assistance and low-interest credit would be given to groups of ten or more comuneros with adjacent land if they removed their fences and farmed that land in common. Only members of the group would receive the loans, and only they would be responsible for repaying them. Moreover, their personal property—homes, livestock, and so forth—could not be embargoed if they failed to meet their debts. Groups were to elect leaders and draw up an internal charter with government assistance. Once these tasks had been accomplished and the fences torn down, group members could receive loans to drill wells, purchase agricultural equipment, buy seeds and fertilizer, and obtain insurance to protect them against crop failures.

The plan must have seemed like a good one in Mexico City. One of the major problems of the Mexican countryside is *minifundia*, the division of farmland into parcels too small to be cultivated by modern methods. By consolidating fields, the government believed it could help farmers reduce their labor expenditures, improve their yields, and grow crops which the Mexican market demanded. The collective groups were, therefore, an attempt to modernize and mechanize Mexican agriculture within the framework of comunidades and ejidos.

What the bureaucrats failed to anticipate, however, was the depth of attachment individuals felt for their fields. Although they kept silent during the meeting itself, most comuneros vehemently objected to the idea of tearing down their fences and farming in common. No other controversy revealed the disparity between national planning and local needs so dramatically. The collective groups were an idea whose time had certainly not come, at least in Cucurpe.

After the meeting, a young comunero talked long and passionately about his reservations concerning the proposed system. First, he pointed out that most stock raisers have to turn their animals into their fields at one time or another because natural forage is so poor. If fences were removed and everyone was growing the same crops, that subsistence strategy would be eliminated.

Secondly, he expressed concern over the role of the government in the administration of these groups. He believed that if the *Banco Rural* (the financial institution funding such efforts) lent considerable sums of money to the comuneros, it would want to protect its investment by telling them what to raise. "We are going to become workers for the banks," he concluded. Farmers such as he would lose their autonomy and their flexibility. In the past eight years, he had not had to buy "one kilo of beans" for his family, but if the group decided to plant only alfalfa, he would no longer be able to maintain his self-sufficiency. Administrators from the bank would supervise everything.

His sentiments were reiterated in one form or another by most of the other comuneros. Again, they repeated the phrase that expressed their vision of the good life: *Quiero vivir muy agusto con mi milpa y mis animales* (I want to live happily with my field and my animals). That vision definitely did not include collective agriculture. Even the most committed bolshevikis wanted no part of the government's scheme. Cucurpe farmers valued their independence, and they were not about to surrender that independence to some bureaucratic blueprint for the future.

Nevertheless, many of them were intrigued by the possibility of obtaining credit to drill wells, improve their crops, or develop pig-raising and bee-keeping cooperatives. During subsequent meetings, government representatives finally abandoned their demand that comuneros tear down their fences. The officials were realistic enough to recognize that such a plan would never be voluntarily accepted. Instead, they began to encourage members of the comunidad to join together to accomplish more limited objectives.

Once the specter of collectivity was banished, many comuneros responded to the government program, and eventually three groups were formed. But each one of these groups, interestingly enough, was composed of farmers with temporales in side canyons of the San Miguel drainage who wanted to bring irrigation water to those fields. Water was their overriding concern, and the need for water became the motivation that finally brought them into the government's fold.

They never accepted any more constraints on arable land. During the course of the debate, officials occasionally muttered about the backwardness of the comuneros, a stereotype common to development agents across the world. What the bureaucrats failed to realize, however, was that their plan would have destroyed an essential element of Cucurpe's agropastoralist economy: flexibility. The comuneros were by no means obstinate traditionalists. On the contrary, they were eager to modernize their agriculture and diversify their economic base as long as those processes did not violate the economic autonomy of their households. Most wanted credit or pump-powered wells but they were not willing to tear down their fences to obtain them. Their ideal of cooperation had definite limits. Once those limits were reached, they resisted any attempt to breach them, proving that under certain circumstances, they were able to determine their own destinies.

10. Conclusions

THE POLITICAL ECOLOGY OF
THE COMUNIDAD OF CUCURPE

As the preceding analysis indicates, the Comunidad of Cucurpe is not an expression of peasant communal solidarity. On the contrary, it is a complex, conflict-ridden institution composed of individual households who fiercely prize their economic independence. As units of both production and consumption, these households strive to exercise direct control over resources they can exploit with their own labor and capital, particularly arable land. Resources such as rangeland and irrigation water, on the other hand, are beyond their capacity to possess at the household level. Consequently, the comuneros join together to hold grazing land and surface water in common. The resulting mixture of domestic and corporate tenure may seem contradictory at first, but those contradictions evaporate when the economic and ecological characteristics of the different resources are understood.

Resource control in Cucurpe also supports Robert Netting's hypotheses about land tenure discussed in the Introduction. Netting argues that types of land that can be cultivated and improved in small, fixed amounts tend to be owned or controlled by individual households. Land that cannot be dependably exploited in such units, by contrast, is often held under some sort of corporate jurisdiction. Corporate tenure is, therefore, a pragmatic response to resources individual households cannot control on their own.

Grazing land along the semi-arid margins of the Sonoran Desert certainly fits Netting's definition of a resource whose frequency and dependability of exploitation are low. Vegetation cover is sparse, making it necessary for livestock to roam over large areas in order to feed. Moreover, the relative scarcity of forage is aggravated by spotty precipitation patterns and centuries of overgrazing, both of which have reduced the amount of fodder even further. Wealthy private ranchers can afford to purchase the thousands of hectares of *agostadero* they

189

The pueblo of Cucurpe, looking east across the floodplain of the Río San Miguel.

need to run their herds. Comuneros, on the other hand, can only obtain access to enough such land through their corporate community. For that reason, they have battled governments and private ranchers alike to retain control of their corporate grazing lands, lands that have undoubtedly belonged to them and their predecessors for the last three hundred years.

Another resource the Cucurpeños hold in common is surface irrigation water. Cucurpe's desert climate does not permit true dry-farming. And even though local farmers do practice runoff agriculture, irrigation is a much more dependable solution to the problem. As a result, Cucurpeños must provide their crops with water that comes from one of two sources: springs along the surface of the Río San Miguel and its tributaries, or subsurface aquifers. Groundwater pumping, a relatively recent innovation, requires a level of capital investment beyond the pocketbooks of most households. Diverting the surface flow of the San Miguel demands neither money nor sophisticated machinery, but it does call for cooperation among the water users themselves. Consequently, most farmers in Cucurpe have formed comunes de agua to make sure they get their fair share of the San Miguel's flow.

It must be reiterated, however, that the comunes de agua are not isomorphic with the comunidad. On the contrary, they are local associations of water users who elect their own officials and organize their own labor parties to clean and repair their own canals. In that respect, the comunes represent yet another expression of Cucurpeño autonomy: corporate groups that encompass only those households who require access to the resource in question. Again, corporate tenure must be seen for what it is: a limited adaptation to economic need, not an ideological expression of peasant solidarity. In fact, the desire for household autonomy is so strong that groundwater pumping is just beginning to become a corporate endeavor even though private pumps have existed in the area for the last forty years (*see* chapters 3 and 9).

The resource that best reflects Cucurpeño independence, however, is arable land. Peasant households may not be able to own their own ranches or drill their own wells, but they are capable of working a few hectares of milpa or temporal. Moreover, through patience and hard work they can improve that land and intensify their cultivation of it, double-cropping the same irrigated fields year after year. As chapter 3 demonstrates, Cucurpeños devote far more time to their milpas than they do to their livestock or the range their animals graze. Because that range is open, selective breeding and proper range management are difficult to achieve. A careful farmer, in contrast, can increase his yields and diversify his crops. By leveling his land, he can insure that all portions of his field are properly irrigated. By planting fence-rows, he can protect against the erosive power of floods. After years of such labor, it is easy to understand why Cucurpeños resist any effort to limit their control of arable land.

"He who would sell his own land would sell his own mother," one farmer told me, expressing the deep and abiding attachment that many Cucurpeños feel toward their fields. But that attachment is far more than peasant traditionalism in the face of market forces. Milpas are the very foundation of agrarian life in Cucurpe; without them, it would be difficult for small rancher-farmers in the municipio to subsist. And even though livestock form Cucurpe's strongest nexus with the outside world, those animals could not survive drought and an overgrazed range without supplementary fodder, fodder produced in Cucurpe fields.

Opposition to government programs such as the grupos colectivos, then, can only be understood in terms of local ecological and demographic realities. Households at different stages in their developmental cycle have different needs. An older couple whose children have grown and emigrated may no longer have any reason to devote much of their acreage to food crops like beans and potatoes. Furthermore, they may have accumulated more wealth and own more livestock than younger families, increasing their demand for forage rather than food. A younger couple with small children, on the other hand, may have fewer animals but more mouths to feed. Consequently, they may choose beans and potatoes over barley or alfalfa. Neither couple, however, has any desire to tear down their fences and plant in common; collectivization would reduce the freedom and flexibility of both.

One could argue, of course, that the government could impose collectivization on the comuneros if it were willing to use the forces at its disposal. But at present, no state or federal agency is committed enough to the collective groups, to livestock reduction, or to any other program of rural development to risk antagonizing the comuneros in the process. Members of the comunidad may not have the power to completely reject government policies, but they often are able to influence the direction those policies take.

What the government has been able to do, however, is to restrict private tenure over arable land. By transforming private ownership into household usufruct rights, the government is attempting to place much of Cucurpe's farmland in social trust in order to make sure that it does not become a commodity that can be bought and sold on the open market. Indeed, one of the major goals of agrarian reform is to provide a refuge for small holders, to protect them from the processes of alienation that destroyed so many corporate communities before the Mexican Revolution. The present generation of comuneros objects to this transformation. Subsequent generations, in contrast, may come to realize that such policies are their best defense against the concentration of irrigated land in private hands.

At present, however, the controversy over arable land continues to rage, engendering dissension among comuneros and dividing the comunidad against itself. More than any other issue, conflict over the status of farmland reveals the complexity of class divisions in Cucurpe. Comuneros with their own fields resist attempts to make those fields a corporate resource. Landless comuneros, on the other hand, generally tend to view usufruct with greater favor. More to the point, they support the expropriation of arable land belonging to nonmembers because they hope to obtain some land of their own. As a result, two distinct classes exist within the comunidad itself: landed comuneros and those without land. In a sense, the two groups are like the segmentary lineages of the Nuer, battling each other over arable land but uniting whenever private ranchers encroach upon their corporate range.

The politics of resource control in Cucurpe, therefore, follow a number of major fault lines. The first cleavage pits private ranchers against members of the three corporate communities, the second, landed comuneros against their landless brethren. In both cases, the conflict concerns the control of a single major resource. Those households who own their own rangeland square off against those who control grazing land in common. Those with fields contend against those without. In such fashion, household relations to the means of production—arable land and grazing land—directly influence local political struggles.

Finally, there are the households who neither own land nor belong to any of the three corporate communities: cowboys, miners, agricultural laborers. Landless comuneros may not be any wealthier than these individuals and their families, but members of the corporate communities theoretically enjoy access to corporate resources. Like the bolshevikis who occupied Milpa Grande (*see* chapters 8 and 9), they may someday possess fields of their own if they manipulate comunidad politics successfully. Landless nonmembers, in contrast, do not look forward to such possibilities and stand in a different relation to the means of production than do landless ejidatarios or comuneros. To further their own interests, landless nonmembers may adopt one of two strategies. First, they may lobby for the creation of a corporate community of their own, just as the bolshevikis of Ejido 6 de Enero did prior to 1976. If they have steady wage work, however, these same landless laborers may choose a very different strategy, supporting rather than struggling against their *patrones*. That is what the cowboys were doing when they helped their bosses cut the fences of the ejido in January 1981 (*see* chapter 1). Cucurpe's landless laborers cannot be viewed as a unitary class. On the contrary, membership or nonmembership in the corporate communities creates a class distinction with potentially serious ramifications, one which, on occasion, turns the landless against one another.

The Cucurpe class system, then, consists of at least four distinct classes: 1) private ranchers; 2) peasant rancher-farmers; 3) landless members of the corporate communities; and 4) landless nonmembers. If there were more merchants or *profesionistas* in the municipio, they might compose a separate class as well. At present, though, their numbers are too small to make them a force in local politics. It could also be argued that another class is in the process of emerging: the small private ranchers. During the early 1980s, their interests were substantially the same as those of their wealthier counterparts. But if they continue to get squeezed between large ranchers and the corporate communities, they may begin to seek new alliances, emphasizing the fact that they truly are the *pequeños propietarios* Mexican agrarian reform law supposedly protects.[1]

One other player in the game must be discussed before concluding this analysis, however, and that is the Mexican government. As the preceding chapters demonstrate, the government influences every major economic and political development in Cucurpe. During the last years of the Echeverría administration, the federal Department of Agrarian Reform granted legal recognition to the comunidades of Cucurpe and San Javier and the Ejido 6 de Enero after decades of struggle. While Echeverría's successor, López Portillo, was in office, federal rural development programs invested large amounts of money to finance projects such as the ill-fated Canteras de Cucurpe within the comunidad (*see* chapters 5 and 9). Throughout both presidencies, state and federal courts heard a series of lawsuits involving land disputes between the comunidad and its neighbors, ultimately ruling in favor of the comuneros. As the final arbiter of legitimacy, the government holds the balance of power in any major conflict over resource control. In a sense, then, relations to the means of production revolve around relations with the Mexican government, because the government controls access to land through the complicated and murky process of agrarian reform.

That process oscillates between the poles of collectivism and capitalism, usually favoring the private sector. Despite the Revolution, Mexico still does not have a coherent vision of rural society. Proponents of capitalist modernization argue that ejidatarios and comuneros utilize land and labor inefficiently, thereby hindering the development of Mexican agriculture (Yates 1981). Orthodox Marxists concur, believing that peasants are destined to be absorbed by the capitalist sector; any attempt to protect them merely prolongs their misery and slows down their inevitable transformation into proletarians (Bartra 1974). Ironically, advocates of both privatization and collectivization see little future for the peasant households clinging to their small herds and fields.

Nevertheless, peasants like the Cucurpeños have not disappeared. Indeed, if anything, they have demonstrated a remarkable capacity for survival. An estimated 70 percent of Mexico's farm population make their living as ejidatarios or comuneros, while more than half of the *pequeños propietarios*, or private farmers, own less than thirteen acres of land (Yates 1981). In other words, the great majority of households in the Mexican countryside are small farmers or ranchers who have benefitted little, if at all, from Mexico's postwar agricultural boom (Kearney 1980; Stavenhagen et al. 1980; Sanderson 1981; Yates 1981; Hewitt de Alcántara 1982).

A growing number of intellectuals are even beginning to acknowledge the tenacity of Mexico's peasantry, arguing that the nation's rural development depends upon their persistence, not their demise (Redclift 1979). Known collectively as *campesinistas*, scholars like Gustavo Esteva, Arturo Warman, and Angel Palerm have fused Marxian analysis with elements of cultural ecology to emphasize the adaptive strategies of peasants as well as their exploitation by outsiders. In the process, the campesinistas have begun to explore some of the enduring structural characteristics of the peasant mode of production, including household organization and corporate tenure (Hewitt de Alcántara 1984).

Such an approach does not constitute a return to an earlier functionalist paradigm that posits the homogeneity or isolation of peasant communities. Esteva, Warman, and others do not divorce peasants from the webs that enmesh them; on the contrary, they realize that domination and exploitation are realities from which few peasants escape. At the same time, the campesinistas recognize that peasants continue to survive as peasants—that is, as a segment of society which still obtains "from self-provisioning an indispensable part of its subsistence" (Palerm 1980). Rather than viewing wage work as an indication of increasing proletarianization, for example, Palerm argues that peasant households depend upon three different economic strategies— agricultural subsistence, market production, and wage labor—in order to meet their needs. According to Warman (1976:15), "It is possible for peasants to plant onions, tomatoes or sorghum for the market, emigrate as a *bracero* or tranquilly convert to protestantism— all little 'traditional' no doubt—without ceasing to be a peasant."

One of the consequences of *campesinismo* among Mexican scholars has been a renewed commitment to detailed case studies rather than to sweeping theoretical generalizations. If peasants adapt, then those adaptations can only be understood in their regional and historical contexts. And if peasants are to become the vehicles of rural development, then their needs and concerns must be taken into account. In Esteva's (1978:710) words:

> When *campesinista* social scientists add their strength to that of the peasantry, with the object of avoiding its extinction, they leave behind the academic environment of speculative contemplation and argument, in which diverse viewpoints are developed, in order to bring theoretical insights to bear on factual situations, where one has to search for the truth of the transformation, rather than the transformation of the truth.

In a place like Cucurpe, then, it is necessary to understand all the factors acting upon peasant households—not just local ecological and demographic adjustments, not just external political and economic influences, but the intersecting force fields of both. Given certain technologies, different resources impose their own constraints upon the way they can be utilized. At the same time, however, the class structure of local agrarian societies and their relations to different outside forces determine access to the resources themselves. Failure to comprehend either side of the equation produces a distorted image of peasant society, one which swings from the myopic romanticism of the isolated little community to the facile generalizations of the all-embracing world system. Both images seriously misrepresent the complex realities of peasant life. Neither captures the gritty determination of people like the Cucurpeños.

REFERENCE MATERIAL

Appendix A

SOURCES OF DATA

Like most ethnographies, the information in this book comes from a variety of sources including fieldnotes, questionnaires, taped interviews, recordings of comunidad meetings, and documentary material made available by municipal and federal authorities. This appendix describes only the more structured methods of collecting data.

Daily Records of Agrarian Activities

In late December 1980, after living in Cucurpe for a month and a half, I asked the heads of six households to keep short daily records of their agrarian activities during the coming year. I gave each of these six men calendars with space for three or four lines of information under each date. The men were asked to note down the tasks performed by members of their households each day. They were also requested to specify the number of individuals involved and the length of time devoted to each task.

The six households were not chosen at random. Instead, I selected men whom I knew fairly well and whom I thought would diligently complete the daily records. None were paid for their efforts, although I did occasionally give them small gifts or bring them merchandise from the United States. In Cucurpe, my wife and I found that whenever we gave anyone a gift, the person quickly reciprocated, overwhelming us with dozens of jars of candied fruit and a heartfelt appreciation for Sonoran hospitality.

The six households do not represent the range of total wealth in Cucurpe. All belonged to the Comunidad of Cucurpe, and all possessed both land and livestock (0.6–9 ha of irrigated milpa; 12–40 head of cattle). Their indexes of total wealth ranged from 88 to 366, and their decile ranking (in total wealth) varied from five to eight. From the poorest to the richest, those indexes and decile ranking are as follows: Ranker 2: 88 (5); Ranker 4: 213 (7); Ranker 1: 243 (7); Ranker 5: 277 (8); Ranker 3: 288 (8); Ranker 6: 366 (8). The six households, therefore, do not represent either the very rich or the very poor. Nevertheless, they do represent the peasant rancher-farmers who constitute the backbone of the municipio.

In general, records were faithfully kept. Every two or three weeks, I would visit the households to copy information on the calendars and fill in gaps that had been omitted or overlooked. The resulting information yields a fairly accurate picture of the agrarian round. It also provides a rough estimate of the distribution of labor among various agrarian activities such as livestock raising and farming. It is by no means a precise, quantifiable input/output analysis of household economies in Cucurpe, however. A number of daily routines, such as milking cows or caring for horses, pigs and chickens, were rarely noted. On the contrary, the household head (or, in some cases, his oldest son or daughter) only wrote down what they considered to be the most important tasks performed that day: whether household members planted, cultivated, or harvested their crops or rode into the countryside to care for their cattle. As such, the records underestimate the total range and amount of household labor. Moreover, the records rarely mention chores carried out by female members, since girls and women do not usually work in the fields or ride the range.

Despite these limitations, however, the daily records were important sources of information. They provided precise dates for the planting and harvesting of all major crops. They also elicited a wide range of agrarian terminology, since the household heads described in their own words what tasks they carried out. If an ethnographer was primarily interested in domestic economies and was willing to devote more time to the daily records, those records would undoubtedly yield more extensive data. Because my major areas of concern lay elsewhere, however, I was content with the information I received. The daily records systematized what otherwise would have been impressionistic information on cropping patterns, the distribution of agrarian labor, and the seasonal round.

Questionnaire No. 1 (N = 251)

My first questionnaire was a household survey that asked for a wide range of economic and demographic information including land tenure, livestock ownership, emigration, and the age/sex composition of the household. No sampling strategy was developed; instead, I tried to administer the questionnaire to every household in the municipio. The total number of households interviewed was 251, approximately 90–95 percent of all households in Cucurpe in 1981. The 5–10 percent I did not interview consisted of families or individuals living on isolated ranches and in mining areas. Of the sample, 103 households belonged to the Comunidad of Cucurpe, 34 to Comunidad San Javier, and 19 to Ejido 6 de Enero. Eighty-six households did not belong to any of the peasant organizations. Nine were households who either divided their time between Cucurpe and other municipios, or whose residential status was unclear. Total number of resident households, then, was 242.

The questionnaire proved to be a flexible and comprehensive instrument with which to elicit a considerable amount of information in a relatively short space of time. Whenever possible, I interviewed the household head. If that was not feasible, I talked to another adult member of the household. Interview time ranged from thirty minutes to several hours depending upon the complexity of the household and the receptivity of household members. Because of the size of the municipio and the nature of its terrain, I visited some of the more remote ranches and mines only once. Nevertheless, only one individual refused to be interviewed.

Questionnaire No. 2 (N = 74)

Questionnaire No. 2 was developed in order to elicit more detailed information from households belonging to the Comunidad of Cucurpe. I chose a 75 percent random sample of the 103 households who had responded to the first questionnaire. Seventy-four households were interviewed; the remaining two interviews could not be carried out.

In general, I felt that the second questionnaire was not as well-designed as the first. First of all, it attempted to cover too many topics. Secondly, it included a series of open-ended questions on political issues facing the comunidad which did not work well in the interview format. If I were to redesign the questionnaire, I would replace the open-ended questions with ones eliciting definite responses. People freely shared their political opinions with me under informal circumstances. When asked point-blank how they felt about the comunidad, however, they often gave vague or ambiguous answers, making it clear that they were uncomfortable with the context in which the questions were asked.

Nonetheless, Questionnaire No. 2 provided detailed information on the household economies of the 74 households, especially in regard to sources of income and patterns of land transmission. Even though the open-ended questions did not yield responses that were easily quantifiable, the answers offered considerable insight into the local politics of resource control.

Absentee Elite Questionnaire

Toward the end of my fieldwork, I developed a questionnaire designed to obtain economic data concerning the amount of land and livestock in Cucurpe controlled by private ranchers living outside the municipio. The questionnaire also solicited opinions regarding the comunidades and the ejido. I administered the questionnaire to fourteen individuals, most of whom resided in the regional center of Magdalena, thirty miles from the pueblo of Cucurpe. Their answers yielded information on the holdings of twenty-eight ranchers. I also asked the respondents to estimate what percentage of their total annual income came from their Cucurpe enterprises.

The small sample was not randomly selected and therefore is not representative of the absentee elite in any strict statistical sense. Absentee landowners in Cucurpe are scattered across Sonora, and it would be extremely time-consuming to track many of them down. Nevertheless, the questionnaire still provided considerable information on the range and scope of the absentee elite's business interests in the municipio. It also elicited some interesting perceptions, usually negative, of the municipio's corporate communities.

State Livestock Censuses

Muncipios in Sonora are divided into livestock zones. Each zone is the responsibility of an appointed livestock inspector, whose major task is to make sure all livestock leaving the municipio receive transit permits, for which the owners or cattle buyers pay a small fee. Such a system is designed to prevent rustling as well as to collect what amounts to a tax on livestock sales. The livestock inspectors also organize the annual fall roundups, or *corridas*, specifying when and where such roundups are to take place. Once the livestock have been gathered in a central location, the livestock inspector is supposed to count the number and types of animals (cows, bulls, calves, steers, horses, mules, etc.) running under different brands.

In Cucurpe, there are three livestock zones administered by three different livestock inspectors whose devotion to duty vary considerably. For example, one man who has held the job for nearly twenty years rarely counts the livestock himself. Instead, he relies upon individual owners to give him the figures. Since there is no tax involved in the roundups, the tallies seem to be relatively accurate representations of the number of animals collected in any given roundup.

Nonetheless, the livestock censuses do not reflect the total number of animals on Cucurpe ranges. Municipal terrain is extremely rugged, and individual corridas rarely last for more than a day. Consequently, not all animals are rounded up, so the livestock censuses underrepresent the size of Cucurpe herds, perhaps by as much as 20 percent.

Appendix B

INDICES OF TOTAL WEALTH AND WEALTH IN LIVESTOCK

In order to compile the Indices of Total Wealth and Wealth in Livestock, I needed to weigh the most important forms of wealth in Cucurpe's agrarian economy—land, livestock, and machinery—according to their approximate value in 1980–81 pesos. I based this weighing upon the price information given me during the course of my fieldwork. The comparative accuracy of such weighing differs from category to category. In general, land is under-valued in comparison to livestock and machinery.

I collected considerable data on the prices of animals sold by Cucurpeños. As expected, prices varied considerably depending upon the age and weight of the animal, the time of year it was sold, and who bought it. Cows and bulls, for example, often brought their sellers more than three times the number of pesos as calves, despite the fact that calves sold for a higher price per kilo. The figures presented below, therefore, represent rough averages of prices per animal:

Type of Animal	Average Price (pesos)	Weight in Index
Cattle	5,000	5.0
Horses	5,000	5.0
Pigs	1,500	1.5
Goats	700	0.7

It was extremely difficult to assess the true market value of arable land because so little of it is sold in Cucurpe. Most farmers I asked estimated that a hectare of floodplain land was worth about 15,000 pesos (U.S. $600) while one hectare of temporal was worth 5,000 pesos (U.S. $200). Since rangeland was selling for $2,000 pesos (U.S. $80) per hectare during 1980–81, Cucurpe farmers were clearly underestimating the value of their cultivated fields. One of the more commercially sophisticated Cucurpeños told me he would not sell a hectare of irrigated land for 50,000 or even 100,000 pesos. Nevertheless, I chose to accept the figures given to me despite their low range. Land may be undervalued, but at least the underevaluation is systematic.

Type of Land	Average Price (pesos)	Weight in Index
Irrigated	15,000	15
Temporal	5,000	5
Range	2,000	2

Although some Cucurpeños own relatively new vehicles or farm machinery, most purchase used machines ranging from old cars and pickups that can barely run to well-maintained tractors and balers. Again, then, the following figures are rough estimates of average value and the actual variation within any category is extensive.

Type of Machine	Average Price (pesos)	Weight in Index
Car	75,000	75
Pickup	100,000	100
Ton truck	200,000	200
Tractor/Farm equipment	350,000	350

Utilizing the above weighted values, Indices of Total Wealth were calculated for every household surveyed with Questionnaire No. 1. Indices of Wealth in Livestock were computed for all livestock owners interviewed with Questionnaire No. 1 or listed in the 1981 livestock censuses. The resulting indices, therefore, furnish a farily accurate and systematic base for comparing household wealth within the municipio of Cucurpe.

Notes to the Chapters

Introduction

1. For discussions of the role peasant corporate communities played in various pre-modern rural societies, see: Bloch (1966) for France, Blum (1971) for Russia, Vassberg (1974, 1980, 1984) for Spain, Rambo (1977) for Vietnam, Skinner (1971) for China, Gibson (1964) for central Mexico, and Wolf (1955, 1957) for Mesoamerica and Java. For discussions of peasant corporate communities that still exist in areas of the world today, see Stavenhagen (1969), Figueroa (1970), and Reyes Osorio et al. (1974) for Mexico, Keatinge (1973), Orlove (1977a), and Guillet (1981) for Andean South America, Netting (1976, 1981) for Alpine Europe, and Freeman (1970) for Spain.

2. In an article concerning types of Latin American peasantry, Wolf (1955) delineates ten general characteristics of the corporate community. These include psychological manifestations such as "defensive ignorance" and a "cult of poverty" as well as structural variables like economic/ecological marginality, wealth redistribution, and the corporate control of scarce, necessary resources, especially land. A later article comparing corporate communities in Mesoamerica and Java stresses the characteristic of closure: corporate communities not only exercise jurisdiction over important natural resources but also restrict access to those resources to members born into the community (Wolf 1957). Despite his later assertion that peasant society is not a "closed system or homeostatic machine" (Cole and Wolf 1974:20), Wolf's model is clearly an equilibrium one, predicated on the maintenance of economic equality and cultural homogeneity within the corporate community itself. According to Wolf:

> The distinctive characteristic of the corporate peasant community is that it represents a bounded social system with clear-cut limits, in relation to both outsiders and insiders. It has structural identity over time. Seen from the outside, the community as a whole carries on a series of activities and upholds certain "collective representations." Seen from within, it defines the rights and duties of its members and prescribes large segments of their behavior (1955:456).

Nevertheless, Wolf clearly recognizes that the corporate community is a response to particular historical forces, not a universal stage on the folk-urban continuum. These communities do not reflect a more primitive stage of human communism, nor do they evolve in isolation. Instead, they represent the reaction of dominated peoples to certain specific types of political and economic pressure originating outside their communities.

3. Altitudinal zonation, of course, is not the only environmental variable influencing the development of corporate tenure among peasants. Throughout western and central Europe during the late middle ages, the ecological necessities of a mixed grain farming/pastoral economy, combined with increasing population pressure on a relatively fixed land base, led peasants to organize themselves into corporate communities (Bloch 1966; Blum 1971; Cole and Wolf 1974; Vassberg 1980). By the late sixteenth century, such communities were losing many of their ancient privileges and prerogatives in western Europe and Spain as feudal and later capitalist estates gradually encroached upon their land (Bloch 1966; Vassberg 1980). But in highland areas, the ecological constraints operating upon mountain agriculture prevented great estates from taking root (Cole and Wolf 1974).

The closure of the community to outsiders was a corporate response to population pressure which threatened to upset the intricate patterns of the agropastoralist economy. In Törbel, this closure was formalized in a written charter as early as the fifteenth century (Netting 1981), in the village of St. Felix in the Tyrol by 1600 at the latest (Cole and Wolf 1974). The strategy of closure was adopted in Alpine Europe, not only to prevent the alienation of community resources to noblemen or powerful capitalists, but also to halt the immigration of other peasants into the mountain valleys. In fact, it appears that population control rather than defensive retrenchment was the major motivating force in the decision to become a "closed" corporate community.

4. Of the four major research traditions in the sociological study of community identified by Effrat (1974), Wolf's concept of the corporate community falls within the category of the "compleat territorial community." According to Effrat:

> The main assumption of most of the research of this type is that small towns, villages, etc., constitute communities that can be considered 'mini' social systems. In these places, everyone knows everyone else at least by sight, and social relations are informal. In other words, it is assumed that residents comprise a community that is a relatively self-contained social environment supplying its members with a wide range of services (1974:5).

The tradition of the "compleat territorial community" has been sharply criticized by many sociologists who point out that social scientists cannot uncritically assume that a spatially bounded aggregate of people depend upon one another for the most important relationships in their lives. They may have more vital economic, political, and psychological ties with people or institutions outside the local area. The importance of local relationships must be empirically determined rather than taken for granted. Only in this fashion will comparable, quantitative data on community dynamics and intercommunity relationships be achieved (Pahl 1968; Stacey 1969).

Nevertheless, Pahl and others who have concentrated their attention on modern industrial societies go too far when they completely disregard the notion of the "compleat territorial community" or the community study. In many rural areas of the world, the local hamlet or village does seem to encompass many of the most important relationships of its inhabitants, or at least it did so in the past. People in those communities fed their families from local resources, and rates of village endogamy were often quite high. In some areas, geographic mobility was limited, immigration rates low, and family lines persisted in the same communities for centuries (Netting 1981).

More recently, similar criticisms have been leveled at anthropological tribal and peasant studies by scholars influenced by Wallerstein's (1974:348) argument that "most entities usually described as social systems—'tribes,' communities, nation-states—are not in fact total systems." As Nash points out, however:

> The advances made in our understanding of how countryside is linked to the city, urban centers and industries related to the nation, and sometimes directly to the world market, have come about as a result of decades of intensive case studies. We should not lose sight of these nor underestimate their value in the enthusiasm for the world system approach (1981:408).

Later in the same article, Nash adds:

> The tendency to take the emergence and dominance of the capitalist system as a foregone conclusion, to assume passive acceptance by peripheral and semi-peripheral regions to the imposed will of core nations can be corrected by methods and findings of ethnographers past and present (1981:417).

5. After an initial period of trial and error, the Spaniards made the creation of nucleated Indian pueblos a cornerstone of their colonial program. In the densely settled areas of central and southern Mexico, they established the policy of *congregación*, under which Indian groups depopulated by Old World diseases were amalgamated and settled in organized villages (Gibson 1964). A similar policy called *reducción* prevailed in many parts of northern Mexico where missionaries and civil officials attempted to concentrate dispersed and often nomadic groups into mission communities. Once such settlements were established, Indian tribute could be collected, Indian labor apportioned under the *repartimiento* system, and Spanish-style civil government imposed.

At the same time, Spanish authorities also instituted a series of laws to protect the land base of these Indian communities from encroachment. In 1532, a royal *cédula*, or decree, affirmed the rights of Indian communities to arable land and pasturage. In 1573, another cédula stipulated that Indian towns were entitled to an *ejido*, or common grant of land, of one square or circular league. Laws promulgated in 1588 and 1598 forbade all land grants prejudicial to Indian communities. A 1713 cédula reaffirmed this legal tradition, stating:

> Indian towns shall be given a site with sufficient water, arable lands, woodlands, and access routes so that they can cultivate their lands, plus an ejido of one league for the grazing of their cattle (Taylor 1972:67).

By setting up royal safeguards to assure the autonomy of Indian towns, Spanish officials hoped to curb the power of aggressive colonists and maintain economic and political control of Spain's New World dominions. Despite these royal efforts, however, Indian communities in areas of intensive Spanish settlement such as the Valley of Mexico steadily lost land to their conquerors. Laws were subverted or ignored. Lands left vacant by declining Indian populations passed into the hands of Spanish ranchers and wheat farmers. The Spaniards had destroyed Indian government above the level of the local community, and the communities found themselves fighting a prolonged but losing battle against Spanish commercial interests, especially the great haciendas that developed in the seventeenth and eighteenth centuries (Wolf 1956; Gibson 1964).

6. Discussions of economic and political inequality within peasant corporate communities can be found in Lewis (1951), Cancian (1965), Goldkind (1965, 1966), Bloch (1966), Keatinge (1973), Brandes (1975), Orlove (1977b), Dow (1977), and Stern (1983).

7. For a trenchant summary of this research, see Greenberg (1981).

8. Even though Marx based his theory of history on class struggle, he devoted little effort to defining the concept of class itself. Nevertheless, his ideas about class emerge clearly, if somewhat diffusely, from his writing. According to Marx, classes are composed of those members of society who share the same relation to the "productive forces." Shaw (1978:10) defines productive forces as "those elements which are both basic and essential to the productive process, not in the wide sense of including all activities or factors which are necessary for society to carry on production, but in the narrower sense of the simple factors of the labor process—that is, those elements which analysis reveals as part of the immediate production process itself."

In other words, the productive forces include "instruments of labor" such as machinery, beasts of burden, canals, and even the land itself; "objects of labor" such as crops, livestock (which can also be instruments of labor when used to produce other animals or animal products), timber, and mineral wealth; and "labor power," that is, the human capacity to produce something of value utilizing both instruments and objects (Shaw 1978:10–20).

Chapter 1. Cucurpe in Historical Perspective

1. In contrast to both the comunidades of Cucurpe and San Javier, Ejido 6 de Enero dates back to the 1960s rather than the colonial period. The organization originated when a group of campesinos occupied an upland valley called Agua en Medio in the northeastern portion of the municipio. There they erected ocotillo jacales, planted nonirrigated (*temporal*) fields of maize and beans, and began to raise goats, pigs, and chickens. They also petitioned the federal government to grant them ejido status, a process permissible under Mexican agrarian reform law wherever private farmers or ranchers possess more than the legal limit of land. Not surprisingly, local ranchers objected to the settlers and fought to protect their property. Given the politics of the time, they were soon able to mobilize the state judicial police to drive the would-be ejidatarios out.

The result was perhaps the most brutal episode in modern Cucurpe history. Descending upon Agua en Medio, the state police arrested all the men and threw them in the Magdalena jail. Then the judiciales burned their jacales, bulldozed their crops, and slaughtered their livestock. Women and children were not harmed, but they were forced to leave Agua en Medio and move to Magdalena, where they had to provide food and clothing for the imprisoned men as well as for themselves. Before they were finally released, several members of the group, including an agrarian activist from an organization called the *Vieja Guardia Agraria*, had spent more than a year in jail.

Under the presidential administration of Luis Echeverría, however, the political climate changed. Agrarian populism experienced a temporary resurgence, and in 1976, the Ejido 6 de Enero was created. Agua en Medio was declared a *nuevo centro de población* (new center of population), and 8,000 ha of rangeland and temporal were expropriated from surrounding ranchers and given to the ejidatarios. Nevertheless, conflict between the ejidatarios and their neighbors did not cease with the presidential declaration or federal recognition. Surrounding ranchers, several of them quite wealthy, petitioned for redress. When legal suits bogged down, they took matters into their own hands, as the vignette at the beginning of chapter 1 describes. The municipal *síndico* later determined that the ejido's fence had been cut in forty-two places. When I left Cucurpe at the end of 1981, neither the ranchers nor their accomplices had been tried for their acts.

2. Unfortunately, the historical record concerning Cucurpe is not particularly detailed. The municipal archives themselves consist of a few boxes of unorganized documents dealing almost entirely with the post-World War II period. It is possible that an intensive search of colonial and state archives might yield more primary documentation about the region, but the information readily available in secondary sources or the computerized indexes of the Documentary Relations of the Southwest division of the Arizona State Museum does not suggest that an extensive and systematic body of historical data about Cucurpe exists.

3. Padre Luis Velarde al Padre Visitador Joseph María Genovese, Dolores, May 9, 1722, Archivo Histórico de Hacienda (AHH), Legajo 278, Expediente 38, Mexico. Vecinos de Nacozari, n.d., AHH, 278, 11. The first document, by a Jesuit, details a series of complaints about Tuñón y Quirós' corruption. The second document, written by Spanish settlers including Juan Mateo Manje, reiterates Velarde's accusations.

4. Spicer (1962) suggests that Opata speakers were pushing into Pima territory from the northeast during late prehistoric times. It is possible, therefore, that the middle portion of the river was occupied by Pimans prior to a Eudeve intrusion. Regardless of the distribution of aboriginal ethnic groups, however, one significant fact is clear: the San Miguel was not a self-contained social and geographic unit oriented north-south along the riverbed. On the contrary, various portions of the watershed were populated by human groups who were culturally and linguistically affiliated with people to the east or west in other Sonoran river valleys. This geographic segmentation of the drainage continued throughout the colonial period and still exists today, reflected in contemporary political units, marketing patterns, and transportation networks (Felger, Nabhan, and Sheridan 1976).

5. Padre Juan de Almonajiz, Matape, January 4, 1689. AHH, Legajo 278, Expediente 12. Archivo General de la Nación, Mexico City. Documentary Relations of the Southwest (DRSW) Master Index 60–131.

6. Gerónimo García de Terán, Bacanuche, February 1, 1684. AHH, Legajo 325, Expediente 87. DRSW Master Index 60–97.

7. Autos de informaciones hechas contra Francisco Montes, alias El Pintor, de nación Pima, a pedimento de el común Pueblo de Cucurpe, ante el general don Juan Antonio Fernández de la Cabada, Juez Visitador General en esta provincia de Sonora para su Majestad. Archivo de Hidalgo del Parral, microfilm reel 1723B, frames 655–688, University of Arizona Main Library. DRSW Master Index 100–1465.

8. Juan Bautista Quigue, Cucurpe, no date (1723). Ibid.

9. Juan Comabur, Cucurpe, July 16, 1723. Ibid.

10. Francisco Juamori, Cucurpe, July 16, 1723. Ibid.

11. Report of Antonio María de los Reyes, O.F.M., 1772. Translated by Kieran McCarty. Manuscript on file in the library of the Arizona Historical Society, Tucson.

12. Padrón de los Vecinos y Yndios de esta Misión de los Santos Reyes de Cucurpe y su visita el Pueblo de Tuape. Tuape, October 14, 1796, Manuel de Legarra. Archivo del Gobierno Eclesiástico de la Mitra de Sonora, Catedral de San Agustín, Hermosillo, Sonora. Quoted in Dobyns (1976).

13. Plano de los Egidos (sic) de Cucurpe, Cucurpe, July 23, 1882. Copy on file in the office of Bienes Comunales, Secretaría de la Reforma Agraria, Hermosillo, Sonora.

14. According to modern Cucurpeños, a detachment of Cucurpe militia helped defeat North American filibusterer Henry Crabb at Caborca in 1857.

15. According to a Sonoran entrepreneur who used to work for the organization, the Cerro Prieto Mining Company began extracting gold and silver ore on a small scale in 1895 and rapidly expanded its operations the following decade. Located in the mountains northeast of the pueblo of Cucurpe, the Cerro Prieto stamp mills processed up to 1,500 metric tons of ore a day. The company also built an electric plant and pumped water up to the mines from the distant Río Saracachi. In the process, Cerro Prieto became a unique multiethnic community in the municipio, employing North American administrators and Mexican and Oriental laborers.

16. During the Mexican Revolution, one of the local *caudillos*, or revolutionary leaders, was a Cucurpeño named Joaquín Núñez. Like many such leaders, Núñez had a reputation for arbitrary violence that survives today. One old man, in fact, said he was "a great killer, a pig" ("*un matazón, un puerco*"). After the revolution was over, Núñez outlived his usefulness to the government. At the instigation of the owner of Agua Fría and his first cousin, who owned the adjoining Rancho Santo Domingo, Núñez was lured to Agua Fría where he was greeted warmly and a dinner held in his honor. Before dining, however, all the guests were requested to disarm and Núñez, lulled by the cordiality, complied. Soldiers hidden from view then burst into the room and grabbed the chieftain, tying him up and mounting him on a horse to be taken to Cucurpe. But Núñez, ever the *macho*, proclaimed, "Cucurpe is my pueblo. I

will never enter my pueblo bound. Better that they kill me." (*Cucurpe es mi pueblo. Nunca entro mi pueblo amarrado. Mejor que me maten.*) Riding down the canyon of the Río Saracachi, Núñez carried out his threat, spurring his horse away from the soldiers and galloping up a hillside until their bullets cut him down.

Now a part of local legend, Núñez' capture and death demonstrates the power and influence the owner must have exercised in the region.

17. *Gomi* was an Opata kickball game involving two teams. Each team attempted to kick a small wooden ball over a lengthy course faster than the other (Sobarzo 1984). In Cucurpe, this game was played during Holy Week and usually pitted the *viejos* (old men) against the *jovenes* (young men).

18. Reversing the provisions of Ley Lerdo incorporated into the Constitution of 1857, Article 27 of the Constitution of 1917 guaranteed the right of communities to corporately control land, forests, and water. Article 27 also called for the restitution of lands that had been illegally alienated. These provisions set in motion a program of agrarian reform guided by a complex body of rules and regulations known as the Federal Law of Agrarian Reform.

19. The Mexican government has largely favored the development of private livestock raising rather than encouraging comunidades and ejidos to engage in commercial cattle production. In 1937, for example, Lázaro Cárdenas issued a presidential decree protecting millions of hectares of private range from expropriation for a period of twenty-five years. A decade later, the administration of Miguel Alemán amended Article 27 of the Constitution to allow individual private ranchers to possess enough land to support 500 head of cattle. This change from an absolute to a relative limit on rangeland, coupled with the freedom from expropriation, revealed just how deeply Mexico was committed to the expansion of the private ranching sector (Peña and Chávez 1985).

20. Similar shifts in cropping patterns, especially from the production of food to forage grains, have occurred throughout Mexico. DeWalt (1985) calls this shift Mexico's "second Green Revolution," and argues that the increasing cultivation of sorghum for animal feed has left much of Mexico's population undernourished as the nation has gone from being a food-exporting nation in the 1960s to a food-importing one today.

21. Even though Article 27 of the 1917 Constitution overturned Ley Lerdo and guaranteed the right of communities to control land, forests, and water corporately, Mexico's commitment to agrarian reform has varied from presidential administration to administration. Presidents such as Lázaro Cárdenas (1934–1940) and, to a lesser extent, Adolfo López Mateos (1958–1964) and Luis Echeverría (1970–76), redistributed millions of hectares of land and occasionally attempted to provide peasant farmers with the credit and capital they needed to modernize their operations. Other administrations, in contrast, demonstrated much more support for large-scale capitalist agriculture, encouraging it with both financial and technological assistance. The result has been a profoundly ambiguous agrarian policy, one that protects peasants on some occasions while championing the private sector on others (Kearney 1980; Sanderson 1981; Hewitt de Alcántara 1982).

Chapter 2. Modern Agrarian Society in Cucurpe

1. Not all Spaniards or Latin Americans, of course, followed this urban pattern. Settlement in the Basque provinces of northern Spain, for example, was less nucleated than in the Castiles or Andalusia. And on the far northern frontier of New Spain, the recalcitrant Spanish colonists of New Mexico repeatedly resisted official attempts to concentrate them into villages rather than isolated *ranchos,* despite the danger from hostile Apaches and Comanches (Jones 1979).

2. The nature of the celebration determines the way fresh meat is prepared in Cucurpe. The most frequent social event is the *carne asada,* which is held in conjunction with family gatherings or *velorios* (all-night vigils) involving small groups of neighbors. All three types of livestock—cattle, pigs, and goats—are slaughtered, and the meat is roasted over an open fire and then served with tortillas, salsa, and raw, chopped cabbage. The constant refrain at carne asadas is *"Come carne!"* (Eat more meat!) as guests are encouraged to consume as much meat as they want. Carne asadas, therefore, accompany events involving people with close friendship or kinship ties.

Barbacoas, on the other hand, characterize large gatherings such as baptisms, weddings, or the arrival of visiting dignitaries such as the state governor. Because of the number of people who have to be fed, cattle are the only animals butchered. The meat is pit-barbecued or simmered in large pots, rather than being roasted, and then ladled onto plates with beans or salad. In other words, portions are determined by the hosts, not the guests, and the phrase *"Come carne!"* is no longer heard. Consequently, the exchange of meat is more generalized and more controlled, symbolizing the looser ties of community rather than the bonds between family members and neighbors (Szuter 1984).

3. Detailed critiques of homeostatic models and the ecosystem concept in anthropology can be found in Moran 1984. Netting, for example, notes:

> This common anthropological error involves an overemphasis on functional integration, stability, and regulatory mechanisms within the community and a relative neglect of disequilibrium, changes emanating from more inclusive political-economic systems, and instances of evolutionary maladaptation. The nature of long-term resident field research, our reverence for an holistic perspective, and the romantic mystique of the self-sufficient, autonomous, emotionally rewarding "little community" all perpetuate our proclivity to learn a lot about a very limited group (1984:225).

Chapter 3. Agriculture and Water Control

1. Precipitation data at Saracachi was collected for five years (1942–46) and at San Javier for thirty-five years (1923–41; 1943–58) (Hastings and Humphrey 1969). Average annual rainfall for Cucurpe is based upon eight years of data (1972–79) available at the Magdalena office of the Secretaría de Agricultura y Recursos Hidráulicos (SARH).

2. The amount of precipitation alone is not a particularly sensitive indication of aridity. A far more accurate measure of the impact of climate upon agriculture is the magnitude of evapotranspiration, that is, the quantity of moisture lost by plants and the soil through transpiration and evaporation. The climatologist C.W. Thornthwaite developed the concept of "potential evapotranspiration" to specify the amount of water which would be evaporated or transpired in any given microclimate if the ground were continuously supplied with water and covered with green plants (Strahler and Strahler 1978). Utilizing this concept, Thornthwaite Associates (1964) were able to estimate the water needs and water budgets for areas across the world, including the agricultural community of Carbó along the lower San Miguel watershed.

At Carbó, potential evapotranspiration (PE) far exceeds actual precipitation (P). Carbó, which lies at an elevation of 464 m, never experiences a water surplus during the year. December, a relatively wet month with the coolest mean monthly temperature, is the only period when no water deficit (potential evapotranspiration [PE] minus actual evapotranspiration [AE]) normally occurs. Employing Thornthwaite's moisture index (Im), it is clear that Carbó with an Im of −75.54 possesses a truly arid (E) climate (Thornthwaite and Mather 1957; Hastings and Humphrey 1969).

The lowest elevations in the municipio of Cucurpe, on the other hand, are 350 m higher than Carbó, a variable affecting both temperature and potential evapotranspiration. Calculating the moisture index for the pueblo of Cucurpe, by contrast, yields an Im of −58, well within the semiarid range (−33.3 to −66.7) according to Thornthwaite Associates (1964). Throughout the municipio, then, semiarid conditions prevail along the floodplain of the San Miguel drainage and most of the intermontane basins. More humid conditions exist in the northern uplands and in the mountains, but little arable land is available there. Semiaridity, therefore, characterizes most of the microenvironments that can be cultivated in Cucurpe.

3. The term *tarea* is a traditional measure of the amount of land that can be worked within a certain amount of time, usually a day (Santamaría 1974). According to one Cucurpeño, a tarea consists of 25 *"pasos perdidos en cuadrado."* In contrast to a *paso natural*, or single pace, a paso perdido is two paces, one with one leg, one with the other leg. Therefore, a tarea is the amount of ground covered by 50 square paces.

Chapter 4. Livestock Raising

1. Bennett (1969) notes that ranching and horsemanship exercise similar holds on the imaginations of the rural inhabitants of the Canadian Great Plains. And in the United States, of course, the cowboy, not the farmer, is the favorite mythical figure of the past.

2. A. Aguirre Martínez and F. Gutiérrez Araiza. Informe de la Secretaría de la Reforma Agraria, August 23, 1975. Copy on file in the offices of Bienes Comunales, Secretaría de la Reforma Agraria, Hermosillo, Sonora.

Chapter 5. Nonagrarian Economic Activities

1. Proyecto de la Planta Laminadora de Cantera de Cucurpe, Sonora, Secretaría de Programación y Presupuesto, Hermosillo, Sonora, October, 1979.

2. Mescal technology and terminology vary somewhat across Sonora. For detailed descriptions of two other moonshine stills in eastern Sonora, see Bahre and Bradbury (1980), and Nabhan (1985). Both focus upon mescal makers who primarily utilize the narrow-leafed *Agave pacifica* to make *bacanora*, the most popular Sonoran mescal. Bahre and Bradbury conclude that mescal-making has endangered only a few local populations of agave. Nabhan, on the other hand, is more pessimistic. In his words:

> A diligent mescalero such as Joaquin needs to harvest about 1600 agaves during favorable seasons to distill the 320 to 400 gallons he sells each year. Most mescal makers in his area harvest considerably fewer plants, perhaps only averaging a single run each year. Yet there may be as many as a thousand to two thousand of these part-time bootleggers in rural Sonora. Considering the wild harvests of both the occasional and the more active mescaleros, on the order of half a million agaves may be harvested each year in Sonora. In wild stands near pueblos and ranches, harvesters probably cut most of the soon-to-bloom agaves they can reach (Nabhan 1985:45).

Chapter 6. Economic Inequality and the Organization of Resource Control

1. The Gini coefficient is a measure of relative inequality. It calculates the proportion of total area lying between a diagonal 45-degree line representing conditions of equal distribution and a Lorenz curve measuring the actual distribution itself. What the Gini does not measure, however, is the shape of the curve; hence, it gives no information about how or where wealth is distributed within a social group. The method for computing the Gini employed in this analysis is discussed in Shryock, Siegel, and Associates (1973).

A selected range of Gini coefficients reported in the anthropological literature (Davis 1977, Cancian 1979, Galt 1980, McGuire and Netting 1982) is as follows: Sarakantsani, Macedonia (.22); Chiapas, Mexico (.32); Orasac, Yugoslavia (.32); Uttar Pradesh, India (.39); Pantelleria, Italy (.43); Missouri, United States (.45); Taichung, Taiwan (.45); Philippines (.48); Törbel, Switzerland (.343–.495); Andra Pradesh, India (.55); Al Karak, Jordan (.58); Genuardo, Sicily (.69); Belmonte, Spain (.70); Vila Velha, Portugal (.75); Alcala, Spain (.87).

2. The candidate imposed in place of the school principal was a retired schoolteacher who had been born in Cucurpe but who had not lived in the municipio for more than twenty years. This man was perceived as the candidate of the local private ranchers and was said to have close ties with the four individuals who were battling the comunidad to retain control of their lands within comunidad boundaries (*see* chapters 8 and 9).

Chapter 7. The Ideology of Resource Control

1. The leader of this faction is a former president of the municipio who also works for the president of the Comunidad of Cucurpe on his restoration projects across the state of Sonora (*see* chapter 8). Consequently, the young man is politically influential among many comuneros, even though he was not yet a member of Comunidad San Javier in 1981.

2. There is also much less of a relationship between female virtue and family honor. Although Cucurpe households supervise their young women and hold virginity in high esteem, women who stray from the norm are not cast out of society or consigned to a permanent position of contempt. One woman who had an illegitimate child by a comunero from San Javier lives on the main street of Cucurpe next door to two of her brothers. She is also married to another man and has several children by him. Neither the men nor the women of her community treat her any differently from other married women. When the subject of her illegitimate child was broached, one of her brothers shrugged and said, "She had an adventure (*aventura*) when she was younger." Her status in Cucurpe has apparently suffered no permanent damage from her youthful indiscretion.

The case of another woman is even more dramatic. Middle-aged now, the woman was a great beauty in her day and has had children by several different men. In 1981, she was living with a man much older than herself, a relatively prosperous stockman and cattle buyer whose wife had died several years before. Tall, confident, and aggressive, with a voice that automatically commands respect and terrorizes umpires who call close ones against the Cucurpe Broncos, the woman is the most dynamic female in the area, the only one who regularly speaks up at comunidad meetings and other community functions. Moreover, she is one of the handful of women who keep Cucurpe's religious traditions alive by leading the services of Holy Week (*Semana Santa*). Her sexual mores clearly do not prevent her from acting as a social and religious leader. And even though people love to talk about her escapades, she is not shunned by anyone. When her name came up in a conversation, one farmer laughed and said, "She likes the happy life (*la vida alegre*)." Amused tolerance rather than moralistic disapproval seems to characterize the attitudes of most Cucurpeños toward her.

Chapter 8. The History and Structure of the Comunidad of Cucurpe

1. G. Echeverría, Ures, October 4, 1878. Expediente "Ejidos de Cucurpe," Archivo del Tesorero General del Estado de Sonora. Copy on file at Bienes Comunales, Secretaría de la Reforma Agraria, Hermosillo, Sonora (herein after cited as Bienes Comunales).

2. Juan Denton Hall, Ursulo Ramos, Leonides Altamirano, Sauturnino Sinohui, Estolano Quijada, Francisco Jiménez, Cucurpe, October 21, 1878. Bienes Comunales.

3. Plano de los Egidos (sic) de Cucurpe, P. López, Cucurpe, July 23, 1882. Bienes Comunales.

4. Manuel Alegría Borboa al Presidente de la República, Cucurpe, May 20, 1963. Bienes Comunales.

5. Antonio Cano Miranda and Aquilino León Ruíz, Cucurpe, March 27, 1955. Bienes Comunales.

6. Eduardo Sinohui al Roberto Barrios, Cucurpe, February 11, 1959. Bienes Comunales.

7. Ibid.

8. Alegría al Presidente, May 20, 1963. Bienes Comunales.

9. Mario Cano Cano al Augusto Gómez Villanueva, México, January 19, 1973. Bienes Comunales.

10. Comité Pro-Defensa de los Antiguos Terrenos de la Comunidad del Pueblo de Cucurpe, Sonora, March 7, 1965. Bienes Comunales.

11. Comité al Norberto Aguirre Palancares, Cucurpe, March 7, 1965. Bienes Comunales.

12. Cuerpo Consultivo Agrario, México, August 15, 1975. Bienes Comunales.

13. Manuel Alegría Borboa al Augusto Gómez Villanueva, Cucurpe, n.d. Bienes Comunales.

14. Cuerpo Consultivo Agrario, August 15, 1975. Bienes Comunales.

15. Gonzalo Aguirre Beltrán al José Pacheco Loya, México, February 11, 1972. Bienes Comunales.

16. Cano Cano, January 19, 1973. Bienes Comunales.

17. *Ley Federal de la Reforma Agraria*, Libro Quinto, Título Cuarto, Capítulo I. México: Editorial Porrúa, 1981.

18. Dictamen, Departamento de Asuntos Agrarios y Colonización, María del Carmen Jiménez Arreola, n.p., n.d. Bienes Comunales.

19. Cuerpo Consultivo Agrario, August 15, 1975. Bienes Comunales.

20. Luis Echeverría Alvarez, México, September 22, 1975. Published in the *Diario Oficial*, December 15, 1975. Bienes Comunales.

21. *Ley Federal de la Reforma Agraria*, Libro Primero, Capítulo II, Artículo 23. Op. cit.

Chapter 10. Political Ecology of Cucurpe Comunidad

1. There have been a number of general discussions of class in the Mexican countryside, including those of Stavenhagen (1969), Bartra (1974), and Esteva (1980). Because all of those authors are talking about class on the national level, they recognize certain class distinctions that do not exist in Cucurpe while compressing other distinctions that do. What my analysis does is to demonstrate the divisions of class that affect one economically marginal municipio in Sonora. General models may be necessary starting points, but they cannot be applied uncritically to local situations. On the contrary, the actual processes of conflict and exploitation must be determined empirically, on a case by case basis, in order to refine or reject larger schemes.

Glossary of Spanish Terms

Acequia: irrigation canal.

Adelantado: individual responsible for the conquest of a new frontier in sixteenth-century and early seventeenth-century Latin America.

Agostadero: grazing land.

Bacanora: famous Sonoran mescal, distilled from the caudices of *Agave pacifica*.

Becerra: female calf.

Becerrada: international calf market.

Becerro: male calf.

Caballo: full-grown male horse.

Cabecera: community which serves as administrative headquarters of a district or municipio.

Campesinista: supporter of the campesino movement. Agrarian populist.

Caudillo: military and political leader, usually with the connotations of a local strongman rather than an authority legitimatized by law.

Científico: positivist advisor or government official under President Porfirio Díaz.

Común: organization of peasants holding certain basic resources such as land and water in common. Term replaced by *comunidad* in Mexico but still used in parts of Spain.

Común de agua: organization of water users.

Comunidad: organization of peasants holding certain basic resources such as land and water in common. In Mexico, comunidades differ from ejidos in that they trace their origins back to a pre-Revolutionary past.

Congregación: policy of congregating different Indian populations, especially those decimated by epidemics of Old World diseases, into single nucleated settlements.

Ejido: in modern Mexico, the most common form of peasant corporate landholding organization. Ejidos differ from comunidades in that they may be entirely new creations rather than associations predating the Mexican Revolution.

Encomendero: one who received a grant of *encomienda*.

Encomienda: a Spanish colonial institution in which the Crown granted individuals the right to extract labor or tribute from specified groups of Indians. In return, the *encomendero* was supposed to provide for the spiritual welfare of the Indians and their instruction in Catholicism.

Estancia: landed estate devoted to raising livestock.

Hacendado: owner of a hacienda.

Hacienda: large, landed estate.

Indigenista: Latin-American intellectual who supported, studied, and often romanticized Native-American culture.

Latifundia: large, landed estate. Term usually associated with pre-Revolutionary Mexico, especially during the *Porfiriato*.

Lechuguilla: locally distilled mescal, usually made from the caudices of *Agave palmeri*.

Milpa: irrigated farmland.

Municipio: in Mexico, roughly analogous to a U.S. county. The next administrative unit below a state.

Novillo: steer or young bull.

Peso: basic unit of Mexican currency. In 1980–81, one U.S. dollar was worth about twenty-five pesos.

Porfiriato: period of Mexican history (1876–1910) when Porfirio Díaz dominated Mexican politics.

Ranchería: Native-American settlement characterized by scattered households, in contrast to the more nucleated *pueblo*.

Real de minas: mining community. Called a "royal" settlement because the Spanish Crown was entitled to a share of all mining revenues, usually the "royal fifth" (*quinto real*).

Reducción: program of concentrating dispersed Native-American groups into a centralized location where they could be missionized and controlled.

Repartimiento: labor system whereby Native Americans were required to work for a certain individual for a specified period of time.

Represa: diversion weir.

San Francisco: St. Francis Xavier. Most important Catholic supernatural in the Sonoran Desert region. Feast and pilgrimage held in Magdalena, Sonora, on and around October 4.

San Isidro: St. Isidore of Madrid, who died there in 1130 A.D. Patron saint of farmers whose feast day is celebrated on May 15.

San Juan: St. John the Baptist, whose feast day is June 24, the day when the summer rains (*las aguas*) traditionally arrive.

Santo Niño de Atocha: manifestation of the child Jesus. According to legend, the Santo Niño appeared in the guise of a small child in Atocha, Spain, where he served Christian prisoners of the Moors water and bread.

Tarea: a measure of land roughly equal to fifty square paces.

Tauna: animal-powered milling stones.

Temporal: nonirrigated farmland.

Toro: bull.

Vaca: cow.

Vaquilla: young cow, one to two years old.

Vara: measure of length equal to 2.74 feet.

Velorio: religious vigil.

Yegua: mare.

Bibliography

Almada, Francisco
  1983 *Diccionario de Historia, Geografía y Biografía Sonorenses*. Hermosillo: Gobierno del Estado de Sonora.
Arensberg, Conrad, and Solon Kimball
  1940 *Family and Community in Ireland*. Cambridge: Harvard University Press.
Bahre, Conrad, and David Bradbury
  1980 "Manufacture of Mescal in Sonora, Mexico." *Economic Botany* 34(4):391–400.
Balmori, Diana, Stuart Voss, and Miles Wortman
  1984 *Notable Family Networks in Latin America*. Chicago: University of Chicago Press.
Bannon, John
  1955 *The Mission Frontier in Sonora, 1620–1687*. New York: United States Catholic Historical Society.
  1974 *The Spanish Borderlands Frontier, 1513–1821*. Albuquerque: University of New Mexico Press.
Bartra, Roger
  1974 *Estructura agraria y clases sociales en México*. México: Editorial Era.
Batteau, Alan
  1982 "Mosbys and Broomsedge: the Semantics of Class in an Appalachian Kinship System." *American Ethnologist* 9(3):445–66.
Bennett, John
  1969 *Northern Plainsmen*. Atherton: Aldine Publishing Company.
Bloch, Marc
  1966 *French Rural History*. Berkeley: University of California Press.
Blum, J.
  1971 "The European Village as Community: Origins and Functions." *Agricultural History* 45(3):157–78.
Brandes, Stanley
  1975 *Migration, Kinship and Community: Tradition and Transition in a Spanish Village*. New York: Academic Press.
Brody, H.
  1973 *Inishkillane: Change and Decline in the West of Ireland*. London: The Penguin Press.

Brush, Stephen
 1976 "Introduction to Cultural Adaptations to Mountain Ecosystems."
       Human Ecology 4:125–34.
Cancian, Frank
 1965 *Economics and Prestige in a Maya Community.* Stanford: Stanford
       University Press.
 1979 *The Innovator's Situation: Upper Middle-Class Conservatism in Agricul-
       tural Communities.* Stanford: Stanford University Press.
Chambers, Erve, and Philip Young
 1979 "Mesoamerican Community Studies: The Past Decade." *Annual Re-
       view of Anthropology* 8:45–69.
Chevalier, Francois
 1963 *Land and Society in Colonial Mexico.* Berkeley: University of California
       Press.
Cline, Howard
 1952 "Mexican Community Studies." *Hispanic American Historical Review*
       32:212–42.
Cole, John, and Eric Wolf
 1974 *The Hidden Frontier: Ecology and Ethnicity in an Alpine Valley.* New
       York: Academic Press.
Cooke, Ronald, and Richard Reeves
 1976 *Arroyos and Environmental Change in the American South-West.* Oxford:
       Clarendon Press.
Crosby, Alfred
 1972 *The Columbian Exchange.* Westport: Greenwood Publishing.
Cumberland, Charles
 1974 *Mexican Revolution: Genesis Under Madero.* Austin: University of
       Texas Press.
Davis, J.
 1977 *People of the Mediterranean.* London: Routledge and Kegan Paul.
Decorme, Gerard, S.J.
 1941 *La Obra de los Jesuitas Mexicanos durante la Epocha Colonial,* Tomo II.
       México: Antigua Librería Robredo de José Porrúa e Hijos.
Deeds, Susan
 1981 "Rendering unto Caesar: The Secularization of Jesuit Missions in
       Mid-Eighteenth Century Durango." Ph.D. dissertation. Tucson:
       The University of Arizona.
 1985 "Land Tenure Patterns in Northern New Spain." *The Americas*
       41(4):446–61.
DeWalt, Billie
 1979 *Modernization in a Mexican Ejido: A Study in Economic Adaptation.*
       London: Cambridge University Press.
 1985 " Mexico's Second Green Revolution." *Mexican Studies* 1(1):29–60.
Dobyns, Henry
 1951 "Blunders with Bolsas." *Human Organization* 10(1):25–32.
 1966 "Estimating Aboriginal American Population." *Current Anthropol-
       ogy* 7(4):395–416.

1976   *Spanish Colonial Tucson: A Demographic History*. Tucson: The University of Arizona Press.
1981   *From Fire to Flood: Historic Human Destruction of Sonoran Desert Riverine Oases*. Ballena Press Anthropology Papers No. 20, Socorro, N.M.: Ballena Press.
Dow, James
1973   "On the Muddled Concept of Corporation in Anthropology." *American Anthropologist* 75(3):904–08.
1977   "Religion in the Organization of the Mexican Peasantry." In *Peasant Livelihood*, edited by Rhoda Halperin and James Dow. New York: St. Martin's Press.
Dunne, Peter
1940   *Pioneer Blackrobes on the West Coast*. Berkeley: University of California Press.
Durrenberger, R.W., and X. Murrieta
1978   Clima del Estado de Sonora, Mexico. *Climatological Publications, Mexico Climatology Series* No. 3. Tempe: Office of the State Climatologist, Arizona State University.
Effrat, M.
1974   *The Community: Approaches and Applications*. New York: Free Press.
Escandón, Patricia
1985   "La nueva administración misional y los pueblos de indios." *Historia General de Sonora* II. Hermosillo: Gobierno del Estado de Sonora.
Esteva, Gustavo
1978   "Los campesinos y la crisis agrícola." *Narxhi-Nandha*, Nos. 8, 9, 10.
1980   *La Batalla en el México Rural*. México: Siglo Veintiuno.
Farriss, Nancy
1984   *Maya Society Under Colonial Rule*. Princeton: Princeton University Press.
Federal Law of Agrarian Reform
1981   *Ley Federal de Reforma Agraria*. México: Editorial Porrúa.
Felger, Richard, Gary Nabhan, and Thomas Sheridan
1976   *The Ethnobotany of the Río San Miguel*. Report prepared for the Centro Noroeste, Instituto Nacional de Antropología e Historia.
Figueroa Valenzuela, Alejandro
1985   "Los indios de sonora ante la modernización porfirista." *Historia General de Sonora* IV:140–63. Hermosillo: Gobierno del Estado de Sonora.
Figueroa, F.
1970   *Las Comunidades Agrarias*. México: Editorial Morales.
Florescano, Enrique
1971   *Estructuras y problemas agrarios de México, 1500–1821*. México.
Freeman, Susan
1970   *Neighbors: The Social Contract in a Castilian Hamlet*. Chicago: University of Chicago Press.
Freyre, G.
1964   *The Masters and the Slaves: A Study in the Development of Brazilian Civilization*. New York: Alfred Knopf.

Galt, A.
  1980   "Social Stratification on Pantelleria, Italy." *Ethnology* 19:405–26.
Gibson, Charles
  1964   *The Aztecs Under Spanish Rule.* Stanford: Stanford University Press.
Gilmore, D.
  1982   "Anthropology of the Mediterranean Area." *Annual Review of Anthropology* 11:175–205.
Goldkind, Victor
  1965   "Social Stratification in the Peasant Community: Redfield's Chan Kom Reinterpreted." *American Anthropologist* 67:863–84.
  1966   "Class, Conflict and Cacique in Chan Kom." *Southwestern Journal of Anthropology* 22:325–45.
Gracida Romo, Juan José
  1985a   "Génesis y consolidación del porfiriato en sonora." *Historia General de Sonora,* IV:19–74. Hermosillo: Gobierno del Estado de Sonora.
  1985b   "El sonora moderno." *Historia General de Sonora* IV:77–138. Hermosillo: Gobierno del Estado de Sonora.
Greenberg, James
  1981   *Santiago's Sword: Chatino Peasant Religion and Economics.* Berkeley: University of California Press.
Guillet, David
  1981   "Land Tenure, Ecological Zone, and Agricultural Regime in the Central Andes." *American Ethnologist* 8(1):139–56.
Gunder Frank, André
  1969   *Capitalism and Underdevelopment in Latin America.* New York: Monthly Review Press.
Hardin, Garrett
  1968   "The Tragedy of the Commons." *Science* 162:1243–48.
Hastings, J. and R. Humphrey
  1969   "Climatological Data and Statistics for Sonora and Northern Sinaloa." *Technical Reports on the Meteorology and Climatology of Arid Regions,* No. 19. Tucson: The University of Arizona Institute of Atmospheric Physics.
Hewitt de Alcántara, Cynthia
  1982   *La Modernización de la Agricultura Mexicana.* México: Siglo Veintiuno.
  1984   *Anthropological Perspectives on Rural Mexico.* London: Routledge & Kegan Paul.
Hollingshead, August
  1949   *Elmstown's Youth.* New York: J. Wiley.
Hrdlička, Aleš
  1904   "Notes on the Indians of Sonora, Mexico." *American Anthropologist* 6(1):51–89.
Hu-DeHart, Evelyn
  1981   *Missionaries, Miners, and Indians: History of the Spanish Contact with the Yaqui Nation of Northwestern New Spain, 1533–1820.* Tucson: The University of Arizona Press.

1984   *Yaqui Resistance and Survival: The Struggle for Land and Autonomy,*
       1821–1910. Madison: University of Wisconsin Press.
Hutchins, Wells
1928   "The Community Acequia: Its Origins and Development." *South-*
       western Historical Quarterly 3:261–84.
Hyden, Goran
1980   *Beyond Ujamaa in Tanzania: Underdevelopment and an Uncaptured Peas-*
       antry. London: Heinemann.
Janvry, A. and C. Garramón
1977   "The Dynamics of Rural Poverty in Latin America." *The Journal of*
       Peasant Studies 4:206–16.
Jones, Oakah
1979   *Los Paisanos: Spanish Settlers on the Northern Frontier of New Spain.*
       Norman: University of Oklahoma Press.
Kearney, Michael
1980   "Agribusiness and the Demise or the Rise of the Peasantry." *Latin*
       American Perspectives 7(4):115–24.
Keatinge, Elsie
1973   "Latin American Corporate Communities: Potential for Mobiliza-
       tion and Political Integration." *Journal of Anthropological Research*
       29:37–58.
Kessell, John
1976   *Friars, Soldiers, and Reformers: Hispanic Arizona and the Sonora Mission*
       Frontier, 1767–1856. Tucson: The University of Arizona Press.
Lafaye, Jacques
1976   *Quetzalcóatl and Guadalupe: The Formation of Mexican National Con-*
       sciousness, 1531–1813. Chicago: University of Chicago Press.
Laslett, Peter
1972   "Introduction: The History of the Family." In *Household and Family in*
       Past Time, edited by Peter Laslett. Cambridge: Cambridge Univer-
       sity Press.
Le Roy Ladurie, Emmanuel
1974   *The Peasants of Languedoc.* Urbana: University of Illinois Press.
Lewis, Oscar
1951   *Life in a Mexican Village: Tepoztlán Restudied.* Urbana: University of
       Illinois Press.
MacLachlan, Colin, and Jaime Rodríguez
1980   *The Forging of the Cosmic Race: A Reinterpretation of Colonial Mexico.*
       Berkeley: University of California Press.
McCarty, Kieran
1981   *A Spanish Frontier in the Enlightened Age: Franciscan Beginnings in*
       Sonora and Arizona, 1767–1770. Washington: Academy of American
       Franciscan History.
McGuire, Thomas
1986   *Politics and Ethnicity on the Río Yaqui: Potam Revisited.* Tucson: The
       University of Arizona Press.

McGuire, Randall, and Robert Netting
  1982 "Leveling Peasants? The Maintenance of Equality in a Swiss Alpine Community." *American Ethnologist* 9:269–90.
Machado, Manuel
  1981 *The North Mexican Cattle Industry, 1910–1975.* College Station: Texas A&M University Press.
Margolis, M.
  1973 *The Moving Frontier.* Gainesville: University of Florida Press.
Menegus Bornemann, M.
  1980 "Ocoyoacac—Una Comunidad Agraria en el Siglo XIX." *Historia Mexicana* 30(1):33–78.
Meyer, Michael
  1984 *Water in the Hispanic Southwest.* Tucson: The University of Arizona Press.
Meyer, Michael, and William Sherman
  1979 *The Course of Mexican History.* New York: Oxford University Press.
Mintz, Sidney
  1973 "A Note on the Definition of Peasantries." *The Journal of Peasant Studies* 1:91–106.
Moran, Emilio, ed.
  1984 *The Ecosystem Concept in Anthropology.* Boulder, Colorado: Westview Press.
Murra, John
  1972 "El 'Control Vertical' de un Máximo de Pisos Ecológicos en la Economía de las Sociedades Andinas." *Visita de la Provincia de León de Huanuco* (1562) 2:249–76.
Nabhan, Gary
  1985 *Gathering the Desert.* Tucson: The University of Arizona Press.
Nabhan, Gary, and Thomas E. Sheridan
  1977 "Living Fencerows of the Río San Miguel, Sonora, Mexico: Traditional Technology for Floodplain Management." *Human Ecology* 5(2):97–111.
Nash, June
  1981 "Ethnographic Aspects of the World Capitalist System." *Annual Review of Anthropology* 10:393–424.
Navarro García, Luis
  1964 *José de Gálvez y la Comandancia General de la Provincias Internas.* Seville: Escuela de Estudios Hispano-Americanos.
Naylor, Thomas, and Charles Polzer, ed.
  1986 *The Presidio and Militia on the Northern Frontier of New Spain,* vol. I, 1570–1700. Tucson: The University of Arizona Press.
Nentvig, Juan
  1971 *Descripción Geográfica de Sonora.* México: Archivo General de la Nación.
Netting, Robert
  1972 "Of Men and Meadows: Strategies of Alpine Land Use." *Anthropological Quarterly* 45:132–44.

1976 "What Alpine Peasants Have in Common: Observations on Communal Tenure in a Swiss Village." *Human Ecology* 4(2):135–46.

1981 *Balancing on an Alp: Ecological Change and Continuity in a Swiss Mountain Community.* Cambridge: Cambridge University Press.

1984 "Reflections on an Alpine Village as Ecosystem." In *The Ecosystem Concept in Anthropology,* edited by Emilio Moran. Boulder, Colorado: Westview Press.

Orlove, Benjamin

1977a *Alpacas, Sheep, and Men: The Wool Export Economy and Regional Society in Southern Peru.* New York: Academic Press.

1977b "Inequalities Among Peasants." In *Peasant Livelihood,* edited by Rhoda Halperin and James Dow. New York: St. Martin's Press.

Orlove, Benjamin, and Glynn Custred

1980 "The Alternative Model of Agrarian Society in the Andes: Households, Networks, and Corporate Groups." In *Land and Power in Latin America,* edited by B. Orlove and G. Custred. New York: Holmes & Meier Publishers, Inc.

Orozco, W.

1975 *Los Ejidos de los Pueblos.* México: Ediciones Los Caballito.

Ortega Noriega, Sergio

1985 "El sistema de misiones jesuiticas: 1591–1699." In *Historia General de Sonora,* II. Hermosillo: Gobierno del Estado de Sonora.

Owen, Roger

1959 "Marobavi: A Study of an Assimilated Group in Northern Sonora." *Anthropological Papers of the University of Arizona,* no. 3. Tucson: The University of Arizona Press.

Pahl, R.

1968 *Readings in Urban Sociology.* Oxford: Pengamon Press.

Palerm, Angel

1980 "Articulación campesinado-capitalismo: sobre la fórmula M-D-M." In *Antropología y marxismo,* edited by Angel Palerm. México: Editorial Nuevo Imagen.

Peña, Elsa, and J. Trinidad Chávez

1985 "Ganadería y agricultura en la sierra, 1929–1980." *Historia General de Sonora* V. Hermosillo: Gobierno del Estado de Sonora.

Pfefferkorn, Ignacio

1983 *Descripción de la Provincia de Sonora.* Hermosillo: Gobierno del Estado de Sonora.

Polzer, Charles

1972a "The Evolution of the Jesuit Mission System in Northwestern New Spain, 1600–1767." Ph.D. dissertation. Tucson: The University of Arizona.

1972b "The Franciscan Entrada into Sonora, 1645–1654: A Jesuit Chronicle." *Arizona and the West* 14(3):253–78.

1976 *Rules and Precepts of the Jesuit Missions of Northwestern New Spain.* Tucson: The University of Arizona Press.

Powell, Philip Wayne
  1952   *Soldiers, Indians, and Silver: The Northward Advance of New Spain, 1550–1600.* Berkeley: University of California Press.
  1977   *Mexico's Miguel Caldera.* Tucson: The University of Arizona Press.
Radding de Murrieta, Cynthia
  1977   "The Function of Market in Changing Economic Structures in Mission Communities of Pimería Alta, 1768–1821." *The Americas* 34(2): 155–70.
  1979   "Las estructuras socioeconómicas de la Pimería Alta, 1768–1850." In *Noroeste de México,* no. 3. Hermosillo: Instituto Nacional de Antropología e Historia, Centro Regional del Noroeste.
Rambo, A.
  1977   "Closed Corporate and Open Peasant Communities: Reopening a Hastily Shut Case." *Comparative Studies in Society and History* 19:179–88.
Ramírez, José Carlos, and Ricardo León
  1985   "El último auge." *Historia General de Sonora* V. Hermosillo: Gobierno del Estado de Sonora.
Ramírez, José Carlos, Ricardo León, and Oscar Conde
  1985   "Cárdenas y las dos caras de la recuperación." *Historia General de Sonora* V. Hermosillo: Gobierno del Estado de Sonora.
Rea, Amadeo
  1983   *Once A River: Bird Life and Habitat Changes on the Middle Gila.* Tucson: The University of Arizona Press.
Redclift, Michael
  1979   "Agrarian Populism in Mexico—the 'Via Campesina.'" *Journal of Peasant Studies* 7(4):492–502.
Ressler, John
  1966   "Spanish Mission Water Systems, Northwest Frontier of New Spain." Master's thesis. Tucson: The University of Arizona.
Reyes Osorio, S., R. Stavenhagen, S. Eckstein, and J. Ballesteros
  1974   *Estructura Agraria y Desarrollo Agrícola en México.* México: Fondo de Cultura Económica.
Roca, Paul
  1967   *Paths of the Padres Through Sonora.* Tucson: Arizona Pioneers' Historical Society.
Rodríguez, Richard
  1982   *Hunger of Memory.* Toronto: Bantam Books.
Romanucci-Ross, Lola
  1973   *Conflict, Violence, and Morality in a Mexican Village.* Palo Alto: National Press Books.
Rowland, Donald
  1930   "The Elizondo Expedition against the Indian Rebels of Sonora, 1765–1771." Ph.D. dissertation. Berkeley: University of California.
Sanderson, Steven
  1981   *Agrarian Populism and the Mexican State.* Berkeley: University of California Press.

Santamaría, Francisco
  1974 *Diccionario de Mejicanismos*. México: Editorial Porrua, S.A.
Sauer, Carl
  1932 "The Road to Cibola." *Ibero-Americana*, no. 3. Berkeley: University of California Press.
Schwartz, Norman
  1978 "Community Development and Cultural Change in Latin America." *Annual Review of Anthropology* 7:235–61.
Shaw, William
  1978 *Marx's Theory of History*. Stanford: Stanford University Press.
Sheridan, Thomas
  1979 "Cross or Arrow? The Breakdown in Spanish-Seri Relations, 1729–1750." *Arizona and the West* 21(4):317–34.
  1981 "Prelude to Conquest: Yaqui Population, Subsistence, and Warfare During the Protohistoric Period." In *The Protohistoric Period in the North American Southwest, AD 1450–1700*, edited by David Wilcox and Bruce Masse. Arizona State University Anthropological Research Papers, no. 24.
  1986 *Los Tucsonenses: The Mexican Community of Tucson, 1854–1941*. Tucson: The University of Arizona Press.
Sheridan, Thomas, and Gary Nabhan
  1978 "Living with a River: Traditional Farmers of the Río San Miguel." *Journal of Arizona History* 19(1):1–16.
Shreve, Forrest, and Ira Wiggins
  1964 *Vegetation and Flora of the Sonoran Desert*, vol. I. Stanford: Stanford University Press.
Shryock, Henry, Jacob Siegel and Associates
  1973 *The Methods and Materials of Demography*, vol. I. Washington, D.C.: U.S. Department of Commerce.
Silverman, Sydel
  1966 "An Ethnographic Approach to Social Stratification: Prestige in a Central Italian Community." *American Anthropologist* 68:899–921.
Simmons, Marc
  1972 "Spanish Irrigation Practices in New Mexico." *New Mexico Historical Review* 47(2):135–50.
Simpson, Leslie Byrd
  1929 *The Encomienda in New Spain: Forced Native Labor in the Spanish Colonies, 1492–1550*. Berkeley: University of California Publications in History, vol. 19.
  1938 "The Repartimiento System of Native Labor in New Spain and Guatemala." *Ibero-Americana*, no. 13. Berkeley: University of California Press.
  1967 *Many Mexicos*. Berkeley: University of California Press.
Skinner, G. William
  1971 "Chinese Peasants and the Closed Community: An Open and Shut Case." *Comparative Studies in Society and History* 13:270–81.

Slatyer, R., and J. Mabbutt
  1964 "Hydrology of Arid and Semiarid Regions." In *Handbook of Applied Hydrology*, edited by V. Chow. New York: McGraw-Hill.
Sobarzo, Horacio
  1984 *Vocabulario Sonorense*. Hermosillo: Gobierno del Estado de Sonora.
Spicer, Edward
  1962 *Cycles of Conquest*. Tucson: The University of Arizona Press.
  1980 *The Yaquis: A Cultural History*. Tucson: The University of Arizona Press.
Stacey, M.
  1969 "The Myth of Community Studies." *British Journal of Sociology* 20:134–47.
Stavenhagen, Rodolfo
  1969 *Las clases sociales en las sociedades agrarias*. México: Siglo Veintiuno.
Stavenhagen, Rodolfo, Fernando Paz Sánchez, Cuauhtémoc Cárdenas, and Arturo Bonilla
  1980 *Neolatifundismo y Explotación*. México: Editorial Nuestro Tiempo.
Stern, Steve
  1983 "The Struggle for Solidarity." *Radical History* 27:21–45.
Strahler, A., and A. Strahler
  1978 *Modern Physical Geography*. New York: John Wiley & Sons.
Szuter, Christine
  1984 "Come Carne! The Social Dimensions of Butchering and Meat Distribution in Northwestern Mexico." Paper presented at the 83rd Meeting of the American Anthropological Association.
Tannenbaum, Frank
  1933 *Peace By Revolution*. New York: Columbia University Press.
Taylor, William
  1972 *Landlord and Peasant in Colonial Oaxaca*. Stanford: Stanford University Press.
Thornthwaite Associates
  1964 "Average Climatic Water Balance Data of the Continents, Part IV: North America (Excluding United States)." *Publications in Climatology* vol. 27, no. 2. Centerton, N.J.: Drexel Institute of Technology.
Thornthwaite, C., and J. Mather
  1957 "Instructions and Tables for Computing Potential Evapotranspiration and the Water Balance." *Publications in Climatology*, vol. 10, no. 3, Centerton, N.J.: Drexel Institute of Technology.
Treutlein, Theodore, ed.
  1949 *Pfefferkorn's Description of Sonora*. Albuquerque: University of New Mexico Press.
Vassberg, David
  1974 "The *Tierras Baldías*: Community Property and Public Lands in 16th Century Castille." *Agricultural History* 48(3):383–401.
  1980 "Peasant Communalism and Anti-Communal Tendencies in Early Modern Castille." *Journal of Peasant Studies* 7(4):477–91.

1984   *Land and Society in Golden Age Castille.* Cambridge: Cambridge University Press.

Villa, Eduardo
  1984   *Historia del Estado de Sonora.* Hermosillo: Gobierno del Estado de Sonora.

Voss, Stuart
  1982   *On the Periphery of Nineteenth-Century Mexico: Sonora and Sinaloa, 1810–1877.* Tucson: The University of Arizona Press.

Wallerstein, Immanuel
  1974   *The Modern World System,* vol. I. New York: Academic Press.

Warman, Arturo
  1976   *Y venimos a contradecir.* México: Ediciones de la Casa Chata.

Weber, David
  1982   *The Mexican Frontier, 1821–1846: The American Southwest Under Mexico.* Albuquerque: University of New Mexico Press.
  1986   "Turner, the Boltonians, and the Borderlands." *American Historical Review* 91(1):66–81.

West, Robert
  1949   "The Mining Community in Northern New Spain: the Parral Mining District." *Ibero-Americana,* no. 30. Berkeley: University of California Press.

Wolf, Eric
  1955   "Types of Latin American Peasantry." *American Anthropologist* 57:452–471.
  1956   "Aspects of Group Relations in a Complex Society: Mexico." *American Anthropologist* 58:1065–78.
  1957   "Closed Corporate Peasant Communities in Mesoamerica and Central Java." *Southwestern Journal of Anthropology* 13(1):1–18.
  1982   *Europe and the People Without History.* Berkeley: University of California Press.
  1986   "The Vicissitudes of the Closed Corporate Peasant Community." *American Ethnologist* 13(2):325–29.

Yates, P. Lamartine
  1981   *Mexico's Agricultural Dilemma.* Tucson: The University of Arizona Press.

Index

234   *Index*

Food preservation, 32
Forage crops, 24, 58, 59, 61, 64, 75, 77, 79, 87, 90, 192, 211n. 20
Franciscans, 7, 8, 15, 16
French: intervention in Mexico, 18, 19; threat to New Spain, 14

Gibson, Charles, and analysis of Aztec society, xxi
Gil Robles, Francisco Xavier, 154
Gini coefficient, 124–132, 214n. 1
Goats, 90–92, 101, 212n. 2
Gomi, Opata kickball game, 22, 211n. 17
González, Manuel, 17, 18, 20, 151
Grazing land: value of, 203, 204. *See also* Corporate grazing lands; Private grazing lands
Greenberg, James, xviii
Groundwater, 71–74, 190, 191. *See also* Water control; Wells: pump-powered
Guillet, David, xx
Guzmán, Nuño de, 6
Gálvez, José de, 15

Haciendas: Cucurpe, 20, 38–39, 144; Mexico, 4. *See also* Agua Fría
Harvesting, 64. *See also* Agriculture: agricultural mechanization; Tractors
Hijuela system, 68. See also *Comunes de agua*; Water control
Hollingshead, August, 137
Holy Week, 26, 27, 40, 112, 172, 211n. 17, 215n. 2
Honor, 145, 215n. 2
Horizontality, concept of, 48
Household autonomy, 48–49, 80, 81, 93–95, 176–178, 187–196
Household labor, 76, 77, 187, 199, 200
Household organization, 35–37
Household wealth, 122–125
Households (peasant): Andean South America, xxi, basic unit of society, xxii, xxiv, unit of production, xxi. *See also* Mode of production (peasant); Peasants
Housing, 34. *See also* Adobe, as basic building material; Dual residence
Hrdlička, Aleš, 22

Ibarra, Francisco, 6
Immigration of Cucurpeños. *See* Emigration
Indian labor: competition for, 9, 10, 15,

16, 17, 19, 20; control of, 12; in missions, 8
Indian lands: competition for, 15; control of, 7–10, 13, 15, 16, 20; protection of, 207, 208n. 5. *See also* Missions
Indian rebellions: in Sonora, 10, 11, 12, 14, 18
Inheritance, 37–39, 143
Instituto Nacional Indigenista. *See* Mexican Indian Institute
Intercropping, 75

Jesuits, 7, 8, 9, 10, 24; expulsion of, 15. *See also* Missions
Jironza Petrís de Cruzat, Domingo, 12
Johnson grass, 75

Kino, Eusebio Francisco, 13, 16, 63
Kinship, networks of, 35–37

La Brisca, 107, 108
La Calera, 29, 31
Labor force, 44–47, 121: in mining, 20, 142, 210n. 15; Orientals in, 210n. 15; in rural Mexico. *See also* Occupational structure; Wage work
Land grants, 7, 98, 99. *See also* Comunidad of Cucurpe, history; Comunidad San Javier, recognized by government; Ejido 6 de Enero, recognized by government; Torreón: as private holding
Land tenure: of arable lands, 79–81. *See also* Agrarian Reform; Comunidad of Cucurpe; Household autonomy
Laslett, Peter, 35
Latifundias, 19. *See also* Haciendas
Lechuguilla, 2, 85, 104–106, 112–117. See also *Bacanora*; Mescal-making
Lentils, 60, 64
Ley Lerdo, 19, 211nn. 18, 21
Lipan Apaches, 14
Livestock: breeding, 77, 94; censuses, 125, 202; inspectors, 47, 83, 84, 202; marketing, 100–103; regulation, 92–95, 99, 100, 175, 184. *See also* Cattle: prices; sales
Livestock distribution: on Comunidad of Cucurpe, 92; on Comunidad San Javier, 93; on Ejido 6 de Enero, 93; on private ranches, 96–100
Livestock industry: Mexico, 211n. 19; Sonora, 22, 23, 120
Livestock numbers: on Comunidad of

Poultry, 33
Private grazing lands, 95–100
Private ranchers (resident): 130. *See also*
Absentee elite
Provincias Internas, 15
Pueblo Indians, 9

Quarrying, 109, 110. *See also* Cantera;
Canteras de Cucurpe
Quigue, Juan Bautista, 12, 13

Rainfall, in Cucurpe, 53–54, 212n. 1
(chapter 3), 213n. 2 (chapter 3)
Ranching heritage, 89, 213n. 1
Range management, 77, 87, 92–95, 98–
100, 175, 176, 184. *See also* Comunidad
of Cucurpe; Corporate grazing lands;
Overgrazing; Private grazing lands
Redfield, Robert, xviii
Reducción, Spanish policy of, 11
Religion. *See* Fiestas; San Isidro; Velorios;
Virgen de Guadalupe
Repartimiento system, 12, 207n. 5. *See
also* Indian labor
Revillagigedo, Conde de (viceroy), 154
Reyes, Antonio de los, 15
Riparian woodland, 86
Rivera, Pedro de, 9, 10
Rodríguez, Richard, 40
Rodríguez Gallardo, Rafael, 10
Roppher, William, 153
Roundups, 82–84. *See also* Livestock: in-
spectors
Rubi, Marqués de, 15
Rural Bank, 187
Russians: emigration to Cucurpe, 168,
180; threat to New Spain, 14
Rye grass, 60

Sacramento, California, 40
San Bruno, 99, 100
San Isidro (patron saint of farmers), 170–
172
San Miguel (river), xv, 11, 55, 61, 68, 73,
190
San Miguel (valley), 10, 209n. 4
Santo Domingo (rancho), 22, 31, 210n. 16
Saracachi (rancho), 150
Saracachi (*real de minas*), 12, 16, 20, 106
Saracachi (river), 11, 38, 53, 55, 67, 70,
210n. 15
Sauer, Carl, 6
Secretaría de Programación y Pre-
supuesto. *See* Department of Planning
and the Budget

Secretaría de Agricultura y Recursos
Hidráulicos. *See* Department of Agri-
culture and Water Resources.
Seed availability, 60
Seep willow, 62, 66
Semana Santa. See Holy Week
Seri Indians, 4, 11, 14, 18, 144
Settlement patterns, 29–32; in Andalusia,
212n. 1; in Basque provinces, 212n. 1;
in Castile, 212n. 1; in New Mexico,
212n. 1. *See also* Dual residence
Sexual morality, 215n. 2. *See also* Honor;
Women, attitude toward
Soil fertilization, 61, 63. *See also* Living
fencerows
Sonora, 154; agricultural development,
58, 107; history of, 7, 17, 19, 21; wild-
food gathering in, 112
Sonoran Consolidated Mining Company,
107
Sonoran Desert, 53, 85, 189
Sorghum, 24, 61
Spain, 144, 145, 214n. 1
Spicer, Edward, 209n. 4
Squash, 46, 56, 64, 75, 79
St. Felix, Tyrol, 206n. 3
Stockmen's association (Cucurpe), 127,
175
Suma Indians, 9
Szuter, Christine, 33

Tarahumara Indians, 9, 12, 61
Tarea, 68, 213n. 3
Taylor, Walter, xxi
Television, 34
Thornthwaite, C. W., 213n. 2
Threshing, 57, 63, 64
Törbel, xix, xxi, xxiii, 129, 152, 172, 206n.
3, 214n. 1
Torreón: land/animal unit ratio, 99; as
private holding, 16, 98; and range
management, 99, 100, 153, 154, 156,
157, 159
Tractors, 58, 64, 65, 75, 76, 204. *See also*
Agriculture: agricultural labor, agricul-
tural mechanization; Draft animals
Tree tobacco, 66
Tuape, 11, 10, 12
Tubutama, 168

Ujamaa, program in Tanzania, xxiv
Upper Pimas, 11

Vassberg, David, 151
Vegetation types, 85–87. *See also* Desert

About the Author

Tom Sheridan has carried out fieldwork in northwestern Mexico since 1971, and in the municipio of Cucurpe, Sonora, since 1975. He holds his Ph.D. in anthropology from the University of Arizona and has been Assistant Curator of Ethnohistory at the Arizona State Museum since 1985. He is also the author of *Los Tucsonenses: The Mexican Community of Tucson, 1854–1941* (Tucson: The University of Arizona Press, 1986).